Literature and Philosophy

Literature and Philosophy

A Guide to Contemporary Debates

Edited by

David Rudrum

palgrave
macmillan

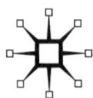

First published 2006 by
PALGRAVE MACMILLAN
Houndmills, Basingstoke, Hampshire RG21 6XS and
175 Fifth Avenue, New York, N.Y. 10010
Companies and representatives throughout the world

PALGRAVE MACMILLAN is the global academic imprint of the Palgrave
Macmillan division of St. Martin's Press, LLC and of Palgrave Macmillan Ltd.
Macmillan® is a registered trademark in the United States, United Kingdom
and other countries. Palgrave is a registered trademark in the European
Union and other countries.

ISBN-13: 978–1–4039–4773–4 hardback
ISBN-10: 1–4039–4773–2 hardback

This book is printed on paper suitable for recycling and made from fully
managed and sustained forest sources.

A catalogue record for this book is available from the British Library.

Library of Congress Cataloging-in-Publication Data
Literature and philosophy: a guide to contemporary debates / edited by
    David Rudrum.
      p.   cm.
    Includes bibliographical references and index.
    ISBN 1–4039–4773–2
    1. Literature—Philosophy.   I. Rudrum, David, 1974–
    PN49.L49995 2006
    01—dc28   2006044295

10   9   8   7   6   5   4   3   2   1
15   14   13   12   11   10   09   08   07   06

Printed and bound in Great Britain by
Antony Rowe Ltd, Chippenham and Eastbourne

For Tracey,
at last

Contents

Acknowledgements

First and foremost, my thanks go to the many contributors to this volume, whose interest, enthusiasm, and expertise have been a constant source of inspiration and encouragement – and, I am unashamed to confess, envy. To them alone belongs the credit for whatever merit this book holds.

My single biggest debt is undoubtedly to Robert Eaglestone, at whose suggestion I began working on this book. Without his initial impetus, and his unstinting subsequent support and advice, this project would never have come to fruition.

My thanks also go to everyone at Palgrave, in particular to Paula Kennedy, Helen Craine, Vidya Vijayan, Emily Rosser, and Eleanor Byrne, for their help and patience throughout the long gestation period of this book.

I am grateful to Blackwell Publishing for permission to quote from Ludwig Wittgenstein's *Philosophical Investigations*.

Finally, having been far too self-absorbed to do so earlier, I would like to thank my friends, my family, especially my parents, and above all my wife, for being such stalwarts throughout. They have borne me up along the way, which I suspect has probably been a harder task than mine.

Notes on Contributors

Andrew Benjamin is Professor of Critical Theory in Design and Architecture at the University of Technology, Sydney. He was previously Professor of Philosophy and Director of the Centre for Research in Philosophy and Literature at Warwick University. An internationally recognized authority on contemporary French and German critical theory, he has been Visiting Professor at Columbia University in New York and Visiting Critic at the Architectural Association in London. His many books include *What is Deconstruction?* (1988), *Art, Mimesis and the Avant-Garde* (1991), *Philosophy's Literature* (2001), and *Disclosing Spaces: On Painting* (2004). He also edited *The Lyotard Reader* (1989), *Abjection, Melancholia and Love: The Work of Julia Kristeva* (1990), *Walter Benjamin's Philosophy: Destruction and Experience* (1993), and *Walter Benjamin and Romanticism* (2002).

Brett Bourbon is the author of *Finding a Replacement for the Soul: Meaning and Mind in Literature and Philosophy* (2004). He is also the author of *Crucifixion Can Seem Like Standing in Air: Poetry, Love, Death, and the Rationality of Description* and *The Apprehension of Power*, with Miguel Tamen (both under consideration at Harvard University Press). He received his B.A. from U.C. Berkeley and his Ph.D. from Harvard University. He has been awarded a Mellon postdoctoral fellowship to Stanford University and a Fulbright Visiting Scholar award to the Program on Literary Theory at the University of Lisbon. He is an assistant professor and Director of the English Undergraduate Honors program in the Department of English at Stanford University.

Josh Cohen is Senior Lecturer in English and Comparative Literature, Goldsmiths College, University of London. He is the author of *Spectacular Allegories: Postmodern American Writing and the Politics of Seeing* (1998); *Interrupting Auschwitz: Art, Religion, Philosophy* (2003); *How to Read Freud* (2005), as well as many articles on modern literature, continental philosophy, and aesthetic theory. He is currently working on a book provisionally entitled *The Ironic End of Art*.

Robert Eaglestone works on contemporary and twentieth-century literature, literary theory, and philosophy at Royal Holloway, University of London. His publications include *Ethical Criticism: Reading after Levinas*; *Doing English*; *The Holocaust and the Postmodern*, as well as articles on contemporary philosophy, the philosophy of history, and literature.

Michael Eskin teaches German and comparative literature at Columbia University, New York. He is the author of *Nabokovs Version von Puskins Evgenij Onegin: Zwischen Version und Fiktion – eine übersetzungs-und fiktionstheoretische Untersuchung* (1994) and *Ethics and Dialogue in the Works of Levinas, Bakhtin, Mandel'shtam, and Celan* (2000), as well as of essays on Levinas, Celan, Bakhtin, Grünbein, Nabokov, and others. He has edited a special issue of *Poetics Today* on ethics and literature. He is currently working on a book on Paul Celan, Durs Grünbein, and Joseph Brodsky.

Jennifer Anna Gosetti-Ferencei is Associate Professor of Philosophy at Fordham University in New York City. She is the author of *Heidegger, Hoelderlin, and the Subject of Poetic Language*; a co-translation (with M. Fritsch) of Heidegger's *Phenomenology of Religious Life*; and a book of poems, *After the Palace Burns*.

Garry L. Hagberg is the James H. Ottaway, Jr Professor of Philosophy and Aesthetics at Bard College, where he is also director of the Program in Philosophy and the Arts. He is the author of *Art as Language: Wittgenstein, Meaning, and Aesthetic Theory* and *Meaning and Interpretation: Wittgenstein, Henry James, and Literary Knowledge* (both from Cornell University Press), and he has contributed numerous articles, essays, and reviews to various journals, collections, and reference works. He is also Editor (jointly with Denis Dutton) of *Philosophy and Literature*, and he guest-edited a special issue of *The Journal of Aesthetics and Art Criticism* on Improvisation in the Arts.

Richard J. Lane is Professor of English at Malaspina-University College, British Columbia, Canada. He specializes in twentieth-century British and Canadian fiction, and twentieth-century theory. His book publications include *Jean Baudrillard* (2000), *Mrs. Dalloway: Literary Masterpieces* (2001), *Beckett and Philosophy* (ed., Palgrave, 2002), *Contemporary British Fiction* (co-ed., 2003), *Functions of the Derrida Archive* (2003), and *Reading Walter Benjamin: Writing Through The Catastrophe* (2005). Lane also writes the 'Canada' section of *The Year's Work in English Studies* for The English Association.

Anthony Larson is Maître de Conférences in English Studies at the Université du Maine in Le Mans, France, where he teaches American literature and literary theory. He is the author of articles on Deleuze, Derrida, poststructuralist French philosophy, and American literature. He is currently at work on a book-length study of the issues developed in his contribution to this collection.

Simon Malpas is Lecturer in English Literature at Edinburgh University. He is the author of *The Postmodern* (2005) and *Jean-François Lyotard* (2003); and editor of *The New Aestheticism* (2003, with John Joughin), *Postmodern Debates* (Palgrave, 2001), and *William Cowper: The Centenary Letters* (2000), as well as articles on aesthetics, Romanticism, continental philosophy, and the post-modern.

Mary C. Rawlinson is Associate Professor of Philosophy and Comparative Literature at Stony Brook University in New York. Her publications include articles on Proust, literature and ethics, Hegel, and French feminism. She is the editor of *Breasts and Medicine* (2005) and the co-editor of *Derrida and Feminism* (1997), as well as the editor of five issues of the *Journal of Medicine and Philosophy*, including *Foucault and the Philosophy of Medicine*, *The Future of Psychiatry*, and *Feminist Bioethics*. She is currently completing a book on agency that explores detective fiction as a genre of moral philosophy.

Rupert Read is a leading British advocate of the 'resolute' reading of Wittgenstein. See his *The New Wittgenstein* (2000), and his essays in the journals *Philosophy, Philosophical Investigations*, and *Philosophical Psychology*. His other books are *Kuhn* (2002) and *The New Hume Debate* (2000). He has edited a volume entitled *Film as Philosophy* (2005) and working on the relationship between Buddhism and Wittgenstein. He is also working jointly with Jon Cook on Wallace Stevens's poetry considered from a philosophical point of view.

Jonathan Rée holds visiting positions at Roehampton University and the Royal College of Art; his books include *Philosophical Tales* and *I See a Voice*.

David Rudrum teaches at London Metropolitan University. He has published articles in a number of journals, including *Philosophy and Literature* and *Angelaki*. He works on the relationship between literature and philosophy, and is currently preparing a book on *Wittgenstein and the Theory of Narrative*.

Ralph Strehle is Visiting Lecturer at Royal Holloway, University of London, where he teaches Modern and Postmodern Critical Theory. His research interest lies in German and French phenomenology, ethics, and reader-response criticism. He is looking forward to singing and studying Opera at the Royal Scottish Academy of Music and Drama this autumn.

Derval Tubridy lectures in English and Visual Culture at Goldsmiths College, University of London. Her research interests lie in the relationships between contemporary philosophy, theory, the visual arts, and literature. She also works on Samuel Beckett and on Thomas Kinsella. Besides numerous journal articles, she is the author of *Thomas Kinsella: The Peppercanister Poems* (2001), and is currently preparing a monograph on Beckett.

Bryan Vescio is Assistant Professor of English and Humanistic Studies at the University of Wisconsin-Green Bay, where he teaches American literature, film, literary theory, and interdisciplinary courses in the humanities. He has published literary criticism on such figures as Nathanael West and John Steinbeck, as well as introductions to the works of philosophers such as William James and Ludwig Wittgenstein. In his theoretical writing, he has focused on the intersections between literary studies and philosophy from both the Continental and the analytic traditions. He is particularly interested in the possibilities for reconciling these two traditions in the work of neo-pragmatists such as Donald Davidson and Richard Rorty. In addition to his work in literary theory, he has also written on film theory from a neo-pragmatist perspective.

Introduction – Literature and Philosophy: The Contemporary Interface

David Rudrum

'The separation of philosophy from literary studies has not worked to the benefit of either.' An uncontentious statement, surely, and perhaps even a disarming or conciliatory one. Who, after all, would think that segregating literature from philosophy could do anything but delimit and restrict both? And yet, within its original context, this statement formed part of a controversy that would rage for many years. It is taken from the introduction to *Deconstruction and Criticism* (Hartman, p. ix), a manifesto heralding the arrival and ascendancy of deconstructive thought in America, which featured contributions from all the leading 'Yale School' critics (Paul de Man, J. Hillis Miller, Geoffrey Hartman, and Harold Bloom), and from Jacques Derrida himself. Its publication marked the opening salvo in some of the most notorious debates in the so-called 'theory wars' of the 1980s.

Looking back, from the distance of a quarter of a century, what is striking about Hartman's preface is the attempt he makes to tag deconstruction, and literary theory in general, onto a venerable tradition stemming from German Romanticism that thrives on the intersection between philosophy and literature.[1] 'Without the pressure of philosophy on literary texts, or the reciprocal pressure of literary analysis on philosophical writing, each discipline becomes impoverished. If there is the danger of a confusion of realms, it is a danger worth experiencing', he argues (Hartman, p. ix). It seems curious today that this move should have been so controversial, even allowing for the vociferous, bitter, and often eccentric climate of polemic surrounding the theory wars. Some critics feared that this harnessing of philosophy would bring a sterile abstraction and theoretism to the study of literature, destroying literature's vitality. Others felt that the kind of philosophy that underpinned deconstruction was too destabilizing: it was both antifoundational and antihumanist. Still others objected to what amounted to interdisciplinary posturing on the part of the deconstructionists: 'Hartman

1

acts as if no one before him had ever connected the two disciplines', wrote one commentator (Dasenbrock, p. 4), whereas in fact, philosophy and liter-ature have almost always been in close proximity to one another, from Plato and Aristotle through Voltaire and Rousseau to the Romantics and Existentialists.

At the time, however, Hartman's proposed deconstructive alliance between literary and philosophical studies initially failed to materialize. As literary theory emerged, evolved, and rose to dominance, many of its philosophical aspirations gave way to debating various different techniques, methods, and thematics of reading. Before long, the fascinating thought of philosophers as diverse as, say, Mikhail Bakhtin, J.L. Austin, and Jacques Derrida was being packaged as 'Bakhtinian theory', 'Speech Act theory', and 'deconstructive theory', each offering a particular angle on a particular set of literary themes, genres, or devices – interesting stuff, certainly, and richly productive in terms of literary analysis, but arguably tending to narrow down rather than draw out the philosophical significance of the ideas behind them. Further specializations, giving rise to feminist theory, postcolonial theory, and queer theory, transformed our sense of the classical canon, and politicized the nature of critical debate in many refreshing ways. Yet, with some exceptions – the importance of de Beauvoir, Cixous, Irigaray, and Butler in feminism, for instance, or the ongoing debates between African philosophy and post-colonialism – these theorists have tended to concentrate on 're-evaluating' or 'reclaiming' areas of traditional literary scholarship. They have done so with great success, yet this does not amount to the *rapprochement* between literature and philosophy that theory was supposed to inaugurate. All too often, the broader conceptual questions that literary theory had promised to tackle – philosophical issues about the nature of language, of reading, of ethics, or of the aesthetic – tended to fall through the cracks between the various competing schools of theory.

It could even be argued that at times, theory was actually something that came between literature and philosophy, rather than bringing them together. Those that claim this will typically point to the 1977 confronta-tion between Jacques Derrida and John Searle over the legacy of J.L. Austin.[2] Derrida used deconstructive theory to question some of the assumptions underpinning Austin's philosophy of communication; Searle, its leading advocate at the time, wrote a reply that dismissed many of Derrida's points out of hand; Derrida replied to Searle by playfully deconstructing Searle's every move. It seems, in retrospect, that neither Derrida nor Searle had an adequate grasp of the tradition they were attacking, and that both were basic-ally talking at cross purposes.[3] But in practical terms, the damage had been done: the debate polarized many Anglo-American philosophers, with their predominantly analytic outlook, against new trends in Continental thought, on the assumption that Continental philosophy entailed an ultimately illo-gical, nonsensical view of language.[4] In the aftermath of this exchange, most philosophy departments barred their doors to deconstructionists, and a symptomatic division in the Anglo-American academy became evident: (analytic) Philosophy and (empirical) Literary Criticism remained distinct, unrelated disciplines.

However, the philosophy department's loss was to be the literature department's gain. New directions in literary theory and in Continental philosophy had a great deal more in common with each other – not least their struggle to secure academic acceptance – as became evident during the advent of deconstructive literary criticism and the ensuing theory wars. In other words, the gulf that opened up between Anglo-American and Continental philosophy during the Searle/Derrida affair forced the latter into an alliance with literary theory. Only two years after the controversy of 1977, the Yale School manifesto of 1979 was proclaiming Derrida's work to be a 'new dawn' in literary criticism (Hartman, p. ix), and the theory wars were about to begin in earnest.

By the 1980s, then, the deconstructionists had largely been aligned with the project of literary theory rather than philosophy. This pattern would repeat itself throughout the reception of many more 'Continental' thinkers, including Foucault, Lyotard, Baudrillard, Deleuze, and Levinas. That this constituted an enrichment of literary studies rather than an impoverishment (let alone a threat) is something I take here as self-evident. However, the full richness of any potential interaction between literature and philosophy was all too often compromised by the tendency to dilute challenging, radical philosophical ideas and concepts into 'theories', which could then be applied to texts to produce 'readings' of them, most of which readings illuminated the theory behind them as much as they did the text itself. In other words, the parameters of traditional literary theory might not have been the best place to develop a fully-fledged relationship between literary and philosophical studies, for these parameters can confine both disciplines by reducing them to neat theories, or to sets of theoretical terms. This is not in any way to downplay the achievements of literary theory in bringing together two highly complex bodies of scholarship, nor to disparage its impressive interdisciplinary achievements. Many literary theories have built sophisticated networks of bridges that span the divide between literature and philosophy, but the traffic that flows across these bridges tends to be regulated. To speak metaphorically, these border crossings work as patrolled checkpoints where texts and ideas can receive an entry clearance, but first they must be stamped as 'theory', and thereby subjected to certain import and export restrictions.

The project of literary theory, however, has not gone unchallenged. Throughout the 1980s, on both sides of the Atlantic, a steady stream of books and collections appeared which challenged and polemicized with the problematic status of the theoretical project. Titles like *Against Theory*, *The Resistance to Theory*, *The Limits of Theory*, and *The Failure of Theory*[5] paradoxically became focal points for theoretical discussion and formulation. In the

1990s, though, a rather different accentuation emerged with books entitled *After Theory* (two of these), *Reading After Theory, Life After Theory, Post Theory*, and so on[6] – the implication being that theory itself was no longer something problematic, controversial, or threatening, nor something that needed challenging, but something that had actually come to an end.

Of course, this much-vaunted 'end of theory' has been the source of a further torrent of theorizing about the end of theory. What might such an end of theory mean? Clearly the end of theory does not mean the end of theoretical thought – more people are writing about figures from Adorno to Zizek than ever before, and certainly more theories that theorize the end of theory are being mooted than ever before. Indeed, it has even been argued that the end of literary theory is coterminous with the triumph of literary theory, insofar as theory is no longer separable nor distinguishable from the mainstream of literary studies. Yet whatever, if anything, the end of theory means – and there is not room to explore that fully here – there are good indications that it marks the beginnings of a promising new period in the often stormy relations between literature and philosophy.[7]

Over the past decade or so, literary theory, traditionally the ally of Continental philosophy, has come in for far more sophisticated scrutiny and scepticism than greeted its arrival during the theory wars. But the response to this has been an encouraging turn to the philosophical thought that underpinned so much of recent literary theory in the first place: Heidegger, Wittgenstein, and Adorno, for example, are now widely debated by literary critics. Simultaneously, many philosophers have begun to pay attention to the intricacy of philosophical discourse, and to approach philosophical texts with a sophisticated awareness of their textuality – they have, in short, recognized the importance of ideas and methods associated with literary criticism.

Much recent work has addressed itself towards the growing relationship between the areas of literature and philosophy, constituting one of the most innovative of contemporary cross-disciplinary interactions for both fields.[8] Interest comes from both directions, making this a well-rounded interdisciplinary encounter. There is even some evidence that this developing *rapport* is being reflected in the structure of the university. At the pedagogical level, the current tendency in higher education to merge academic departments now means that literature and philosophy are sometimes being taught and studied in the same department. Doubtless this owes as much to economic necessity as to the intellectual *rapprochement* between the two, but it is nevertheless instructive that within the university, philosophy is now often located alongside literature as opposed to, say, science, mathematics, theology, social science, or politics. The basis for this realignment is borne out by some of the most productive contemporary scholarship and research in both disciplines.

A growing sense has emerged within contemporary literary studies that traditional critical theories should begin to engage more fully with issues such as ethics, identity, pragmatism, or aesthetic truth. These issues are traditionally located within the provenance of philosophy. Accordingly, a 'post-theoretical' generation of critics is turning increasingly to the philosophical and aesthetic thought that engendered literary theory in the first place. For example, it is now at least as common to find younger academics (and their students) working on Heidegger or Nietzsche than on Paul de Man, and probably more common to find them working on Adorno or Benjamin than working on Terry Eagleton. A case in point here would be the debates around the 'New Aestheticism', in which Continental thought on the nature of the aesthetic has been taken up and reused by Simon Malpas and others to re-evaluate the significance of this traditional philosophical category.[9]

Simultaneously, Anglo-American philosophy departments – dominated for so long by the analytic tradition – have gradually begun to open their doors to the Continental thought that informed literary theory. Thinkers such as Derrida, Adorno, and Levinas are now being read and accepted far more widely by the anglophone philosophical community. This development has compelled many philosophers to reconsider the stance that philosophy has taken towards literature, and to re-examine the ground it shares with contemporary literary theory. Some have followed the example of Stanley Cavell in using readings of literature to exemplify and refine points about language, aesthetics, and so on. Others, following Jonathan Rée's lead, have taken up the challenge of reading philosophy itself as literature.[10]

If literary theory once acted as a bridge to facilitate traffic between philosophical and literary studies, then its task has been successfully achieved, perhaps to the point of rendering such a bridge redundant. In the intervening period between the arrival of theory and the so-called 'end' of it, traditional boundaries have gradually been broken down, and interdisciplinary thought has grown instead. It is therefore, at last, a timely moment to stage a full-scale face-to-face encounter between literary and philosophical studies, one that is not obliged to make the traditional detour through critical theory. To literary critics who have raised questions about the end of theory and what should succeed it, the reciprocally informative relationships between literature and philosophy offer a plausible answer.

Such is the background and genesis of the lively set of debates encapsulated in this book. What follows is divided into six parts. The first half of the book explores encounters between literature and the three principal schools of Western philosophy, with each of the first three parts dedicated to the relationship between literature and, respectively, French, Anglo-American, and German philosophy. In the second half of the book, Part IV ('Literature and Philosophy: The Question of Ethics'), Part V ('Reading Philosophy as Literature'), and Part VI ('Approaching the End') explore more specific issues. Each of these parts contains essays from a variety of philosophical backgrounds, with a view to showing how different philosophies interact with literature over similar issues, thereby charting a breadth of approaches to the subject, and encapsulating the diversity of the literature/philosophy interface. Part IV examines how the question of ethics is explored at the intersection of philosophy and literature; Part V engages in various aspects of reading philosophy as literature; and, by way of a conclusion, Part VI debates the notion of the end of art and its implications for literature.

Each of these six parts is introduced with a brief expository essay, which maps out the field under discussion, describing the major aspects of the literature/philosophy dialogue in the area in question. These introductory essays chart the origins and consequences of this dialogue, as well as pointing towards important new developments in both literary and philosophical scholarship. They are intended not only to introduce the key philosophical movements and thinkers to literature students, but also to provide something of a bibliographical essay for those who wish to read further in any of these areas. It should be emphasized that this aspect of the introductory essays is just that – introductory. They are aimed at undergraduate students rather than advanced students or researchers, and are by no means comprehensive or exhaustive.

Finally, the book as a whole is an attempt to represent the burgeoning field of 'literature and philosophy' at its most diverse. It does not attempt to offer nor to advance any particular philosophy of literature, nor to philosophize any particular aspect or body of literature, nor to dragoon philosophy into the service of literary criticism or *vice versa*. Its aim is to appeal to philosophers and literary critics or theorists of every stamp and shade of opinion, without privileging either discipline (or any of their countless sub-disciplines) over the other, and to provide a guide to the vast spectrum of thought involved in the contemporary debates between literature and philosophy.

Notes

1. The best recent discussion of this tradition is Bowie (1997).
2. For the essence of this debate, see Derrida (1988). The consequences of what eventually became a heated controversy are explored by Dasenbrock (1989).
3. See Dasenbrock, and also Stanley Cavell's 'What Did Derrida Want of Austin?' and 'Seminar on "What Did Derrida Want of Austin?" ', in his *Philosophical Passages*.
4. For an interesting re-evaluation of this position, see Wheeler.
5. As can be seen from these titles, challenges to theory came from a variety of different perspectives. Respectively, W.J.T. Mitchell (1985) debates a pragmatist approach; Paul de Man (1986) is the classic deconstructive engagement with it; Thomas M. Kavanagh's collection (1989) contains a broad spectrum of opinion on the subject, while Patrick Parrinder's position (1987) is basically a Marxist polemic. For an interesting discussion of the various rejections of theory, see Robert Eaglestone's engagement with the issue (1997).
6. Once again, the sheer breadth of opinion on this subject can be gauged from the distance between the authors of the two books entitled *After Theory* – Thomas Docherty (1996), an avowed post-Marxist, and Terry Eagleton (2003), the Marxist

stalwart. The contributors to *Life After Theory* (2003) are no less diverse, ranging between Jacques Derrida, Frank Kermode, Toril Moi, and Christopher Norris. Finally, the distance between the theorists theorizing the end of theory in McQuillan *et al.*'s collection *Post-Theory* (1999), and Valentine Cunningham's approach to the same problem in his *Reading After Theory* (2002), is just as great.

7. To clarify: I am not trying to claim here that the dialogue between literature and philosophy has only opened up in recent times. After all, the respected journal *Philosophy and Literature* was established as far back as 1976, and is still going strong (this volume includes a contribution from its co-editor, Garry Hagberg). Furthermore, throughout the 1980s there appeared numerous collections of interesting interdisciplinary work, such as Griffiths (1984), Cascardi (1987), and Dasenbrock (1989). Nor is my point that, to hijack a phrase from Barthes, the birth of a literature/philosophy dialogue must be at the cost of the death of literary theory; on the contrary, debates around literary theory continue to be productive, fruitful, and important. Rather, the idea of the end of theory – the rumours of which may well yet turn out to be largely unsubstantiated – has created the perfect conditions for philosophers, critics, and theorists to re-examine how their disciplines meet and interact.

8. See, amongst many other more specialized accounts, the following general orientations: Zima (1999), New (1999), Skilleås (2001), and John and Lopes (2004). Andrew Benjamin's *Philosophy's Literature* (2001) can be singled out as a particularly stimulating interdisciplinary engagement by a master of both fields.

9. See Joughin and Malpas (2003).

10. See Rée (1987).

Works cited

Benjamin, Andrew, *Philosophy's Literature* (Manchester: Clinamen Press, 2001).

Bowie, Andrew, *From Romanticism to Critical Theory: The Philosophy of German Literary Theory* (London: Routledge, 1997).

Cascardi, Anthony J. (ed.), *Literature and the Question of Philosophy* (Baltimore: Johns Hopkins University Press, 1987).

Cavell, Stanley, *Philosophical Passages: Wittgenstein, Emerson, Austin, Derrida* (Oxford: Blackwell, 1995).

Cunningham, Valentine, *Reading After Theory* (Oxford: Blackwell, 2002).

Dasenbrock, Reed Way (ed.), *Redrawing the Lines: Analytic Philosophy, Deconstruction, and Literary Theory* (Minneapolis: University of Minnesota Press, 1989).

De Man, Paul, *The Resistance to Theory*, foreword by Wlad Godzich (Minneapolis: University of Minnesota Press, 1986).

Derrida, Jacques, *Limited Inc* (Evanston, IL: Northwestern University Press, 1988).

Docherty, Thomas, *After Theory* (2nd ed. Edinburgh: Edinburgh University Press, 1996).

Eaglestone, Robert, *Ethical Criticism: Reading After Levinas* (Edinburgh: Edinburgh University Press, 1997).

Eagleton, Terry, *After Theory* (New York: Basic Books, 2003).

Griffiths, A. Phillips (ed.), *Philosophy and Literature* (Cambridge: Cambridge University Press, 1984).

Hartman, Geoffrey, 'Preface' to *Deconstruction and Criticism*, ed. Harold Bloom (London: Routledge, 1979).

John, Eileen and Dominic McIver Lopes (eds), *Philosophy of Literature – Contemporary and Classic Readings: An Anthology* (Oxford: Blackwell, 2004).

Joughin, John and Simon Malpas (eds), *The New Aestheticism* (Manchester: Manchester University Press, 2003).

Kavanagh, Thomas M. (ed.), *The Limits of Theory* (Stanford: Stanford University Press, 1989).

McQuillan, Martin, Robin Purves, Graeme MacDonald, and Stephen Thomson (eds), *Post-Theory: New Directions in Criticism* (Edinburgh: Edinburgh University Press, 1999).

Mitchell, W.J.T. (ed.), *Against Theory: Literary Studies and the New Pragmatism* (Chicago: University of Chicago Press, 1985).

New, Christopher, *Philosophy of Literature: An Introduction* (London: Routledge, 1999).

Parrinder, Patrick, *The Failure of Theory: Contemporary English Criticism and Fiction* (Brighton: Harvester, 1987).

Payne, Michael and John Schad (eds), *Life After Theory* (London: Continuum, 2003).

Rée, Jonathan, *Philosophical Tales: An Essay on Philosophy and Literature* (London: Methuen, 1987).

Skilleås, Ole Martin, *Philosophy and Literature: An Introduction* (Edinburgh: Edinburgh University Press, 2001).

Wheeler, Samuel C., *Deconstruction as Analytic Philosophy* (Stanford: Stanford University Press, 2000).

Zima, Petr, *The Philosophy of Modern Literary Theory* (London: Athlone Press, 1999).

Part I
Encounters with Literature in French Philosophy

Introduction

Literature and philosophy have been particularly close neighbours in the French academy, and in French culture in general. Their proximity dates back at least to the 1930s and 1940s, when Jean-Paul Sartre (1905–80), Albert Camus (1913–60), and Simone de Beauvoir (1908–86) epitomized this *entente cordiale*. All three enjoyed success both as novelists and as philosophers, to the extent that dubbing their works as either 'philosophy' or 'literature' is, at best, making an arbitrary distinction, and registering assumptions about clear-cut disciplinary boundaries that their works do not share. Sartre's essays on literature, for example, seem particularly resistant to this kind of academic pigeonholing. See his *'What is Literature?' and Other Essays* (Cambridge, MA: Harvard University Press, 1988).

If the existentialism of Camus and Sartre is sometimes thought of as dominating post-war French thought, it did so only superficially. Equally interesting, and ultimately more influential on contemporary literary studies, are the much bleaker writings of their contemporaries Georges Bataille (1897–1962) and Maurice Blanchot (1907–2003). Like Camus and Sartre, Bataille and Blanchot also wrote in both literary and philosophical genres, but once again it would be hard to draw a neat line separating their writings into 'literature' and 'philosophy'. Unlike Camus and Sartre, whose existentialism offered an essentially humanist vision of individual freedom and responsibility, Bataille's and Blanchot's writings are considerably less upbeat. Bataille, briefly associated with the surrealist movement, probed the limits of both literary and philosophical boundaries by exploring pornography, violence, and excrement (see *The Bataille Reader*, ed. Fred Botting and Scott Wilson [Oxford: Blackwell, 1997] and *Georges Bataille: Core Cultural Theorist* by Paul Hegarty [London: Sage, 2000]). Blanchot's writings valorize literature for its anti-philosophical qualities. The literary, for Blanchot, is a space of extreme otherness, an interrogative challenge to traditional philosophical categories and to our understandings of, for instance, the nature of

9

death or of the human subject (see *The Station Hill Blanchot Reader: Fiction and Literary Essays* [Barrytown, NY: Station Hill, 1999]). Good discussions include *Blanchot: Extreme Contemporary* by Leslie Hill (London: Routledge, 1997) and *Maurice Blanchot: The Demand of Writing*, ed. Carolyn Bailey Gill (London: Routledge, 1996). Blanchot's work was influenced by that of his friend and colleague Emmanuel Levinas (1906–95), a philosopher whose emphasis on the ethics of otherness, and especially on the irreducible alterity of the other, has assumed a formative influence on debates about the ethics of literature and literary criticism. See Part IV for a fuller discussion.

There were several other successors to the existentialist tradition of French thought. Like Bataille and Blanchot, Maurice Merleau-Ponty (1908–61) found himself increasingly suspicious of Sartre's emphasis on individuality and liberty. His solution was to return to the phenomenological thought of Husserl and Heidegger from which existentialism had originated (see Part III). Merleau-Ponty's writings on the importance of the body and his rethinking of the phenomenology of interpretation and perception are coming to be appreciated as an important source for much contemporary critical thought on these subjects. Another return to phenomenology is evident in the thought of Paul Ricoeur (1913–2005), who revisited the questions of time and selfhood, and developed Husserl's and Heidegger's suggestion that the two notions are interrelated. Ricoeur's conclusion – that narrative is one of the fundamental forms of understanding, and that identities are constructed through narrative – has shaped a great deal of subsequent thought in both literary theory and philosophy (see his vast three-volume study *Time and Narrative*, trans. Kathleen McLaughlin and David Pellauer [Chicago: University of Chicago Press, 1984–88]).

Ultimately, however, the single most influential movement that succeeded Sartrean existentialism was structuralism, which came to dominate virtually all aspects of the humanities, from anthropology to psychology and from linguistics to film studies. Literary criticism was by no means exempt from its influence, which was particularly strong in the fields of narrative form and poetics. The structuralist analysis of narrative came to be known as narratology, and besides being a particularly sophisticated and ambitious application of structuralist methodology, it also drew on the philosophy of Ricoeur in exploring the extent to which narrative underwrites a vast range of forms of thought – such as the structures of philosophical systems, or of subjectivity itself – as much as it does literary texts. Good representatives of structuralist narratology include Gérard Genette's *Narrative Discourse* (trans. Jane E. Lewin. Oxford: Blackwell, 1980), Tzvetan Todorov's *The Poetics of Prose* (trans. Richard Howard. Oxford: Basil Blackwell, 1977), and the early works of Roland Barthes (1915–80). Strictly speaking, structuralism was not a philosophical movement: its origins lay in linguistics and communication theory. Nevertheless, its conceptual rigour and interdisciplinary methodology bear favourable comparison with those of many approaches derived from philosophy.

Both phenomenology and structuralism were crucial influences on what has arguably been the single most important current of thought in bridging the literature/philosophy divide – deconstruction. Jacques Derrida (1930–2004), whose views on language are developed in attentive readings of both literary and philosophical texts, has done more than anyone else to call the division between these two disciplines into question. His emphasis on aporia and paradox, his unearthing the traces of residual or poten-tial alternative meanings, and his diagnosis of *différance* – the apparently endless deferrals and differentiations inherent in signification – have clear and fruitful applications to literary study. Furthermore, by championing writing (as opposed to speech), and by approaching philosophy as a body of texts requiring scrupulously close reading (as opposed to a body of abstract thought), Derridean deconstruction introduced a new 'textualism' into tradi-tional philosophy. Deconstructive criticism, which soon spread to America and the 'Yale school', embraced Derrida's vision of undecidability, indeterm-inacy, and free play with the text. Its exponents, for instance Paul de Man (1919–83), deconstructed the works of philosophers such as Nietzsche or Rousseau as well as established works of literature. Rarely uncontroversial, deconstruction was one of the formative influences on contemporary literary theory, and simultaneously the *bête noire* of both traditional criticism and traditional philosophy during the so-called 'theory wars' of the 1980s. Since then, however, Derrida's work has continued to develop and to interrogate itself. His later works discuss themes related to ethics, responsibility, forgive-ness, morals, politics, and religion. For a discussion of these, see Herman Rapaport, *Later Derrida: Reading the Recent Work* (London: Routledge, 2003).

The reception of Derrida's ideas has opened the gates to a great deal of commerce between French philosophy and literary studies since the 1970s. The historical approach of Michel Foucault (1926–84), the vision of post-modernism set out by Jean-Francois Lyotard (1924–98), the notion of the disappearance of reality gnomically prophesied by Jean Baudrillard (1929–), and the stress on difference and desire in the rhizomatic thought of Gilles Deleuze (1925–95) have all made substantial and lasting impressions on the shape of literary theory and criticism. Indeed, it might seem as if French philosophy has been the mainstay of critical theory in recent times. This is not, however, because of any one overarching method or particularly incisive technique it has brought to the reading of literary texts. On the contrary, a variety of different emphases, nuances, and opinions abound, without any clear methodological consensus, and there is so little unity of approach that some might argue the very term 'French philosophy' suggests a coherent, canonical movement that is not borne out in actual practice. However, the ensuing breadth of outlook and diversity of approach has been one of the great strengths of French philosophy, and arguably the principal reason for the extent of its success in influencing so many aspects of literary studies. The most interesting and challenging of the many phases in the development of literary theory have been intimately wedded to developments in French thought over the past generation or so. More recently, the philosophies of Philippe Lacoue-Labarthe, Alain Badiou, and Jean-Luc Nancy have been mooted by some literary theorists as successors to this tradition.

The essays in this section chart the impact of various currents of French thought on the reading of literature. Anthony Larson opens the collection by considering some of the practical implications of the relationship between literature and philosophy in a world that appears to have ever less time and space for both. Taking F. Scott Fitzgerald's classic *The Great Gatsby* as an object lesson, he shows how Deleuze's work helps develop our understanding of this dynamic relationship. Derval Tubridy's essay provides an extensive survey of the broad diversity involved in French philosophy by comparing how a wide range of thinkers in this tradition have read the works of Samuel Beckett. The spectrum of opinion that arises in respect to this controversial writer conveys a good sense of the variety of perspectives that French thought has brought to bear on literature in recent times.

David Rudrum

1

First Lessons: Gilles Deleuze and the Concept of Literature

Anthony Larson

For students of literature – beginners or old hands – the obligatory detour through theory and philosophy has always been dangerous. This is not simply because of the importance that Continental thought and philosophy have assumed in the past forty years in literary studies; generations of readers had to maneuver through the philosophical influences of aesthetic theory, for example, before the arrival of Derrida and the philosophical tradition he represented. It is, rather, the negotiation between disciplines that makes this passage difficult. Tied to the beginner's question of why such a move through another discipline rather than one's own is the more practical one: how can philosophy say something about literature and vice versa? How can one tradition, with its concepts, problems and history possibly help us understand another? Framing the question in these terms – in terms of the question 'How?' – is a practical move. Such a manner of approaching the question might cause more than one reader to grimace, since, after all, from the point of view of the education world, practical questions seem always to be the best way to put an end to studies in literature and philosophy. So often, the practical question of students echoes that of their parents (who pay the bill for such practically minded students' education) and administrators: How can something as quaint as literature and philosophy be of any use to us today? How can we use literature and philosophy today when everything seems to point away from such disciplines and towards the means–end relationship of business? The danger in such an approach towards the question of philosophy and literature is one of the question itself putting an end to any possible further discussion. This would be misleading and an error.

From the very beginning of his work, with his study of the constitution of the subject in the work of Hume, to his last published essay on the consequences of situating thought on the plane of immanence, the work of Gilles Deleuze was always placed within a practical framework. For Deleuze, the work of philosophy was that of the creation of a concept – a concept that responded to a particular problem's set of questions. In this sense, philosophy endlessly asked the practical question 'How?' – How can we understand a particular problem through the creation of a concept or, to render the Nietzschean undertones of such an approach more explicit, 'Given a proposition, what is the mode of existence of s/he who pronounces it, what mode of existence must one have in order to be capable of pronouncing it?' (Deleuze, 2003, p. 188).[1] One of the places in which Deleuze exercised this particular form of practical philosophy was in literature itself and he was the author of book-length studies of Proust, Kafka, and Sacher-Masoch. However it is Deleuze's preoccupation with Anglo-American literature that perhaps best responds to our question of philosophy and literature and their practical use. As is well known, a chapter of his conversations with Claire Parnet in *Dialogues* is entitled 'On the Superiority of Anglo-American Literature', and the majority of authors treated in his last collection of texts dealing with literature (*Critique et clinique*) are Anglo-American.

At first glance, such a declaration regarding Anglo-American literature's superiority seems surprising. For if it is a certain open-ended, deterritorialized or schizophrenic writing that Deleuze is seeking then there are doubtless other traditions that produce the same style of writing (Proust and Kafka, for example, as well as the very rich and splendid Russian tradition). This however would be to misread Deleuze's use of the term 'Anglo-American literature', for he is not discussing a literary tradition in terms of literary history but in terms of a concept. For Deleuze, literature achieves a certain greatness when it exceeds closed, psychological, or personal narratives and opens itself up onto the endless conditions of its creation (what he calls the 'stuttering' of language). Literature which responds to this condition achieves the form of a concept since it responds to the problem of its own creation and in this sense the term 'Anglo-American literature' is no longer personal or historical but impersonal and conceptual.

If we think of literature in such conceptual and practical terms, then we are brought back to our original question concerning the interaction between philosophy and literature, for a conceptual reading of literature would teach us as much about philosophy as about literature and how we can use each of them today. And it is just this pedagogical aspect of the two disciplines which interests readers of this collection and gives this article its title. When speaking of philosophy and its relation to the concept, Deleuze and Félix Guattari underline the supremely pedagogical role of the concept:

If the three ages of the concept are that of the encyclopedia, pedagogy and professional training, only the second can prevent us from falling from the heights of the first into the absolute disaster of the third – an absolute disaster for thought whatever the given social benefits from the point of view of universal capitalism'. (Deleuze and Guattari, p. 17)

The hypothetical means–ends questions posed at the beginning of this article clearly belong to this third age of the concept but it will be my goal in the next few pages to take Deleuze at his word and apply a pedagogical reading of the concept of literature, to offer a practical lesson concerning literature and philosophy. To do so, I propose to make the task even more overtly practical and to treat a text often read and mis-read by beginning students of literature: F. Scott Fitzgerald's *The Great Gatsby*. By orienting what follows in such pedagogical and practical terms, I hope not only to be able to shed light on the particularly Deleuzian response to the question of philosophy and literature but also to be able to open literary texts up to some very practical and philosophical consequences.

The choice of Fitzgerald's text as an example is not by chance. He is often mentioned in Deleuze's texts on literature, most specifically the autobiographical essay on writing and alcoholism, *The Crack-Up*. When reading that text, it is not hard to see what attracted Deleuze since the piece opens with a discussion of how the small, almost molecular changes (in opposition to what Fitzgerald calls the 'big sudden blows') that occur in life are the greatest and most powerful changes. In addition, life is characterized there as an endlessly repeating process of 'breaking-down'. Yet this text is an essay and not part of Fitzgerald's collection of fiction. Following his definition of philosophy as the practical creation of concepts, Deleuze identifies one of the most important features of literature as its capacity to turn language into something else – to trace a language within language as a becoming-other of the major language. Quoting Proust, Deleuze declares, '[. . .] literature offers two aspects, to the extent that it operates a decomposition or destruction of the mother tongue, but also the invention of a new language in language, through the creation of a syntax' (Deleuze, 1993, p. 16). *The Great Gatsby* as a creation of fiction not only offers the occasion to examine the double movement of destruction/creation operated on language by the writer, but also, perhaps more importantly, presents a double appearance which serves as a key to our practically inspired Deleuzian investigation. This double appearance is evident from the very first pages of the novel and even from the title. When faced with the book for the first time, many readers are confronted by the odd declaration made by the narrator, Nick Carraway, concerning his previous year's experience with Gatsby: '[. . .] I wanted no more riotous excursions with privileged glimpses into the human heart. Only Gatsby, the man who gives his name to this book, was exempt from my reaction – Gatsby, who represented everything for which I have an unaffected scorn' (Fitzgerald, p. 8). Why, students ask, does Nick give such a contradictory description of Gatsby? Why is he 'great' if the narrator, opening the novel and looking back on his previous summer, already qualifies him as receiving his 'unaffected scorn'? This mystery only deepens as the reader advances in the novel, coming to the increasingly evident truth that Gatsby is a con man, a liar, and small-time gangster. As most critics of the novel have noted, this contradiction/tension is at the heart of the novel and is its driving force.[2]

I would advance the thesis that there are at least two truths in this novel. One is the truth of who Gatsby really is – Jay Gatz, a small-time dreamer from Minnesota. The other truth is that of the text itself, of the invention of Jay Gatsby and not so much of Gatsby's ability to maintain this illusion for himself but of the creation of dreams and/or characters themselves. This is the truth of Nick Carraway and the reason why, despite all evidence to the contrary, Nick loves Gatsby and serves to preserve the dream and not deflate it. The first truth belongs to Gatsby-the-name and the detective work of the reader, focused on finding out who Gatsby really is from Nick's betraying narration in the opening pages. The second truth belongs to Gatsby-the-text and the narrative work of the writer, pushed to the limit of his craft, caught between the dream glimpsed on the horizon, like the green island of Manhattan, and its failure on the preceding pages ('for a transitory enchanted moment man must have held his breath in the presence of this continent, compelled into an aesthetic contemplation he neither understood nor desired, face to face for the last time in history with something commensurate to his capacity for wonder' [Fitzgerald, p. 171] read the famous lines of one of the last paragraphs of the book).

The first truth is then that which leads the reader to consume the text, to find out who Gatsby really is and, consequently, to *judge* him. As Arnold Weinstein has remarked, the reader is almost dared into this critical act, of taking apart the dreams, lies, and illusions surrounding Gatsby in order to finally get at the terrible truth. In this sense, Fitzgerald's novel recalls its realist predecessors in that it sets out to pierce Gatsby's 'great expectations' in order to reach the book's lesson and teach us of 'lost illusions' (Weinstein, p. 132). Fiction, in this context, is used, practically, as a tool for revealing the truth about a world around us; the relationship between fiction and reality is reversed so that it is fiction which serves to better understand and read reality. In other words, Gatsby is read as a moral lesson on the excesses and failures of a certain America and the American dream itself. This is a very typical and even satisfying way of approaching the text and it is often where most readers and students stop.

However, there is a problem with this reading, for the text is the creation of one character: Nick Carraway. Nick is deciding exactly what to add and when, and what to subtract and when, and no amount of narrative trickery can hide this. He might dutifully report the speech and reaction of characters around him, but the number of qualifying statements such as 'I suppose', 'I suspect', or 'as if' quickly sap the power of his what appears to be an objective and realist narrative.[3] Thus, at a crucial point in the narration where Nick relates Gatsby's love for Daisy, his narrative art is telling in its weakness:

> Through all he said, even through his appalling sentimentality, I was reminded of something – an elusive rhythm, a fragment of lost words,

that I had heard somewhere a long time ago. For a moment a phrase tried to take shape in my mouth and my lips parted like a dumb man's, as though there was more struggling upon them than a wisp of startled air. But they made no sound, and what I had almost remembered was uncommunicable forever.[4] (Fitzgerald, p. 107)

In other words, the realist narrative technique that readers so often consume is an illusion and the entire reading strategy associated with this technique (centred on discovering who Gatsby is and, importantly, on *judging* him) is to read the book backwards. This is why the reader is puzzled by Nick's double-cutting declaration at the beginning of the novel, saying that Gatsby was exempt from his reaction to the world of East and West Egg extravagance but was also the one for whom he had 'unaffected scorn'. There are two paths that open in front of the reader: one follows the path of judgement, while the other follows the construction of Gatsby's 'greatness', which is the novel's greater truth.

Thus, one may indeed 'see through' Gatsby's lies, but it is not entirely certain that Nick 'sees' them as lies – or more precisely sees them as lies that must be 'seen through'. It would be fairer to say that Nick allows these lies to continue, that he becomes an accomplice in Gatsby's tales. Never does Nick actually confront Gatsby on his wealth or the impossible stories put together to support it, and this is an important point since Gatsby is Nick's story. Nick does not allow himself to make a final judgement of Gatsby, something he also warns the reader against doing on the opening page, quoting the words of advice offered by his father, 'Whenever you feel like criticizing anyone . . . just remember that all the people in this world haven't had the advantages that you've had', in order to come to the conclusion, 'Reserving judgements is a matter of infinite hope' (Fitzgerald, p. 7). Furthermore, just before making this interesting statement concerning judgement and infinite hope, Nick makes an even more revealing comment. Speaking of how this practice often attracted the confidences of a number of people, he underlines how these tales were often the 'intimate revelations of young men [the terms of which] are usually plagiaristic and marred by obvious suppressions' (Fitzgerald, p. 7) which leads one to wonder how much Nick suppresses from his tale of Gatsby and what the effect of these suppressions is. It seems that the hasty reader fills in these gaps, performing the critical equivalent of a boy who at the end of the tale scrawls an obscene word with a piece of brick on Gatsby's front steps. Tellingly, Nick erases it (see Fitzgerald, p. 171).

None of this is to say that the reader's suspicions should shift in turn from Gatsby to Nick but rather that the real sense or direction of the story is not one in which the reader peers through the lies towards truth but rather one in which those lies and, more crucially, beliefs are extended outwards. Nick is not the stand-in for the critical reader but the one who makes Gatsby 'great', the one who makes Gatsby's lie real. In this perspective, reality is no longer to be found by peering behind Gatsby's (or Nick's) stories but rather in their very invention and propagation, and this is why Gatsby himself takes on such a magnetizing appearance so often in the novel. It is in his endless capacity for invention, for drawing invention out of the narrator/reader that he is described by Nick:

> It was one of those rare smiles with a quality of eternal reassurance in it, that you may come across four or five times in life. It faced – or seemed to face – the whole eternal world for an instant, and then concentrated on *you* with an irresistible prejudice in your favour. It understood you just so far as you wanted to be understood, believed in you as you would like to believe in yourself, and assured you that it had precisely the impression of you that, at your best, you hoped to convey. (Fitzgerald, p. 49)

This, of course, refers not only to the character of Gatsby but also, and most importantly, to the tale itself, to Gatsby-the-work-of-art which the reader holds in her hands. To encounter Gatsby-the-character is to encounter the endless capacity for invention that is language.

It is at this point that a turn to Deleuze becomes fruitful. One of the recurrent ideas in Deleuze's texts is that literature is an 'affair of health'.[5] In other words, literature is the expression of the 'symptoms' of the world to which the writer (she who is afflicted with 'weak health') is especially capable of giving expression:

> Literature appears then as an undertaking in health: not that the writer is necessarily in good health [. . .] but that she/he enjoys an irresistibly weak health that comes from the fact that she/he has seen and heard things that are too great for her/him, too strong and stifling and whose transmission exhausts the writer while nonetheless giving her/him becomings that a dominating and strong constitution would render impossible. (Deleuze, 1993, p. 14)

Deleuze goes on to qualify this 'excessive' definition of literature as 'writing as fabulating' in the sense that the writer, by expressing something which had heretofore remained unexpressed, 'invents' or 'fabulates' a people-to-come, capable of seeing and hearing these things of which, for the moment, only the writer is capable (Deleuze, 1993, p. 14). In this sense, it is perhaps useful to return to the short excerpt cited earlier where a breakdown in Nick's narrative technique and the appearance of a different kind of writing in Fitzgerald's text was detected.

It is at this point in the text that the 'fabulating' function of the novel is laid bare insofar as one is confronted with the fact that this text is an invention that is as great or greater than Gatsby's. Here we go beyond the personal tale of Gatsby-the-character to what might be termed the 'impersonal' of the text itself, to a certain stuttering of language in that Nick hears something and tries to articulate it, only to lose it, so that what is expressed is only what cannot be expressed. This moment recalls Deleuze's reading of literature as an 'affair of health' and, more precisely, with the aforementioned Deleuzian concept of 'stuttering'. According to Deleuze, literature decomposes language to the extent that it invents a new syntax – a new language – within a language so that the entire linguistic system is brought up against its limits, '[. . .] an outside or flipside consisting in Visions and Sounds which are no longer of any language' (Deleuze, 1993, p. 16). Deleuze goes on to declare that these visions are not simply fantasies but rather Ideas that the writer sees and hears in the interstices of language itself (Deleuze, 1993, p. 16). The passing from one reading of Fitzgerald's text to another is exactly that passing which Deleuze describes as being so important in literature itself: 'It is a process, that is to say the passing of Life which traverses the liveable and the lived' (Deleuze, 1993, p. 11). One moves from a narrative (and a narrative strategy) that is based on a character and the personal, to a narrative that is based on textuality and the impersonal. Just as reading Fitzgerald's novel in order to determine who Gatsby is and to judge him is to read the text backwards, Deleuze affirms that to understand the 'fabulating function' of language as a substitute for the first or second person is a mistake, a reverse reading of literature. That is, the visions that characters see in texts elevate them to singular and impersonal appearances:

> Admittedly, literary characters are perfect individuals and are neither vague nor general, but all of their individual traits raise them to a vision which carries on into an undefined, like a becoming that is too powerful for them. [. . .] [T]he fabulating function does not consist in imagining or projecting an ego. Rather, it reaches these visions; it rises up to these becomings or powers. (Deleuze, 1993, p. 13)

A reading of this aspect of Fitzgerald's text as 'impersonal' and Deleuze's more precise evocation of the 'powers' of such a text finally allow us to take up the practical aspects of this particular text and this particular reading of literary texts.

Earlier I mentioned the Nietzschean overtones of a practically-oriented reading of literature and philosophy but the question of what mode of existence allows us to make certain propositions also contains hints of Spinoza. In his short study of Spinoza, importantly entitled *Spinoza: Philosophie pratique*, Deleuze examines the famous question of the body in the *Ethics*. He explains there that if one takes Spinoza at his word and understands the body, on the one hand, as an infinite collection of particles in movement and, on the other hand, as the power both to be affected by other bodies and to affect other bodies, the implications for thought are radical. No longer is a life conceived in terms of a form or of a subjective interiority but as a relation of acceleration and deceleration: one enters into relations that give more or less consistence to one's form; one slides between one body and another. Furthermore, this movement between bodies is conditioned by the power to affect and to be affected: one finds the right or wrong 'harmony' of movement depending on whether one affects and is affected positively or negatively (see Deleuze, 1981, pp. 165–6). In everyday terms, we enter into relations that strengthen our bodies (such as the fruitful intellectual stimulation of a work of philosophy or a loving relationship with another) just as we also enter into relations that diminish our bodies (such as a relationship in which one is exploited by another or a drug or alcohol addiction).

As Deleuze notes, an ontology of this sort poses a specific set of practical problems:

> How do individuals compose themselves in order to form a superior individual, infinitely? How may a being take another into her/his world while keeping and respecting each individual's own relations and world? And in this respect, for example, what are the different types of sociability? What is the difference between a society of men and a community of reasonable beings? (Deleuze, 1981, p. 169)

It is well known that in Spinoza these problems are solved in terms of cultivating joyful passions, particularly passions that allow one to contemplate God in the infinity of his being. As one passes through the different passions (moving from the sad passions that decompose relations to the relatively joyful passions of the body to the higher ones of the mind), one experiences different intensities as one 'extends' one's being and is filled with a greater and greater capacity for being affected and in turn actively affecting those around us. This intensity comes, in particular, from one's gradual liberation from all illusions that lead one to believe that there is always something *exterior to* or *outside of* the plane of life such as values of Good or Evil, sin, hatred, *ressentiment*, fear, despair, redemption, salvation, and even hope or security. These are the sad passions that separate one from life in that they serve as values from which one might judge life, and in this manner they are *transcendent* categories. For Spinoza and Deleuze, the task (and difficulty) of an ontology 'of the middle', of immanence, is that the process of composition must seize itself through itself and in itself without recourse to any 'supplemental' or transcendent category. Deleuze explains this difficult manoeuvre in terms of desire *à la* Spinoza: 'We must find a real definition of desire which shows at the same time the "cause" by which consciousness is carved, as it were, into the process of appetite' (Deleuze, 1981, p. 32). According to Spinoza, each being extends itself in an attempt at self-preservation, and this movement of self-preservation changes with the different bodies it encounters (enabling or disabling encounters). Objects or bodies with which one is capable of entering into relation allow one to form a greater and more adequate idea of the plane of being, just as bodies or objects with which one is incapable of entering into relation or which damage one's being reduce one's idea of the plane of being (see Deleuze, 1981, pp. 28–43, 164–75). Quite simply put, one becomes stronger or weaker according to what one encounters, and becoming stronger is always a moment of intensity while becoming weaker is a reduction in one's intensity of being.[6] The stakes of such a philosophy are in arriving at an idea of being that is adequate with its infinite parts.

Gatsby and the concept of literature that he represents allow us to take a step in that direction, by passing through a first and naïve reading of the text that turns around discovering the truth about Gatsby to a second reading that focuses on how Gatsby's own lies or inventions are linked to the greater enterprise of writing as an invention or lie. In this movement, one gains a greater and more adequate idea of the relation not only between two bodies in the text, Gatsby-the-character and Gatsby-the-text, but also between oneself and life. Fitzgerald's text offers an odd echo to Deleuze's praise for Spinoza's *Ethics*. For Deleuze, part of the greatness of Spinoza's thesis is how it works at two levels: one, the 'geometrical' proof that builds slowly to its conclusion, and another, the scholia attached to the proofs which openly and violently hammer at religion and Cartesian philosophy. Together, they flow into one another, each adding to the intensity of the other.[7] In the same way, there are two texts, two intensities, at work in *The Great Gatsby*. The first is in the grasp of transcendence: a value of truth or morality guides the reader as she make a judgement concerning Gatsby and his lies. The second pushes the logic of Gatsby's lies and fabulations to their limits, so that the lies and fabulations of the first fold into the second, increasing the power of both (one realizes that the first reading is not only a reading of Gatsby-the-character but also that of Gatsby-the-text, and vice versa). The passage between Gatsby-the-character and Gatsby-the-impersonal-text gives one a glimpse of a greater and more adequate idea of life and this is perhaps the most difficult but most practical aspect of such a conceptual reading of (Anglo-American) literature. Just as importantly, it is the practical reason for continuing to read and write literature.

This final declaration might conceal an echo of unpractical optimism but there are some very important implications for such a reading or use of literature. If we are to take such a concept of literature seriously then our task is to search out conceptual encounters that strengthen our being instead of diminishing it. We are called, quite literally, to follow Nick Carraway in his habit of reserving judgement, 'a habit that has opened up many curious natures to me and also made me the victim of not a few veteran bores' (Fitzgerald, p. 7). Ethically and politically, the consequences of such a 'mode of life' or disposition are fundamental. If one is constantly 'reserving judgement', in an attempt to extend and amplify one's being, then one is constantly situating oneself in what Nietzsche would call the 'untimely' and what Deleuze, following Foucault, terms the '*actuel*'. That is, intensive 'increases' in one's being reveal new ways of thinking of oneself and of the world, ways that were unthinkable before coming into contact with a new body. As Deleuze and Guattari explain,

> When Foucault admires Kant for posing the problem of philosophy not in terms of the eternal but in terms of the Now, he means to say philosophy is not meant to contemplate the eternal nor to reflect on history but to diagnose our actual becomings: a becoming-revolutionary that, according to Kant himself, is not to be confused with the past, the present or the future of revolutions. A becoming-democratic that is not to be confused with the State of law [. . .]. (Deleuze and Guattari, pp. 107–8)

'Reserving judgement' is a resolutely political and ethical posture that demands that one worry less about judging and more about positioning oneself in order to actively extend one's ability in the most positive way.[8] Yet it is in just this perspective, of being able to see how even in the most reprehensible of bodies the 'seeds' of immanence and the errors of transcendence are present, that reserving judgement can be a practical ethical and political practice. Every body, every encounter, carries with it a capacity to change our present situation, and the practical use of literature and philosophy is to situate ourselves in such a way that positive change can be possible. Admittedly, this is a rather optimistic conclusion to our study of American literature, and in this context it rings a little like the inevitable happy ending that is relentlessly forced down our throats in American popular culture. Nothing, of course, guarantees such an optimistic outcome. Indeed, many long pages in Deleuze's study of de- and re-territorialization are devoted to the dangerous 'black holes' of negative and debilitating encounters, distant cousins to Nick Carraway's 'veteran bores'. I must insist, however, on the infinite hope that is so characteristic not only of American literature and this particularly American text but of the concept of literature and the immanence activating it. This is the entire point of Deleuze's short essay on immanence and life published shortly before his death: transcendence is always the product of immanence and our task is to re-introduce immanence back into transcendence, to read Gatsby, as it were, correctly and actively (see Deleuze, 1995, esp. pp. 4–6). Literature and philosophy, when taken through this particular Deleuzian lens, fold back into one another, lifting each to an intensity, a strength, that was not present in either alone. Calling on us to be resolutely aware of our 'deployment' in being and open to encounters that increase our idea of immanence, this practical use of literature and philosophy is eminently active.

Notes

1. When citing Deleuze, page numbers and texts will refer to the original French editions, and translations from the French are mine.
2. Two excellent studies of Fitzgerald's novel are to be found in Tony Tanner, *The American Mystery: American Literature from Emerson to DeLillo* (Cambridge: Cambridge University Press, 2000), pp. 166–200, which also serves as the 'Introduction' in the Penguin 1990 edition of *The Great Gatsby*; and Arnold Weinstein, *Nobody's Home: Speech, Self, and Place in American Fiction from Hawthorne to DeLillo* (Oxford: Oxford University Press, 1993).
3. Tanner counts over 60 occurrences of 'as if' in addition to 'possibly', 'probably', 'perhaps', or 'he seemed to say'. See Tanner, p. 176.
4. This passage, obviously, should be placed in relation to the final paragraphs of the novel.
5. Although references to literature abound in his philosophical texts, the collection *Critique et Clinique* offers some of Deleuze's finest writing on literature, in particular, the opening essay 'La Littérature et la Vie'. The quotes which follow are from this essay. Echoes of the themes evoked in this essay may be found not only in *Dialogues*, but also throughout *Qu'est-ce que la philosophie?* and its chapter on 'Percept, Affect et Concept' (pp. 154–88).
6. It is striking the number of times 'intensity' appears in Fitzgerald's novel, especially in relation to Gatsby himself (often linked to descriptions of his persona or his smile) or Daisy. When one considers what Daisy represents for Gatsby, and the importance that her vision holds in our elaboration above of a Deleuzian concept of literature, this discovery comes as no surprise.
7. See Deleuze, 1981, p. 170, and Deleuze, 1968, pp. 313–22 ('Appendice: Etude formelle du plan de l'*Ethique* et du rôle des scolies dans la réalisation de ce plan: Les deux ethiques').
8. On the history and error of judgment, see Deleuze's *Présentation de Sacher-Masoch* (Paris: Minuit, 1967), pp. 71–9, the chapter entitled 'La loi, l'humour, l'ironie.' Many of the arguments presented there are taken up again and modified with a more overt influence from Spinoza and Nietzsche in the essay entitled 'Pour en finir avec le jugement' in *Critique et clinique*, pp. 158–69.

Works cited

Deleuze, Gilles, *Présentation de Sacher-Masoch* (Paris: Minuit, 1967).
——*Spinoza et le problème de l'expression* (Paris : Minuit, 1968).
——*Spinoza: Philosophie pratique* (Paris: Minuit, 1981).
——*Critique et clinique* (Paris: Minuit, 1993).
——'Immanence: une vie . . .' in *Philosophie*, no. 47 (Paris: Minuit, September 1995).
——'Préface pour l'édition américaine de *Nietzsche et la philosophie*' in *Deux régimes de fous, Textes et entretiens 1975–1995*, ed. David Lapoujade (Paris: Minuit, 2003).
Deleuze, Gilles and Félix Guattari, *Qu'est-ce que la philosophie?* (Paris: Minuit, 1991).
Fitzgerald, F. Scott, *The Great Gatsby* (London: Penguin, 1980).
Tanner, Tony, *The American Mystery: American Literature from Emerson to DeLillo* (Cambridge: Cambridge University Press, 2000).
Weinstein, Arnold, *Nobody's Home: Speech, Self, and Place in American Fiction from Hawthorne to DeLillo* (Oxford: Oxford University Press, 1993).

2
'The Absence of Origin': Beckett and Contemporary French Philosophy

Derval Tubridy

In 1964 Ruby Cohn remarked that 'when Beckett turned from English to French as a writing language, his protagonists turned from a kind of Logical Positivism to a kind of Existentialism' (Cohn, 1964, p. 175). The landscape of Beckett criticism has changed considerably since the 1960s, yet there remains for critics a productive tension in Beckett's work between the empiricist underpinning of Anglo-American analytic philosophy and the more phenomenologically orientated philosophy characteristic of the European continent. The shift that Cohn identifies in Beckett's work runs parallel with the writer's move away from the anxiety regarding the relationship between language and the world that we see particularly in the novel *Watt*, to a greater exploration of the subject that inhabits that world, an exploration given powerful expression in the subsequent trilogy *Molloy, Malone Dies*, and *The Unnamable*. With his increasing focus on the nature of subjectivity, albeit a subjectivity in dissolution, Beckett interrogates the relation between the subject and the body that gives it a place within the impoverished yet enduring world that he has made his own.

Beckett's philosophical background was informed by the writings of René Descartes, Arnold Geulincx, George Berkeley, Arthur Schopenhauer, and Fritz Mauthner. Through these thinkers Beckett explored his attitude to language and to the speaking subject. In turn, Beckett's writing has had significant impact on the development of contemporary thought, particularly in France, where Beckett made his home. The relationship between contemporary French philosophy and Beckett's writing is one of profound influence. Philosophers such as Maurice Blanchot, Gilles Deleuze, Jean-François Lyotard, and Alain Badiou have developed their thought within a context informed by Beckett's writing, and have written perceptively on his prose and drama. Other philosophers have been influenced by Beckett, but have not engaged directly with his writing. In *Acts of Literature*, Jacques Derrida explains that because he feels so close to Beckett, indeed identifies with the author, he has sought to avoid writing directly on him:

> [Beckett] is an author to whom I feel very close, or to whom I would like to feel myself very close; but also too close. Precisely because of this proximity, it is too hard for me, too easy and too hard. (Derrida, 1992b, p. 60)

Critics such as Steven Connor, Leslie Hill, Carla Locatelli, Simon Critchley, and David Watson have elaborated rich and productive readings of Beckett through the philosophies of Deleuze, Blanchot, and Derrida. This work is continued by the criticism of Mary Bryden, Lois Oppenheim, Richard Begam, Anthony Uhlmann, and Andrew Gibson, who have demonstrated the importance of contemporary French philosophy, including the work of Lyotard and Badiou, for our readings of Beckett. Recent publications on Beckett and philosophy include Richard Lane's collection *Beckett and Philosophy* which includes essays that explore Beckett's work in the context of German and French thought, and Lois Oppenheim's collection *Samuel Beckett Studies* which includes a cogent and succinct overview of poststructuralist engagement with Beckett's work, 'Poststructuralist Readings of Beckett', by Leslie Hill.

This chapter examines the productive relationship between literature and philosophy, tracing the key ideas that inform Beckett's work and the ways in which these ideas are central to the French philosophy that developed in Beckett's wake. Forged within a similar cultural nexus, both writer and philosophers pursue questions of epistemology and ontology within an exploration of the nature and function of language. Rather than providing an overview of the philosophical terrain (one that has been excellently mapped in Lane's and Oppenheim's editions) I will focus on a particular topography by arguing that both Beckett and key French thinkers such as Deleuze, Lyotard, Derrida, Blanchot, and Badiou seek to establish an understanding of subjectivity that takes into consideration the somatic and contingent within the context of writing. My analysis will concentrate primarily on readings of *Watt, The Unnamable,* and *Company.*

Beckett's writing explores and embodies the problematics of language conceived as a differential, abstract structure. He develops a distinctive literature which destabilizes language and conflates meaning with manifestation. Gilles Deleuze has responded to Beckett's work on a number of occasions. His praise for Beckett's only venture into film-making, 'The Greatest Irish Film (Beckett's "Film"), analyzes Beckett's engagement with Berkeley's argument that to be is to be perceived (*esse est percipi*) through a cinema characterized by 'action, perception, and affection' (Deleuze, 1998, p. 26). Most significant for Deleuze, however, is Beckett's use of language and the ways in which he complicates the relation between language and reality.

In his essay 'He Stuttered', Deleuze takes Beckett's novel *Watt* as an example of a literary work in which 'the transfer from the form of expression to the form of the content has been completed' (Deleuze, 1994, p. 26). Deleuze cites the mathematical permutations in *Watt* as an example of Beckett's 'art of the inclusive disjunction', an art which 'no longer chooses but rather affirms the disjointed terms in their distance and, without limiting or excluding one disjunct by means of another, it criss-crosses and runs through the entire gamut of possibilities' (Deleuze, 1994, p. 26). The reverse transition from the form of the content to the form of the expression whereby 'people speak as they walk or stumble' (Deleuze, 1994, p. 26) is completed in *Watt* for 'As Watt walked, so now he talked, back to front' (Beckett, 1981, p. 162). Deleuze argues persuasively that it is only a disequilibriated language like Beckett's that can incorporate such inclusive permutations, a language in which '*disjunctions become included and inclusive and connections become reflexive* on the basis of a rolling gait that affects the process of language and no longer the flow of discourse' (Deleuze, 1994, p. 26). The rolling gait with which the protagonist Watt approaches Mr Knott's house (Beckett, 1981, p. 28) is emulated by Beckett's writing so that 'it is as if the entire language had begun to roll from left to right, and to toss from back to front' (Deleuze, 1994, p. 26). In Mr Knott's house Watt's control over the conventional structure of language breaks down. His speech undergoes a fundamental change as grammar and syntax are disregarded. The phonetic subtleties of pronunciation and enunciation are subsumed beneath a flow of speech '*at once* so rapid and so slow' (Beckett, 1981, p. 154). The linguistic transformation of Watt's speech intensifies towards the end of this novel until language itself begins 'to vibrate and to stutter' (Deleuze, 1994, p. 24). The formal organization of language disintegrates and since 'syntax is constituted by means of the curves, links, bends, and deviations of this dynamic line as it passes by positions with a double perspective on disjunctions and on connections', Deleuze concludes that

> It is no longer the formal or superficial syntax that presides over the equilibrium of language, but syntax in the process of becoming, a veritable creation of a syntax that gives birth to a foreign language within language and a grammar of disequilibrium. (Deleuze, 1994, p. 27)

In *Watt*, Beckett begins to subject language to the kind of stress that leads to a progressive and creative disorganization. He starts with a series of permutations, such as the 12 possibilities of Mr Knott's dinner arrangements (Beckett, 1981, p. 86) or the wonderful passage on human sexuality:

> Not that it is by any means impossible for a man to be both a man's man and a woman's man, or for a woman to be both a woman's woman and a man's woman, almost in the same breath. For with men and women,

with men's men and women's men, with men's women and women's women, with men's and women's men, with men's and women's women, all is possible, as far as can be ascertained, in this connexion. (Beckett, 1981, p. 138)

This breathless passage approaches the condition described above by Deleuze as 'the art of the inclusive disjunction' (Deleuze, 1994, p. 26). Though it explores the possible positions of each linguistic element, this passage still maintains the position of each relative to the other. It conserves the structure of elements through which sense is produced, a structure which is, as Deleuze explains in *The Logic of Sense*, 'a machine for the production of incorporeal sense' (Deleuze, 1990, p. 71). In the latter part of this novel Beckett moves towards a more complex series of permutations in which the inner structure of each linguistic element is subject to recombination. These linguistic contortions strain the thin line of sense that separates the corporeal from the incorporeal. The language of *Watt* is, for Deleuze, 'the nonsense of the word devoid of sense, which is decomposed into phonetic elements' (Deleuze, 1990, p. 90). It retains the ability to separate the 'pure "expressed" of words' and the 'logical attribute of bodies' (Deleuze, 1990, p. 91). Although resulting from 'the actions and passions of the body' it differs in nature, being neither action nor passion (Deleuze, 1990, p. 91). Most importantly, it continues to prevent confusion between sonorous language and the physical body. Though it does not possess any particular meaning, this nonsense is opposed to the absence of meaning, it is 'that which has no sense, and that which, as such and as it enacts the donation of sense, is opposed to the absence of sense' (Deleuze, 1990, p. 71). This sense about which Deleuze speaks is not a 'Principle, Reservoir, Reserve' or 'Origin' (Deleuze, 1990, p. 72) which must be rediscovered or restored. It is something 'to produce by a new machinery', something which 'belongs to no height or depth, but rather to a surface effect, being inseparable from the surface which is its proper dimension' (Deleuze, 1990, p. 72).

Through the eyes of Watt's interlocutor Sam we witness the development of a foreign language within language as Watt dislocates linguistic rules and conventions while he advances backwards through the undergrowth of Mr Knott's garden, responding to Sam's cry of concern with the rather disconcerting retort: 'Not it is, yes' (Beckett, 1981, p. 157). This short phrase causes Sam 'more alarm, more pain, than if [he] had received, unexpectedly, at close quarters, a charge of small shot in the ravine' (Beckett, 1981, p. 157). It would seem from this and previous examples that Watt's language has deteriorated into nonsense. The appropriate sounds are still intact, but Watt's disregard for the basic elements of semantic organization would suggest that his speech has become meaningless, as this response indicates, 'ot bro, lap rulb, krad klub' (Beckett, 1981, p. 163). However this is not necessarily so. While at first Watt's sounds are 'devoid of significance' (Beckett, 1981, p. 163) for Sam, gradually they begin to make sense, as he explains how 'soon I grew used to these sounds, and then I understood as well as before, that is to say a great part of what I heard' (Beckett, 1981, p. 163). This pattern of incomprehension and understanding is repeated as Watt processes through eight stages of permutation:

> This further modification Watt carried through with all his usual discretion and sense of what was acceptable to the ear, and aesthetic judgment. Nevertheless to one, such as me, desirous above all of information, the change was not a little disconcerting. (Beckett, 1981, p. 163)

Linguistic communication as a continuous, dynamic process makes possible the dialogue between the characters of Sam and Watt in the latter part of the novel. Watt presents Sam with an initially unintelligible phrase. Sam can choose to ignore or respond to that phrase. Either way, Sam is required to engage with the phrase, to recognize the other even if it is to recognize the radical alterity of the other. This interactive view of language, in which a phrase is something to engage with rather than grasp, is discussed by Jean-François Lyotard in his study *The Differend*. Lyotard proposes a view of language somewhat similar to Wittgenstein's language game. For Lyotard, the elemental unit of an analysis of language is the phrase, which cannot be doubted, 'What escapes doubt is that there is at least one phrase, [. . .]. *There is no phrase* is a phrase' (Lyotard, 1988, p. 65). The phrase cannot be ignored for 'it is necessary to link onto a phrase that happens (be it by silence, which is a phrase), there is no possibility of not linking onto it' (Lyotard, 1988, p. 29). Within this context we understand how Sam must respond to Watt's utterances, even if this response is silence. But the novel allows for no predetermined response. There are no rules of the game, as Lyotard explains, 'to link is necessary; how to link is contingent' (Lyotard, 1988, p. 29). The importance of Lyotard's work for a reading of Beckett lies in his recognition of the necessity of language while dislocating the structure of language. While critics such as Watson and Hill situate Beckett's writing in an impasse caused by its continuous impulse to move beyond language within language, a reading of Beckett through Deleuze and Lyotard makes it possible to argue that the dissolution of a structured discursive language that Beckett effects in his writing does not imply the dissolution of language. On the contrary, it transforms language into a dynamic pragmatics the focus of which is not the transmission of a preexistent meaning, but the development of linguistic interaction which requires the recognition of the other.

In *Watt* Beckett interrogates this concept of language, forcing his protagonist beyond that unitary shared structure in order to, as Beckett writes in his 1937 letter to Axel Kaun, 'get at the things (or the Nothingness) behind it' (Beckett, 1983, p. 171). Watt's passage through Mr Knott's house traces the disintegration of the notion of language as a shared structure of conventions. In *Watt* the separation of sounds from bodies necessary for language is undone. On the ground floor of Mr Knott's house, language loses its powers of designation, manifestation, and signification. On the first floor, the distinction between the linguistic and the physical is blurred. The moment Watt enters Mr Knott's house, his language 'is stripped of its sense, its *phonetic elements* become singularly wounding. The word no longer expresses an attribute of the state of affairs; its fragments merge with unbearable sonorous qualities' (Deleuze, 1990, p. 88). Here, language as a differential, abstracted structure is reincorporated into the physical. The constituents of differentiation – the sentences, words, and syllables – break free from their allocated places within the language. The line of sense which separates propositions from things is erased and a causal connection between the word and the thing is established. The abstract linguistic or semiotic machine breaks down and Watt is faced with a choice: he can either recover meaning, or destroy the word (Deleuze, 1990, p. 88). The former involves an alliance with structure and differentiation; existence on the surface where sound is separated from the body and organized into propositions (Deleuze, 1990, p. 181). The latter transforms 'the word into an action by rendering it incapable of being decomposed and incapable of disintegrating' (Deleuze, 1990, p. 89). It is language without articulation, without differentiation, what Deleuze calls the language of depth. With *Watt* Beckett effects the disintegration of language as an abstract differential structure and indicates a line of development that works towards a use of language which includes the somatic and material aspects of language, and locates the linguistic instance within the particular rather than the abstract.

Watt signals Beckett's development of what Deleuze and Guattari call a 'minor literature'. In this novel Beckett begins to write in a minor language, a language made foreign within itself, a language that flees from any constant relationship of linguistic variables. A minor language makes the major language vibrate, placing it in a state of continuous variation 'as in music, where the minor mode refers to dynamic combinations in a state of perpetual disequilibrium' (Deleuze, 1994, p. 25). This disequilibriated language subverts the major language while subsisting within it. *Watt* marks the beginning of Beckett's movement towards a literature that engages with the material as well as the abstract nature of language. It is a literature which, in Lyotard's terms, incorporates the figural within the discursive, at times privileging the graphic and sonic aspect of language over the significatory aspect. However, this prioritization of the material over the structural aspects of language serves to problematize issues of subjectivity and translation which are central to language and meaning, and fundamental to Beckett's work.[1]

Deleuze refines his approach to Beckett's use of language in a later work, 'The Exhausted', by dividing Beckett's language into three categories that describe the writer's development. Language I is a language of names in which 'enumeration replaces propositions and combinatorial relations replace syntactic relations' (Deleuze, 1998, p. 156). This language, for Deleuze, characterizes Beckett's early work, particularly novels like *Molloy* and *Watt*. Language II is a language of voices rather than names, 'a language that no longer operates with combinable atoms but with blendable flows' (Deleuze, 1998, p. 156). This is the language of Beckett's middle period, beginning with *The Unnamable* and its concern with the exhaustion of words, the attainment of silence. Deleuze proposes that 'to exhaust the possible in this new sense, the problem of exhaustive series must be confronted anew, even if it means falling into an "aporia"' (Deleuze, 1998, p. 157). The third category of language, Language III, is 'no longer a language of names or voices but a language of images' (Deleuze, 1998, p. 159). These images occupy a non-significatory space which prioritizes the material aspect of the word poised between voice and silence. Echoing Olga Bernal's characterization of Beckett's writing as a '*chute hors du langage*' (Bernal, pp. 17–30), Deleuze describes this third language as an 'outside of language' (Deleuze, 1998, p. 160). The paradox of a silence made possible through speech is an aporia that animates much of Beckett's work. Such a silence carries with it a notion of necessary engagement for, as Lyotard emphasizes in *The Differend*, silence is also a phrase which carries the same ethical demands for response (Lyotard, 1988, p. 29). However, the condition of Beckett's silence is also an impossibility since, in John Cage's words, there 'is no such thing as an empty space or an empty time. There is always something to see, something to hear. In fact, try as we may to make a silence, we cannot' (Cage, p. 8).

As Deleuze underlines in 'The Exhausted', the risks of falling into aporia are never more apparent than in *The Unnamable*. The novel is characterized by a rhetoric of paradox and aporia centered on the interrelationship between speech and silence which invokes notions of duty and passage. In *The Other Heading*, Derrida uses the term 'aporia' for a duty which duplicates and negates itself, 'a double, contradictory imperative' (Derrida, 1992a, p. 79). The imperative about which Derrida writes in his study *Aporias* 'puts to test a *passage*, both an impossible and a necessary passage, and two apparently heterogeneous borders' (Derrida, 1993, p. 17). Beckett's aporia is an imperative which involves the passage of language between differential structure and visceral force, a passage which is at once impossible and obligatory. The pensum with which the unnamable has been charged requires him to speak in order to be silent. It requires that 'in this churn of words' (Beckett, 1975, p. 27) he find something, some truth, that has not been said before. It is an epistemological challenge centered on identity in which the speaker must establish 'what I am, where I am, whether I am words among words, or silence in the midst of silence' (Beckett, 1975, p. 106). Words and silence form the boundaries inside which the unnamable tries to 'reconstitute the right lesson' (Beckett, 1975, p. 27). They trace the lines of passage from which the unnamable speaks.

The aporia that Beckett explores in *The Unnamable* can be understood through Derrida, who argues that it is 'not necessarily a failure or a simple paralysis, the sterile negativity of the impasse. It is neither stopping at it nor overcoming it' (Derrida, 1993, p. 32). This aporetic text takes as its point of departure the realization that the abstract systematic structure of language which underwrites meaning and subjectivity is no longer tenable. The opening statement, 'Where now? Who now? When now? Unquestioning. I, say I. Unbelieving', at once affirms the necessity and impossibility of establishing the coordinates of location, identity, and time within a language in which the value of the term depends entirely on the other terms in the system (Beckett, 1975, p. 7). The speaker says 'I', unbelieving, for the first-person pronoun does not have any value in itself within such a system of language. It is only in the act of enunciation that the deictic signifier can operate, and it does so by providing a point of passage between virtual signification and actual designation. This movement from signification to designation disrupts the containment of language and threatens the stability of subjectivity. It is a passage at once necessary and impossible, for in order to posit oneself as a subject one must say 'I', but the very enunciation of this deictic pierces the virtual plane of language and introduces the particular contingencies of location, identity, and time which depend on the body in space.

The aporia about which the unnamable speaks is a duty to transgress the borders between word and world. Yet it is an impossible duty, for in so doing he dismantles the discrete structure upon which his subjectivity is founded. The passage between the virtual and the actual is 'the difficult or the impracticable [...] the impossible passage, the refused, denied, or prohibited passage' (Derrida, 1993, p. 8). It is a passage which threatens the subjectivity of the unnamable and which can only be refused by a rejection of the 'I' which marks its point of entry. But this passage is also a 'nonpassage, which can in fact be something else, the event of a coming' (Derrida, 1993, p. 8). This something else is the opening up of language to the conditions of its emergence. It is the inclusion of the corporeal with the linguistic; an acknowledgement of the inextricability of the visceral and the abstract without which speech and subjectivity are impossible: 'in the midst of silence, its great swell rears towards me, I'm streaming with it, it's an image, those are words, it's a body, it's not I, I knew it wouldn't be I, I'm not outside, I'm inside' (Beckett, 1975, p. 128). It is only when those two poles of aporia, silence and speech, are joined that the unnamable can speak of location, identity, and resolution:

> in the end I'll recognise it, the story of the silence that he never left, that I should never have left, that I may never find again, that I may find again, then it will be he, it will be I, it will be the place, the silence, the end, the beginning [...]. (Beckett, 1975, p. 131)

Maurice Blanchot's influential article on Beckett 'Where now/ Who now?' (1953) brings the questions raised by *The Unnamable* to the heart of literature itself. Conflating author and narrator, Blanchot focuses on the impossibility of authorship arguing that

> the man who writes is already no longer Samuel Beckett but the necessity which has displaced him, [. . .] which has made him a nameless being, The Unnamable, a being without being, who can neither live nor die, neither begin nor leave off, the empty site in which an empty voice is raised without effect, masked for better or worse by a porous and agonizing *I*. (Blanchot, 2000, p. 97)

Blanchot explores the aporetic situation presented by Beckett's writing through the idea of origin which, as Gary Banham explains, 'is the space of the middle between words and world. This space opens and the divide or cut which is experienced through the word as creating the world speaks and says *I*' (Banham, p. 60).

Beckett's late novel *Company* explores the origin of writing. It seeks to reach that point before the artifices of character and story, that point before even the very voice which allows writing to speak. But this movement toward the origin is an impossibility because, as Maurice Blanchot explores in *The Infinite Conversation*, 'the origin itself, excluding in its unrecoverable anteriority all that is born of it, is, not being, but rather what turns away from it – the harsh breach of the void out of which everything arises and into which everything sinks and gives way' (Blanchot, 1993, p. 404). Blanchot's conception of the origin depends upon a repetition and impossibility which is characteristic of Beckett's writing. It is an origin which separates birth and death only by the harsh breach which is life. This breach is described in *Waiting for Godot* by a furious Pozzo who exclaims, 'They give birth astride of a grave, the light gleams an instant, then it's night once more' (Beckett, 1990, p. 83). The origin is conceived by Blanchot as the center which is 'the absence of any center, since it is there that the thrust of all unity comes to be shattered: in some sense the non-center of non-unity' (Blanchot, 1993, p. 404). However, this non-center and non-unity does not cancel out the center and unity, nor does it abolish the origin. Instead, it describes a tension between the absence and presence of these impossible poles, which maintains the origin 'under the harsh interrogation of the absence of origin, which, as soon as the origin poses as the cause, the reason, and the word for the enigma, immediately deposes it and speaks a more profound enigma: the Arising that, as such, sinks down, is engulfed and swallowed up' (Blanchot, 1993, p. 404). This 'harsh interrogation' is played out in Beckett's dramatic works *Play*, *Not I*, and *What Where*. It is the demand that the story be told, the insistence that there is something to tell, the search for 'what' and 'where', all of which will never be realized. Beckett's writing traces the light which gleams an instant, before interminable dark.

Like the words in *Watt* which empty themselves of signification, the words with which this fable is told are 'inane' (Beckett, 1992, p. 51). Whereas the speaker of *The Unnamable* is all words, made of words, the speaker of *Company* seeks the end of words in order, finally, to be alone, to be the singular 'I':

> With every inane word a little nearer to the last. And how the fable too. The fable of one with you in the dark. The fable of one fabling of one with you in the dark. And how better in the end labour lost and silence. And you as you always were. Alone. (Beckett, 1992, pp. 51–2)

But this solitude can only be achieved through words, and indeed, the one who is 'alone' is never alone for there is still, in this last passage of *Company*, a voice which speaks. The 'you' who hears 'how words are coming to an end' is still in the company of the one who speaks those words. The word 'Alone' which announces the solitude of the figure is spoken by another, thereby introducing company. The solitude and silence which the 'I' of Beckett's writing always seeks is an impossibility for, as Blanchot emphasizes, the act of writing makes an other of the 'I': 'to write is to pass from "I" to "he"' (Blanchot, 1993, p. 380). The narrative 'he' marks the intrusion of the other. *Company* seeks to abolish the intrusion of the 'he'. It tries to join the 'you' of the voice with the 'he' of the figure through the utterance of the 'I' in the act of remembrance: 'I remember' (Beckett, 1992, p. 28). To reach the 'I' is to reach the origin of the fable, the point from which the story starts. This point is also the silence which all of Beckett's narrators seek. But writing can never abolish the multiplicity of the 'I' and the other, for it is only through this distinction between the 'I' and that which is other to the 'I' that the act of narration can emerge. Once again, as Leslie Hill points out, the words of *Company* are 'attributed to another, to a voice that cannot be made present and which disperses into a multiplicity of idiom from which unity, in the shape of the first-person pronoun, has been removed, detached, subtracted' (Hill, 1990, p. 160). The narrative voice of *Company* is the voice which in the very act of speaking becomes other. It 'has no place in the work', speaking only from a 'kind of void in the work' (Blanchot, 1993, p. 385). This is the same void from which the narrator of *The Unnamable* speaks, 'Two holes [. . .]. Or a single one, entrance and exit, where the words swarm and jostle like ants, [. . .]' (Beckett, 1975, p. 72), and again, 'there must be a hole for the voices' (Beckett, 1975, p. 76). The origin of writing is this void, and from it comes 'the narrative voice, a neutral voice that speaks the work from out of this place without a place, where the work is silent' (Blanchot, 1993, p. 385).

Alain Badiou's work on Beckett picks up traces of Deleuze's and Blanchot's thought. Echoing both philosophers, Badiou argues that the role of the voice in Beckett's writing 'is to track down – by way of a great deal of fables, narrative fictions, and concepts – the pure point of enunciation' (Badiou, p. 52). The movement of Beckett's voice is dual: it proliferates (as we have seen in *Watt*), or it exhausts itself (as we see toward the end of *The Unnamable*, and *Company*) – 'it stammers, repeats itself, inventing nothing' (Badiou, p. 52). For Badiou, Beckett's writing is characterized by the substitution of 'the question "how are we to name what happens?" for the question "what is the meaning of what is?" ' (Badiou, p. 55). This shift, from the kind of hermeneutic anxiety that we find in *Watt* to a broader engagement with ontological questions as they center around the dilemma of the name (which gains particular focus in *The Unnamable*), is explained by Badiou in terms of what he describes as the event. What happens in Beckett for Badiou is a 'supernumerary, incalculable, indiscernible, undecidable event – irreducible to all established protocols of being, nameable only as something ill seen and ill said, of which all that can be said is missaid' (Hill, 2004, p. 81). Resisting both presentation and representation, the event inaugurates a process of subtraction that approaches the singularity of the name, but is limited by unnamability: it 'becomes possible as a Beckettian process of repudiation, denial and *ascesis* moves towards its completion' (Gibson, 2002, p. 100). Blanchot's non-center or non-unity can be understood also in terms of Badiou's idea of the void which, as Andrew Gibson argues, is closely linked with the idea of infinity: 'Badiou sees Beckett as concerned with "the fictive place of being". He conceives of the "place" as precisely the point at which language arrests what is otherwise the infinite "flight" [*fuite*] of being towards the void' (Gibson, 2005, p. 155). Badiou's idea of the void has particular relevance to my argument about the voice in *Company* as a movement toward a union of the narrator and the act of narration, or the teller and the told, through which literature is possible. In 'Being, Existence, Thought: Prose and Concept' Badiou describes the void as that point of union since

> The void 'in itself' is what cannot be ill said. This is its definition. The void *cannot but be said*. In it, the saying and the said coincide, which prohibits ill saying. Such a coincidence finds its reason in the fact that the void itself is nothing but its own name. (Badiou, p. 99)

Badiou's readings of Beckett depart from those of his precursors in that he swaps meaning for truth, shifting the focus from epistemology to ethics. In this he heralds a new way of thinking about the engagement of philosophy and literature, which is characterized by what Gibson describes as a 'thought of intermittency' most fully explored by Badiou and the writings of Jacques Rancière and Françoise Proust (Gibson, 2005, p. 137). A new direction for a new century.

Note

1. See Jean-François Lyotard's *Discours, figure*. In this important work, Lyotard argues for the co-existence of line and letter, of the plastic and the textual. This holding together of heterogeneous plastic and graphic spaces without privileging either,

Lyotard calls the 'figural'. The figural is not alternative to the textual, for it moves within both textual and visual space. Just as the letter, while repressing its corporeality, cannot function without the line, so the line cannot be reduced to pure corporeality, since it contains the potential for arbitrary signification, by demarcating one space in relation to another (Lyotard, 1985).

Works cited

Badiou, Alain, *On Beckett*, ed. Nina Power and Alberto Toscano (Manchester: Clinamen Press, 2003).

Banham, Gary, 'Cinders: Derrida with Beckett', pp. 55–67 in *Beckett and Philosophy*, ed. Richard Lane (London: Palgrave, 2002).

Bataille, Georges, 'Le silence de Molloy', *Critique*, 7 (15 May 1951), 387–96.

Beckett, Samuel, *The Unnamable* (London: Calder & Boyars, 1975).

——*Watt* (London: John Calder, 1981).

——*Disjecta: Miscellaneous Wrtings and a Dramatic Fragment*, ed. Ruby Cohn (London: Calder, 1983).

——*Samuel Beckett: The Complete Dramatic Works* (London: Faber & Faber, 1986, repr. pbk 1990).

——*Nohow On: Company, Ill Seen Ill Said, Worstward Ho* (London: Calder, 1992).

Begam, Richard, *Samuel Beckett and the End of Modernity* (Stanford: Stanford University Press, 1996).

Bernal, Olga, *Langage et fiction dans le roman de Beckett* (Paris: Gallimard, 1969).

Blanchot, Maurice, *The Infinite Conversation*, trans. Susan Hanson (Minneapolis: University of Minnesota Press, 1993). Originally published as *L'Entretien infini* (Paris: Gallimard, 1969).

——'Où maintenant?, qui maintenant?', *Nouvelle Revue Française*, 2 (octobre 1953), pp. 678–86, repr. in *Le Livre à venir* (Paris: Gallimard, 1959), pp. 256–64. Translated by Richard Howard as 'Where Now?, Who Now?', pp. 141–49 in *On Beckett: Essays and Criticism*, ed. S.E. Gontarski (New York: Grove Press, 1986), repr. pp. 93–8 in *Samuel Beckett*, ed. J. Birkett and K. Ince (London: Longman, 2000).

Bryden, Mary, 'Deleuze Reading Beckett', pp. 80–92 in *Beckett and Philosophy*, ed. Richard Lane (London: Palgrave, 2002).

——'Nomads and Statues: Beckett's Staged Movement', pp. 35–46 in *Drawing on Beckett*, ed. Linda Ben-Zvi (Tel Aviv: Assaph, 2003).

Cage, John, *Silence* (London: Calder & Boyars, 1968).

Cohn, Ruby, 'A note on Beckett, Dante, Geulincx', *Comparative Literature*, 12 (1960), 93–4.

——'Philosophical Fragments in the Works of Samuel Beckett' *Criticism: A Quarterly for Literature and the Arts*, 6 (1964), 33–43.

Connor, Steven, *Samuel Beckett: Repetition, Theory and Text* (Oxford: Basil Blackwell, 1988).

Critchley, Simon, *Very Little . . . Almost Nothing: Death, Philosophy, Literature* (London: Routledge, 1997).

Deleuze, Gilles, *The Logic of Sense*, trans. Mark Lester with Charles Stivale, ed. Constantin V. Boundas (London: The Athlone Press, 1990).

——'He Stuttered', pp. 23–9 in *Gilles Deleuze and the Theatre of Philosophy*, trans. Constantin V. Boundas, eds Constantin V. Boundas and Dorothea Olkowski (London: Routledge, 1994).

——'The Exhausted', pp. 152–74 in *Gilles Deleuze: Essays Critical and Clinical*, trans. Daniel W. Smith and Michael A. Greco (London and New York: Verso, 1998).

——'The Greatest Irish Film (Beckett's "Film")', in *Gilles Deleuze: Essays Critical and Clinical*, trans. Daniel W. Smith and Michael A. Greco (London and New York: Verso, 1998).

Deleuze, Gilles and Felix Guattari, *Kafka: Toward a Minor Literature*, trans. Dana Polan (Minneapolis: University of Minnesota Press, 1975).

Derrida, Jacques, *The Other Heading*, trans. Pascale-Anne Brault and Michael B. Naas (Bloomington: Indiana University Press, 1992a).

——*Acts of Literature*, ed. Derek Attridge (London: Routledge, 1992b).

——*Aporias*, trans. Thomas Dutoit (Stanford: Stanford University Press, 1993).

Gibson, Andrew, 'Beckett and Badiou', pp. 93–107 in *Beckett and Philosophy*, ed. Richard Lane (London: Palgrave, 2002).

——'Badiou and Beckett: Actual Infinity, Event, Remainder', *Polygraph*, vol. 17 (2005), 137–66.

Hill, Leslie, *Beckett's Fiction: In Different Words* (Cambridge: Cambridge University Press, 1990).

——'Poststructuralist Readings of Beckett', pp. 68–88 in *Samuel Beckett Studies*, ed. Lois Oppenheim (London: Palgrave, 2004).

Lane, Richard (ed.), *Beckett and Philosophy* (London: Palgrave, 2002).

Locatelli, Carla, *Unwording the Word: Samuel Beckett's Prose Works after the Nobel Prize* (Philadelphia: University of Pennsylvania Press, 1990).

Lyotard, Jean-François, *Dicours, Figure* (Paris: Klincksieck, 1985).

——*The Differend: Phrases in Dispute* (Manchester: Manchester University Press, 1988).

Murphy, P.J., 'Beckett and the Philosophers', pp. 222–40 in *The Cambridge Companion to Beckett*, ed. John Pilling (Cambridge: Cambridge University Press, 1994).

Oppenheim, Lois, *Samuel Beckett Studies* (London: Palgrave, 2004).

Uhlmann, Anthony, *Beckett and Poststructuralism* (Cambridge: Cambridge University Press, 1999).

Watson, David, *Paradox and Desire in Samuel Beckett's Fiction* (London: Macmillan, 1991).

Part II
Encounters with Literature in Anglo-American Philosophy

Introduction

From the early twentieth century, philosophy in Britain and America came to be dominated by the analytic tradition, to the extent that 'analytic philosophy' and 'Anglo-American philosophy' practically became synonyms. The analytic tradition has consistently tended to focus on linguistic philosophy, which it approaches using methods of analysis derived from logic. Those who practise analytic philosophy apply an almost mathematical exactitude in unpacking the propositions of everyday language. Its earliest advocates included Bertrand Russell (1872–1970), G.E. Moore (1873–1958), and Alfred North Whitehead (1861–1947). W.V.O. Quine (1908–2000), H.P. Grice (1913–88), P.F. Strawson (1919–), and Saul Kripke (1940–), amongst many others, have featured amongst the leading contemporary practitioners of Anglo-American philosophy. Yet despite the foundational importance of figures such as Gottlob Frege (1848–1925) and Ludwig Wittgenstein (1889–1951) – German and Austrian, respectively – analytic philosophy has nevertheless increasingly been contrasted with 'Continental' philosophy, on a shaky assumption that the former is a largely Anglophone enterprise.

With its scrutiny of language in terms of logical forms and structures, its emphasis on ordinary language (which some have opposed to literary language), and its eagerness to resolve all linguistic ambiguity using ever more rigorous logical precision, analytic philosophy might not appear to have a great deal in common with the way most people go about reading literature today. Interestingly enough, though, both analytic philosophy and English literature rose to prominence as academic disciplines at roughly the same time. The Cambridge of Moore, Wittgenstein, and Russell was also the Cambridge of F.R. Leavis. Tellingly, Leavis was particularly adamant that the study of great literature should be kept free from the theoretical, mathematical, and logical models that his colleagues in the Cambridge philosophy department brought to their study of language. Arguably, this was not because of any lack of applicability of analytic methods to the toolkit of literary criticism, but more likely in order to maintain the distinctness of 'English' as an academic subject. Viewed this way, the division between Anglo-American philosophy and literary criticism owes as much to artificial institutional distinctions as it does to any deep-seated differences of methodological approach.

In actual fact, the Anglo-American analytic tradition of thought has made several substantial contributions to the study of literature. For instance, the notion of performativity, first elaborated by J.L. Austin (1911–60) in his classic 1955 lecture series *How to Do Things with Words* (2nd edition, Oxford: Oxford University Press, 1975), has provided literary theorists with a powerful model of how language works that highlights its ability to enact changes on the world, and to transform states of affairs. A useful discussion of how this concept might deepen our understanding of literature can be found in J. Hillis Miller's *Tropes, Parables, Performatives: Essays on Twentieth Century Literature* (London: Harvester Wheatsheaf, 1990). More recently, Judith Butler's description of the construction of sexuality and gender identities through a series of performative acts has probably been the most widely influential use of performativity in literary studies, although her treatment of the concept has been a source of some controversy.

Austin's description of the performative was elaborated and expanded by various Anglo-American philosophers into the body of thought known as Speech Act theory, the clearest articulation of which is probably John R. Searle's *Speech Acts: An Essay in the Philosophy of Language* (Cambridge: Cambridge University Press, 1969). Speech Act theory has in turn exerted a considerable influence over several areas of literary studies (see, for example, Mary Louise Pratt, *Toward a Speech Act Theory of Literary Discourse* [Bloomington: Indiana, 1977]; Shoshana Felman, *The Literary Speech Act* [Ithaca: Cornell University Press, 1983]; Sandy Petrey, *Speech Acts and Literary Theory* [London: Routledge, 1990]; and J. Hillis Miller, *Speech Acts in Literature* [Stanford: Stanford University Press, 2001]). Ironically, however, it was Searle's 1977 confrontation with Jacques Derrida that ultimately polarized the opposition between analytic philosophy and literary theory, the latter being typically viewed by the former as the pursuit of 'Continental' philosophy by other means. The essence of this debate can be found in Derrida's *Limited Inc* (Evanston, IL: Northwestern University Press, 1988), and its aftermath is pondered in Reed Way Dasenbrock's *Redrawing the Lines: Analytic Philosophy, Deconstruction, and Literary Theory* (Minneapolis: University of Minnesota Press, 1989).

In the decades since then, a climate of coldness has subsisted in some quarters between analytic philosophy and literary theory, based largely on mutual misunderstanding. Much has also been done, however, to heal this rift. Two leading contemporary Anglo-American philosophers, Stanley Cavell and Richard Rorty, have taken a serious interest in works of literature and the question of the literary, and have also engaged with thinkers such as Derrida who are central to the project of literary theory. Cavell, in particular, has repeatedly emphasized the problem of tragedy as a crucial issue where philosophy and literature intersect, and has also sought to rectify some of the damage done by the Derrida/Searle exchange. See his *Philosophical Passages: Wittgenstein, Emerson, Austin, Derrida* (Oxford: Blackwell, 1995), *Must We Mean What We Say? A Book of Essays* (Updated edition, Cambridge: Cambridge University Press, 2002), and *The Claim of Reason: Wittgenstein, Skepticism, Morality, and Tragedy* (New edition, Oxford: Oxford University Press, 1999). Aspects of Rorty's thought are discussed by Bryan Vescio in the following chapter.

One of the most distinguished of Anglo-American philosophers, Donald Davidson (1917–2003) is gradually coming to be recognized as a major voice in the philosophy/literature dialogue. His radical views on the nature of metaphor and the process of radical interpretation, for example, contribute to the debate an aporetic, anti-foundational current of thought that has clear applications to literary study. Davidson's ideas are gradually being taken on board by some critics, and two of the essays in this section point towards further ways in which Davidson's interesting blend of analytic method with unsettlingly destabilizing conclusions might well enrich our critical approach to reading literature. Bryan Vescio's piece sets out a vision of what a 'Davidsonian' approach to the study of literature might look like, offering a view that also draws on the pragmatism of Richard Rorty in advocating a methodological pluralism. Garry Hagberg's essay, on the other hand, uses Davidson's philosophy to address the more specific question of memory. Beginning with Wittgenstein's discussions of the practice of reminiscing, it seeks to elaborate the implications that such a viewpoint might have for conceptualizing the nature of autobiographical discourse.

The final chapter in this section, by Brett Bourbon, takes the methodological approach of analytic philosophy and applies it to the work of a problematic writer, Gertrude Stein. Stein's writings are literally nonsensical (i.e. they lack sense), but it is argued that they are nonsensical in various different ways, and that a typology of Steinian nonsense can be constructed. It is not that sense can be made of the nonsense by doing so, but rather that the different ways in which nonsense makes itself manifest produce different literary effects and raise different philosophical questions about the nature and logic of language.

In summary, there exists within Anglo-American thought as broad and diverse a range of opinion regarding questions of literature as can be found in any of the other principal schools of philosophy, although this interest is sometimes expressed in terms alien to (and even hostile to) certain aspects of contemporary literary theory. A good survey of the breadth of current views would take in the pragmatism of Richard Shusterman's *Surface and Depth: Dialectics of Criticism and Culture* (Ithaca: Cornell University Press, 2002), the deconstructive emphasis of Samuel C. Wheeler III's *Deconstruction as Analytic Philosophy* (Stanford: Stanford University Press, 2000), and the rather more conservative coordinates of Reed Way Dasenbrock's *Truth and Consequences: Intentions, Conventions, and the New Thematics* (University Park: Pennsylvania State University Press, 2001). Christopher New's *Philosophy of Literature: An Introduction* (London: Routledge, 1999) maps out some of the basic issues facing an analytic philosophy of literature, while Eileen John and Dominic McIver Lopes' *Philosophy of Literature – Contemporary and Classic Readings: An Anthology* (Oxford: Blackwell, 2004) is a valuable sourcebook of various classic analytic approaches to the subject.

David Rudrum

3
The Pattern that Literature Makes: Davidson, Pragmatism, and the Reconstruction of the Literary

Bryan Vescio

Recent literary theorists influenced by Continental philosophy have maintained that defining literature in terms of formal structures and qualities of language will not work. But they have not provided the alternative definitions of literature in terms of its uses within the culture, its institutional functions, that their positions would seem to entail. Instead, they have largely abandoned definitional questions altogether, and the result has been that those engaged in literary studies still lack an adequate justification for their enterprise that they can offer to skeptical students and administrators. Although it may seem at first glance an unlikely source, analytic philosophy, the other dominant mode in contemporary philosophy, may provide a solution to this problem. As its name suggests, analytic philosophy specializes in analyzing the structure of a phenomenon – breaking it down into its constituent parts – rather than in assessing its utility – placing it within a wider network of social relations. One way to read the later Wittgenstein is to see him as blurring this distinction by suggesting that the only way to understand the structures of language is to examine the social practices in which they are embedded. Donald Davidson is an analytic philosopher who extends this tradition in the philosophy of language. His views on meaning and interpretation are based on the practical exigencies of actual speech situations rather than on anything like their acontextual 'logical form'. This Wittgensteinian tendency in Davidson's writings on metaphor and interpretation, brought out most clearly in Richard Rorty's pragmatist reading of his work, can, I will argue, form the basis for an institutional conception of literature.

Davidson's theory of metaphor, as articulated in 'What Metaphors Mean', is formulated in opposition to the theories of Max Black and others who attribute cognitive content or meaning to metaphors. Davidson stresses that the meanings of metaphorical expressions are derived simply from the literal or ordinary meanings of their words. But for Davidson, while the meanings of such expressions are generally banal – they usually make metaphors merely false statements – they produce *effects* that are not subject to paraphrase the way meanings are. In other words, Davidson distinguishes the meaning or 'content' of a metaphor from its effects or 'what it makes us notice', and he claims that only the latter makes metaphors distinct. Moreover, he argues, the reason metaphors are not paraphrasable is that their content is not limited:

> But in fact there is no limit to what a metaphor calls to our attention, and much of what we are caused to notice is not propositional in character. When we try to say what a metaphor 'means,' we soon realize there is no end to what we want to mention. (Davidson, 1984, p. 263)

In an essay entitled 'Unfamiliar Noises: Hesse and Davidson on Metaphor', Richard Rorty interprets Davidson's distinction between meaning and effect as that between 'the quite narrow (though shifting) limits of regular, predictable, linguistic behaviour' (Rorty, 1991, p. 164) and 'unfamiliar noises' which challenge our expectations for linguistic behavior. This point may also be put in terms of context: most utterances fit nicely and easily into our ready-made contexts for understanding them, but a metaphor sends us on a search for context that remains inconclusive as long as the metaphor remains alive.

This treatment of metaphor is of a piece with the rest of Davidson's philosophy of language, which develops a theory of interpretation with anomaly at its core. His theory of 'radical interpretation' emerges from a consideration of the speech situation in which an interpreter is confronted with the most extreme unfamiliarity, the situation of a field linguist who must build from scratch a translation manual for the marks and noises emitted by members of a newly discovered, isolated community. This theory receives its most provocative elaboration in the essay 'A Nice Derangement of Epitaphs', where Davidson argues that an adequate theory of interpretation must explain how it routinely succeeds even in the face of errors and anomalies like malapropisms. According to Davidson, theories that require speaker and hearer to share a set of rules or conventions fail this test. He distinguishes prior theories, or the expectations about each other's linguistic behavior that speaker and hearer bring to the conversation, from passing theories, or the explanations – derived by revising prior theories in the light of new utterances, malapropisms, and so on – that they ultimately use to understand one another. Only the latter, Davidson argues, need be shared for speaker and interpreter to communicate successfully. But passing theories are not shared sets of conventions, since they vary from conversation to conversation and are the products, not the preconditions, of communication. Neither are prior theories sets of shared conventions, since one will have as many prior theories as one has interlocutors. Davidson concludes that interpretation does not require shared conventions at all, and even that 'there is no such thing as a language' (Davidson, 1986, p. 446) at all, if it is to be identified with such conventions. Interpretations, then, even in the most ordinary conversations, are not derived methodically, but rather are

> derived by wit, luck, and wisdom from a private vocabulary and grammar, knowledge of the ways people get their point across, and rules of thumb for figuring out what deviations from the dictionary are most likely. There is no more chance of regularizing, or teaching, this process than there is of regularizing or teaching the process of creating new theories to cope with new data in any field – for that is what this process involves. (Davidson, 1986, p. 446)

This theory of interpretation makes anomalous utterances like malapropisms and metaphors paradigm cases rather than deviant ones, but a crucial difference remains between the kind of anomaly represented by malapropisms and the kind represented by metaphors. To interpret the former correctly, an interpreter must assign the novel utterance a determinate, though temporary, place within a passing theory, to endow it with a clear meaning. But when the latter has been interpreted correctly, its place within a passing theory must remain somewhat vague – to assign it a determinate meaning beyond the literal meanings of its words is to kill it. Consequently, in 'What Metaphors Mean' the role of the interpreter of metaphors is portrayed somewhat differently than that of the interpreter in 'A Nice Derangement of Epitaphs'. Davidson begins his essay on metaphor, appropriately enough, with the metaphor 'metaphor is the dreamwork of language', and he glosses it by alluding to the creativity involved in the interpretation of both dreams and metaphors:

> The interpretation of dreams requires collaboration between a dreamer and a waker, even if they be the same person; and the act of interpretation is itself a work of the imagination. So too understanding a metaphor is as much a creative endeavour as making a metaphor, and as little guided by rules. (Davidson, 1984, p. 245)

As in ordinary communication, the interpretation of metaphor is not governed by rules, but it seems to involve a degree of creativity that is not always required in interpretation. Davidson concludes the essay by elaborating on the creative role of the interpreter or critic of a metaphor:

> Not, of course, that interpretation and elucidation of a metaphor are not in order. Many of us need help if we are to see what the author of a metaphor wanted us to see and what a more sensitive or educated reader grasps. The legitimate function of so-called paraphrase is to make the lazy

or ignorant reader have a vision like that of the skilled critic. The critic is, so to speak, in benign competition with the metaphor maker. The critic tries to make his own art easier or more transparent in some respects than the original, but at the same time he tries to reproduce in others some of the effects the original had on him. In doing this the critic also, and perhaps by the best method at his command, calls attention to the beauty or aptness, the hidden power, of the metaphor itself. (Davidson, 1984, p. 264)

Because the point of a metaphor is not its cognitive content but what it makes us notice, and because what it makes us notice is endless, the critic can only 'reproduce in others *some* of the effects the original had on him'. The critic must choose one or more contexts for understanding a metaphor from among the endless number the metaphor evokes. This inevitable need for selection must be what Davidson means when he calls the interpretation of metaphor a 'creative endeavour'.

As even Davidson's language suggests, it is tempting to read this distinctly creative role for the interpreter as the difference between literary criticism and ordinary interpretation. But metaphors are not confined to literary texts, nor are they the only form of language associated with the 'literary'. So to identify the distinctive things critics do with metaphors is not yet to identify the distinctive things they do with literary texts, the activities that define literary studies. Davidson's essay, however, suggests a way of extending his analysis of metaphor to literary texts in general. At one point, he quotes four stanzas from T.S. Eliot's poem 'The Hippopotamus' as a case in which 'there [is] neither simile nor metaphor, but what seem[s] to get done [is] just like what gets done by similes and metaphors' (Davidson, 1984, p. 261). What gets done is, in Davidson's terms, 'intimation' rather than determinate meaning, and it is accomplished by an entire text rather than an isolated sentence or phrase. To interpret such a text, presumably, would involve the same sort of 'creative endeavour' of selection among a potentially endless set of applicable contexts that Davidson associates with the interpretation of metaphor. This suggests that Davidson's views on the interpretation of metaphor can indeed be extended to describe the activity of literary criticism in general.

Extending Davidson's theory in this way accounts for many features of the institution of literary studies today. First of all, Davidson's anti-methodological account of interpretation in general explains why literary critics have never agreed on a particular methodology, though at various times in the history of literary studies one or another has dominated. Secondly, Davidson's notion that literary critics are more concerned with what he calls 'intimation' than with what he calls 'meaning' explains why interpretive pluralism has always been the rule in the practice, if not in the theory, of literary studies, and why the institution as a whole has never been particularly troubled about proliferating interpretations even when some both inside and outside the field have been. Davidson's view of literary interpretation as a creative endeavor also squares well with the sense critics have often had that their work should be not merely parasitic on literary texts but rather a genre of literature in its own right. But most importantly, it explains why literary theorists have found it so difficult to define their field by distinguishing a particularly literary kind of language or form in texts. For on Davidson's view, the kinds of language and structure found in such 'literary' devices as metaphors are regularly used in every kind of utterance or text. Literary critics only concern themselves with entire texts that produce these kinds of effects – often, as in Eliot's poem, without actually employing the relevant 'literary' devices or structures – the kinds of texts in which determinate meaning is less important than intimation.

What this implies for the institution of literary studies can be seen by returning to the notion of context. Most utterances and texts receive adequate treatment in one or a small number of conversational contexts, defined by the pragmatic goals of ordinary communication or more specialized professional discourses. But literary texts are clearly not part of any ordinary conversation, nor does placing them within the various disciplinary conversations in the professional or academic world seem to exhaust what we find significant about them. This is not because they have a special context of their own called 'the literary' any more than metaphors have a special meaning called 'metaphorical meaning'. Rather, just as what makes metaphors metaphorical is our inability to exhaust them with our familiar contexts of understanding, so what makes literary texts literary is our inability to account for them with our ready-made disciplinary contexts. To do justice to them, we need a kind of anti-disciplinary discipline where methodological and interpretive pluralism are the central goals. Such an institution of literature is implied by Davidson's views on metaphor.

But to describe the institution of literature this way is still not to justify it, because this description does not yet explain why anyone should place special value on texts that resist our familiar contexts of understanding. As we have seen, Davidson explains the value of metaphors in terms of their 'beauty' and 'power', but these terms beg most of the questions with which literary theory is preoccupied. Social institutions have social purposes, and justifying the institution of literary studies means explaining how its purposes link up with the purposes of the wider community. Pragmatism, which explains and justifies phenomena by making such linkages, would be the logical place to turn for such an explanation, so it makes sense to turn to the work of Richard Rorty, who interprets Davidson's ideas in pragmatist terms, to fill in the details of his conception of literature.

One of the startling conclusions Davidson draws at the end of 'A Nice Derangement of Epitaphs' is that there is no distinction 'between knowing a language and knowing our way around in the world generally'

(Davidson, 1986, pp. 445–6). He reaches this conclusion because he has argued that what defines linguistic competence is not a set of shared rules or conventions, but rather is coextensive with the totality of a speaker's or interpreter's beliefs about the world. In an essay entitled 'Inquiry as Recontextualization: An Anti-Dualist Account of Interpretation', Rorty concludes from Davidson's position that fields of inquiry cannot be divided into two classes, one in which objects are encountered in linguistic context and another in which objects are encountered in themselves. Since identifying an object requires placing it within a linguistic context and thus in relation to other such contexts, inquiry in all fields is equally 'interpretive' in the sense that it is a matter of recontextualization. Rorty pursues this idea further in 'Texts and Lumps', where he explicitly compares the kind of inquiry undertaken in literary criticism with that undertaken in the natural sciences. Both kinds of inquiry involve placing either 'texts' or 'lumps' in a context. What determines which contexts are appropriate in a given field are the 'desiderata' or the purposes inquirers in that field hope to satisfy. As Rorty observes, 'some institutions will appear more internally diverse, more complicated, more quarrelsome about ultimate desiderata than others' (Rorty, 1991, p. 84). He identifies literary criticism as one of these institutions with more diverse purposes and therefore more available contexts for recontextualization, and he lists some of those contexts as a text's 'relation to other texts, or the intentions of its author, or what makes life worth living, or the events of the century in which the poem was written, or the events of our own century, or the incidents of our own lives' (Rorty, 1991, p. 82). This description of the pluralism of literary studies squares with both the conception implied by Davidson's remarks on metaphor and the actual practices of contemporary critics.

In his book *Contingency, Irony, and Solidarity*, Rorty further explains the value of such a pluralistic institution by associating it with certain developments in Western culture. In his first chapter he argues that Davidson's philosophy – and specifically his theory of metaphor – belongs to a tradition that has helped us to see language not as a medium for representing thoughts or the world, but rather as a tool for helping us cope with the world. This in turn has helped us to see the language we use as just as contingent as the other products of Darwinian evolution that help us survive. Rorty suggests that this awareness of contingency has created increasing numbers of intellectuals he calls 'ironists', who have learned to distrust what he calls their 'final vocabularies', the most fundamental terms in which they justify themselves. According to Rorty, the increasing irony of our culture has coincided with an expansion in the scope and prestige of the field of inquiry known as literary criticism. He sees the recent expansion of literary criticism into the realm of theory as extending the field 'to every book likely to provide candidates for a person's final vocabulary' (Rorty, 1989, p. 81). In the current practice of literary criticism, we place less familiar texts and figures in the context of more familiar texts and figures, so that 'we revise our opinions of both the old and the new. Simultaneously, we revise our own moral identity by revising our own final vocabulary' (Rorty, 1989, p. 80). Literary criticism thus functions as a kind of laboratory in which ironist intellectuals can experiment with their final vocabularies. Such an institution requires precisely the kind of interpretive pluralism envisioned by Davidson's theory of metaphor.

The most detailed attempts to appropriate Donald Davidson for literary theory, however, have set his work in opposition to just this idea of the institution of literature. In his book *Truth and Consequences: Intentions, Conventions, and the New Thematics*, Reed Way Dasenbrock derives from Davidson's work a theory of interpretation in which authorial intention functions as a constraint. Central to his argument is the contrast between 'intentionalism', the view he attributes to Davidson, and 'conventionalism', the view he attributes to Rorty, along with Stanley Fish, Barbara Herrnstein Smith, and others. But this distinction breaks down in a number of places, most clearly in his treatment of Fish, whose views on interpretation Rorty endorses in 'Texts and Lumps'. Dasenbrock locates Fish's conventionalism in his notion that 'interpretive communities' constrain interpretation. But how hostile is Davidson's theory of interpretation to Fish's idea of interpretive communities? In his reply to Rorty in *The Philosophy of Donald Davidson*, Davidson emphasizes the existence of a 'speech community', the members of which 'share a host of overlapping, non-identical, habits of speech, and have corresponding expectations about what others in the community will mean by what they say' (Hahn, p. 598). It is not clear how Fish's interpretive communities differ from the communities that produce such expectations, which Davidson goes on to identify with prior theories. Moreover, Fish repeatedly characterizes himself as an intentionalist, as when he says that interpreters 'cannot help positing an intention for an utterance if they are in the act of regarding it as meaningful' (Fish, pp. 116–17). The distinction Dasenbrock attempts to draw between Fish's conventionalism and Davidson's intentionalism appears to be at most a difference in emphasis.

What Dasenbrock really objects to in the theories of Fish, Rorty, and others is the view he calls 'universal intentionalism', the view that any context that makes a text meaningful, not just that of the historical author's intentions, can be described as 'intentional'. We have seen this view in Rorty's description of the various contexts for understanding texts and lumps, and Fish echoes it when he says that the 'intentional agent' posited in interpretation need not be the historical author, but may also be 'the spirit of the age, . . . some transhistorical truth about human nature, or . . . the intentional structure of language' (Fish, p. 119). Dasenbrock finds the specter of relativism in this view and says that in order to quell the proliferation of conflicting interpretations in literary studies, the institution must not only restrict itself to intentions, but also rededicate itself to the pursuit of truth.

He claims, 'Scholarly research becomes an intelligible activity only as long as its purpose remains the pursuit of truth and not a rhetorical veil masking a will to power' (Dasenbrock, p. 199). Again he finds support for this position in analytic philosophy, not only from Davidson but also from Hilary Putnam. And again the target of the argument is a form of 'conventionalism' that holds truth to be relative to a community, a view Dasenbrock attributes to Rorty.

It is not surprising that Dasenbrock almost never quotes Rorty to support this attribution, since Rorty spends much of his time denying that he believes any such thing. Almost the only time Dasenbrock does quote Rorty to this effect is when he cites Rorty's claim in 'Hilary Putnam and the Relativist Menace' that 'the rightness or wrongness of what we see [*sic*]... *is* just for a time and a place' (qtd in Rorty, 1998, p. 47). Dasenbrock leads us to believe that 'rightness or wrongness' in this quotation refers to truth, when in fact the context of the quotation makes it clear that its subject is warranted assertability or justification. Rorty says in the same paragraph, 'If we shift from correctness and warrant to truth, then I suppose we might say, noncontroversially if pointlessly, that the *truth* of what we say is not just for a time or place' (Rorty, 1998, p. 60). For Rorty, truth is as absolute and universal as can be; it is only justification that is relative to a community's values and practices. Dasenbrock is simply wrong to claim that Rorty thinks 'truth-claims are a rhetoric we are better off without' (Dasenbrock, p. 10) and that Rorty has 'a theory of truth' that claims 'there is no such thing as truth' (Dasenbrock, p. 45). Rorty can no more imagine language use without truth or truth-claims than can Davidson or Putnam. But since he believes that a community's practices of justification are the only tests for the presence or absence of truth, he also asserts that truth cannot be a separate goal of inquiry, and this view does, as we have seen, run afoul of Dasenbrock's vision of an institution of literary studies dedicated to 'the pursuit of truth'.

It turns out, however, that all these views held by Rorty on truth are shared by Donald Davidson. In 'Truth Rehabilitated', his contribution to *Rorty and His Critics*, Davidson reiterates a disavowal of the correspondence theory of truth he has often made, writing, 'Truth as correspondence with reality may be an idea we are better off without.... The formulation is not so much wrong as empty...' (Davidson, 2000, p. 66). In a footnote to the same essay, he endorses Rorty's distinction between truth and justification: 'If, as seems right, it *is* a legitimate norm to want to be justified, but not to seek the truth, then there must be a large difference between them' (Davidson, 2000, p. 74). This passage suggests that Davidson also endorses Rorty's more controversial claim that truth is not a goal of inquiry, and he confirms this at another point in his essay, saying, 'Since it is neither visible as a target, nor recognizable when achieved, there is no point in calling truth a goal. Truth is not a value, so the "pursuit of truth" is an empty enterprise . . . ' (Davidson, 2000, p. 67).[1] Nothing in Davidson's thought authorizes the view that a renewed dedication to the 'pursuit of truth' will provide a genuine constraint on interpretation rather than empty rhetoric on the part of literary critics. Dasenbrock's distinction between Rorty's 'conventionalism' about truth and Davidson's 'anti-conventionalism' evaporates as quickly as that between Fish's 'conventionalism' about interpretation and Davidson's 'anti-conventionalism'. Neither distinction proves sufficient to justify the constraints he recommends for literary interpretation.

A corollary of Dasenbrock's views on truth is his view that literary scholars must seek a consensus about their method of research. He begins his book by lamenting the interpretive pluralism currently allowed in literary studies, and later he follows up this complaint with one about the discipline's methodological pluralism: 'Instead, convinced that no such consensus or common ground is attainable or even conceivable, we have agreed to disagree and to leave it there. Methods of literary study, like taste, have become something there is little point in disputing' (Dasenbrock, p. 186). A pragmatist vision of the institution of literature along the lines I am recommending cannot second this criticism, for reasons Rorty makes clear in his essay 'Pragmatism Without Method'. He writes,

> If one takes the core of pragmatism to be its attempt to replace the notion of true beliefs as representations of "the nature of things" and instead to think of them as successful rules for action, then it becomes easy to recommend an experimental, fallibilist attitude, but hard to isolate a "method" that will embody this attitude. (Rorty, 1989, pp. 65–6)

Dasenbrock's objection to methodological pluralism also receives scant support from the work of Davidson, whose theory of interpretation embodies precisely the anti-methodological, 'experimental, fallibilist attitude' endorsed by pragmatism. As Davidson writes of interpretation in general at the end of 'A Nice Derangement of Epitaphs', 'There is no more chance of regularizing, or teaching, this process than there is of regularizing or teaching the process of creating new theories to cope with new data in any field – for that is what this process involves' (Davidson, 1986, p. 446). Surely, that is also what the interpretation of literary texts involves. On this reading, then, Davidson's writings suggest a different view of literary theory than Dasenbrock's: they suggest a view that resembles the 'conventionalist' alternatives provided by Fish and Rorty.

Dasenbrock's most persuasive argument in favor of authorial intention as an interpretive constraint, however, is made independently of Davidson's philosophy. Late in his book, Dasenbrock says that 'the choice among the various interpretive protocols and theoretical systems outlined in this book is finally an ethical one' (Dasenbrock, p. 258). The ethical principle he offers in favor of adhering to authorial intention is 'that our descriptions of others should clash as little as possible with how they might describe themselves' (Dasenbrock, p. 145). Something like this principle is also endorsed in Rorty's work. In *Contingency, Irony, and Solidarity*, he worries about the potential for humiliation in an ironist's redescriptions: 'The redescribing ironist, by threatening one's final vocabulary, and thus one's ability to make sense of oneself in one's own terms rather than hers, suggests that one's self and one's world are futile, obsolete, *powerless*. Redescription often humiliates' (Rorty, 1989, p. 90). On the other hand, Dasenbrock's way of putting the point is far too sweeping, since redescription is indispensable for both moral and intellectual progress. His principle would entail, for example, describing a racist as a member of a superior race and describing a New Critic's espe- cially insightful reading as the discovery of a text's 'organic unity'. Rather, Rorty suggests two ways of guarding against humiliation that are more or less built into the literary institution. In the first place, by forcing acquaintance with lots of alternative final vocabularies, literary studies is more likely to sensitize interpreters to the dangers of humiliation than are other discip- lines. Secondly, because humiliation depends on power, the literary insti- tution is fortunately well insulated from the sources of political power. In Rorty's terms, this means it is located on the private side rather than on the public side of our current institutional arrangements. There is little danger of humiliating Shakespeare by reading him as an existentialist rather than as a neo-Platonist, and at any rate, this is the sort of redescription that no form of inquiry can do without. Literary critics can, as Rorty suggests, safely treat the names of authors as 'abbreviations for a certain final vocabulary' (Rorty, 1989, p. 79) without worrying about whether that vocabulary belonged to a particular historical figure.

Given these objections to Dasenbrock's account of literary interpretation, it comes as something of a surprise to learn from Davidson's own writing on literature that he largely agrees with that account. In his essay 'Locating Literary Language', Davidson is also worried about the specter of 'relativism' in literary interpretation, and he seeks to avoid it by proposing the same constraint Dasenbrock proposes, 'In any case, the intention by the originator that an utterance or writing be interpreted in a certain way is only a necessary condition for that being the correct interpretation; it is also necessary that the intention be reasonable' (Davidson, 1993, pp. 305–306). Why he would come to this conclusion after formulating the pluralistic views on interpret- ation I have quoted becomes clearer when Dasenbrock notes in his book, 'For Davidson, the purpose of interpretation is simple: to understand others' (Dasenbrock, p. 80). For both Davidson and Dasenbrock, 'understanding' seems to name a single, simple purpose. Davidson's views on interpretation are formulated with a situation in mind – that of the radical interpreter encountering an unfamiliar community – in which understanding indeed has a more or less clear and limited set of purposes: to coordinate behavior, to avoid hostilities, and so on. But it is not clear that the purposes involved in understanding a literary text are the same, since we will rarely have anything like the pragmatic, face-to-face dealings with its author that a radical interpreter has with the natives or that we have with our conversation-partners in ordinary communication.[2] A cursory glance at the field of literary studies is enough to demonstrate the diversity of purposes for reading literary texts that exist in practice, and Davidson's philosophy gives us no reason to limit that diversity *a priori*.

Yet Davidson persists in claiming the centrality of authorial intentions in his reply to Dasenbrock in *The Philosophy of Donald Davidson*: 'Of course, there is room for imaginative readings that may or may not have been in the author's mind. But these are interesting only if the author's meaning is also in our minds' (Hahn, p. 379). Why should this be so? This remark seems to rely on a criterion of 'interest' that depends on wider societal purposes. Such 'interests' are precisely what is excluded from the narrowly defined situation on which Davidson bases his theory of interpretation. This feature of Davidson's theory, which leads him to advocate the same constraint on literary interpretation as Dasenbrock when so much in his philosophy works against it, is, I suspect, influenced by his roots in the analytic tradition that prefers talk of structure or form to talk of social context. This is also, I have argued, why a coherent Davidsonian account of the institution of literature needs a bit of help from pragmatism, perhaps in spite of Davidson's own intentions.

In this essay, I have followed the suggestions of Davidson and Rorty in positing the literary institution as one that, in contrast to other fields of inquiry – and in contrast to the institution of literary studies envisioned by Dasenbrock – fosters diversity rather than consensus. Its success is measured not by the amount of truth it produces, but by the number of interesting original selves it produces. This Davidsonian conception of the institution of literature describes what is most valuable in literary studies as it is currently practiced. It does not say why a society should value such an institution, but Rorty's pragmatist reading of Davidson implicitly does. Rorty's pragmatism is inspired by John Dewey's conception of democracy, in which democratic institutions must be combined with a democratic culture that encourages the growth of diverse individuals. The pluralistic institution of literature, as envisioned by Davidson and Rorty, is a vital component of such a democratic culture. From this point of view, the danger for literary studies is not that it will proliferate methodologies or interpretive protocols but that it will restrict itself to one or a few, and the field's currently growing consensus on the protocols of cultural studies may be a sign of stagnation. Like Dasenbrock, I worry that the survival of the institution itself may be at stake, but my reading of Davidson makes me think it is more likely to survive if its self-image is built around interpretive and methodological pluralism than if its self-image is built around the unwarranted methodological constraints Dasenbrock recommends.

Notes

1. These ideas are given further treatment in Davidson's 'Is Truth a Goal of Inquiry?: Discussion with Rorty'.
2. I develop these reservations about Davidson's writing on literature in more detail in 'Donald Davidson, Pragmatism, and Literary Theory'.

Works cited

Dasenbrock, Reed Way, *Truth and Consequences: Intentions, Conventions, and the New Thematics* (University Park: Pennsylvania State University Press, 2001).

Davidson, Donald, 'What Metaphors Mean', pp. 245–64 in *Inquiries into Truth and Interpretation* (Oxford: Clarendon Press, 1984).

—— 'A Nice Derangement of Epitaphs', pp. 433–46 in *Truth and Interpretation: Perspectives on the Philosophy of Donald Davidson*, ed. Ernest LePore (Oxford: Blackwell, 1986).

—— 'Locating Literary Language', pp. 295–308 in *Literary Theory After Davidson*, ed. Reed Way Dasenbrock (University Park: Pennsylvania State University Press, 1993).

—— 'Is Truth a Goal of Inquiry?: Discussion with Rorty', pp. 17–19 in *Donald Davidson: Truth, Meaning and Knowledge*, ed. Ursula Zeglen (London: Routledge, 1999).

—— 'Truth Rehabilitated', pp. 65–74 in *Rorty and His Critics*, ed. Robert B. Brandom (Oxford: Blackwell, 2000).

Fish, Stanley, *Doing What Comes Naturally: Change, Rhetoric, and the Practice of Theory in Literary and Legal Studies* (Durham: Duke University Press, 1989).

Hahn, Lewis Edwin (ed.), *The Philosophy of Donald Davidson* (Chicago: Open Court, 1999).

Rorty, Richard, *Contingency, Irony, and Solidarity* (Cambridge: Cambridge University Press, 1989).

—— *Objectivity, Relativism, and Truth: Philosophical Papers, Volume 1* (Cambridge: Cambridge University Press, 1991).

—— 'Inquiry as Recontextualization: An Anti-Dualist Account of Interpretation', pp. 93–110 in *Objectivity, Relativism, and Truth*.

—— 'Pragmatism Without Method', pp. 63–77 in *Objectivity, Relativism, and Truth*.

—— 'Texts and Lumps', pp. 78–92 in *Objectivity, Relativism, and Truth*.

—— 'Unfamiliar Noises: Hesse and Davidson on Metaphor', pp. 162–72 in *Objectivity, Relativism, and Truth*.

—— 'Hilary Putnam and the Relativist Menace', pp. 43–62 in *Truth and Progress: Philosophical Papers, Volume 3* (Cambridge: Cambridge University Press, 1998).

Vescio, Bryan. 'Donald Davidson, Pragmatism, and Literary Theory', *Philosophy and Literature*, 22, 1 (April 1998), 200–11.

4
Autobiographical Memory: Wittgenstein, Davidson, and the 'Descent into Ourselves'

Garry L. Hagberg

If forced to capture in succinct form the difference between the writing of a biography and an autobiography, we might naturally appeal to the distinctive role of memory played in the latter. While it is true that a biography or memoir of a person we know, or knew, does depend on memory (as does Norman Malcolm's memoir of Wittgenstein,[1] for example), it is of course common to write biographically of a subject we did not know personally (as in Ray Monk's biography of Wittgenstein[2]). In the autobiographical case, unlike that of a biographer, however, it seems impossible to escape this fact: even where the autobiographer relies upon what we will in this context call 'externals' – for example, letters, documents, photographs, diaries, calendars, journals, and countless other bits of data – that data will have a memory-triggering function. That is to say, the autobiographer will use all the assembled materials not, as does the non-personally acquainted biographer, to assemble a mosaic of what the subject must have done and might have experienced. Rather, the autobiographer will use those materials to stimulate, or revivify, memories of the events, actions, and experiences indicated by each bit of assembled data. And if the autobiographer finds himself or herself utterly at a loss to remember the event indicated by a given piece of memorabilia, for example a train ticket, we will doubt (assuming the memory of the autobiographer is otherwise fully intact) the veracity or accuracy of the evidence – in this case that the train journey was taken by the subject. (Perhaps he bought the ticket in his name but for the use of his daughter; perhaps he had to cancel the trip at the last minute, etc.). Clearly, no such criterion of memory applies in the case of biographical writing of the non-personally-acquainted kind. And, while memory may well enter as a criterion in a biography of the personally-acquainted kind, it will of course still not play the distinctive role that it does in the autobiographical case: Malcolm may remember what *he* said or did in connection with Wittgenstein, but the subject of the memoir is *Wittgenstein*, whose memories he of course will not have, as we say in such contexts, from the inside. Only the subject himself or herself can stand in that unique relation (to put it in brief and formulaic terms, a relation of identity between remembering and remembered self); memory functions as a criterion, as we think of it in accordance with our picture of the general distinction between biographical and autobiographical writing in a manner whose uniqueness is preserved by metaphysics. And the philosophical picture of how precisely this autobiographical memory works is hardly unfamiliar.

It was perhaps Locke who most clearly enunciated the conception of the mind as a repository of ideas: here the experience impinges upon the mind (or makes its impression upon the *tabula rasa*). The sensory experience *itself* in life is of course then gone and, as sealed in the past, unrepeatable, but its *image* is retrieved and brought before the inner gaze, before the mind's eye as it is focused upon the memory images of its own past experience. And this, as we shall see below, also corresponds to a picture, or metaphysical model or conceptual template, of how recognition works: we match the present, new sensory impression with an image called up of the old impression; recognition just is, according to the picture, indeed *re*-cognition – recognizing is construed as an act of matching the present impression to its predecessor-image. Locke's successor Hume then saw a problem concerning just how we really distinguish the one from the other (i.e. the present data from the past image), since they match exactly (in a present successful case of recognition). His answer to this was provided, as we know, in terms of differences of force and vivacity – the sensations of the present are distinguishable from presently-called-up images of past sensations because they are more vivid in the mind and make a more forceful impression. And Hume's delayed successor in turn, Russell, kept the underlying conceptual model intact while giving a slightly different answer regarding our capacity to mark the contrast between the present impression and the past impression-image: the past impression-image, as brought into the mind as an *object* of consciousness, carries with it, or induces, a sense of familiarity that marks the contrast between the otherwise indistinguishable mental objects.

All of these specifications of the distinctive experience of memory (or its close cognate, recognition), as further elucidations of the subject's private act of remembering, are thus at the same time further specifications of the autobiographer's self-investigative project. But while familiar, they too, as picture-driven and over-generalized ways of characterizing an involved and intricate set of human self-descriptive phenomena, seriously mislead.

Donald Davidson has written,

There is a picture of the mind which has become so ingrained in our philosophical tradition that it is almost impossible to escape its influence even when its worst faults are recognized and repudiated. In one crude, but familiar version, it goes like this: the mind is a theatre in which the conscious self watches a passing show (the shadows on the wall). The show consists of 'appearances', sense data, qualia, what is given in experience. What appear on the stage are not the ordinary objects of the world that the outer eye registers and that the heart loves, but their purported representatives. Whatever we know about the world outside depends on what we can glean from the inner clues. (Davidson, p. 61)

This picture of the mind and its contents is indeed ingrained in our philosophical tradition. It is a prerequisite to unearthing this picture and criticizing it in the light of day – in the light of our actual variegated practices as they proceed in the stream of life without subservience to the conceptual picture that is created in the attempt to unify them, to give them a general theoretical formulation – that we not only articulate the picture clearly (as Davidson has done), but also, we need, as Wittgenstein has shown (and to whom we shall shortly return), to understand a number of the moves of thought, the images employed, the pressures on our thinking, that taken together generate a false necessity concerning this way of thinking, this picture of the mind.

   This picture powerfully reinforces the very idea of *objects* of consciousness; it is just these that are inspected with the inward-directed act of perceptual scrutiny. And our image of memory – or, perhaps more accurately, our image of the rememberer (as we may see in our initial image of Augustine writing his *Confessions*[3] or our image of Dostoevsky's Underground Man[4] hermetically sealed within a private world of self-reflection) – is assembled around this fundamental idea of memory *object*: in remembering, whatever else may happen (e.g. triggered associations, awakened related memories), the essence of the phenomena is that we retrieve, and bring into the theatre, the particular and determinate object of consciousness that is the memory. Davidson adds, a bit later in his discussion, that the 'solution in the case of mental states' is to 'get rid of the metaphor of objects before the mind'. 'Of course', he adds, 'people have beliefs, wishes, doubts, and so forth; but to allow this is not to suggest that beliefs, wishes, and doubts are *entities* in or before the mind, or that being in such states requires there to be corresponding mental objects' (Davidson, p. 62).

   This last line is particularly significant for our present purposes: a natural but (as we shall increasingly see as this discussion proceeds) deeply misleading image of memory can influence our reflections on autobiographical writing in precisely the same way. People have beliefs, wishes, doubts – and of course memories – but in believing, wishing, doubting, or remembering, there need not be a mental *object* as the center of inward attention and that is necessary for the very cogency of the concept 'memory'.

   The problem with this model or picture of mental content, for Davidson, is two-pronged. First, the dogma, as he calls it, 'that to have a thought is to have an object before the mind' runs afoul in this way (Putnam makes this argument[5]): an object, if at least partly constituted by external relations or relational properties, cannot reliably be held to correspond directly, in one-to-one fashion, to an object in the mind – a thought, as construed on this model – because the thinker of the thought, its possessor, may be wholly or partly ignorant of those identity-determining external relations or properties. Second, Davidson adds that we cannot then look to *another* kind of object – presumably one not partly constituted by external relational properties – because *that* object (insofar, I would add, as we can intelligibly conceive of it in the first place), in not being connected to the world, would not allow us to learn about the object in the world by inwardly contemplating the mental object. It, to further encapsulate the point, would be semantically detached, and thus not able to provide what we fundamentally want in bringing it, the thought-as-mental-object, before the mind's gaze in the first place. The deep significance of our modeling of autobiographical memory in just this way is perhaps apparent: if a remembered event is represented internally by such an allegedly corresponding thought-object, and if that remembered event is in part relationally constituted, then we cannot assume that the event does in fact correspond to the object before the remembering mind. And with this skeptical gap, we would forever be wondering if we, quite literally, knew what we were, if not talking, then thinking, about. And if the memory-object is made wholly knowable by the remembering mind by severing its external relational-connectedness, then it loses what Davidson called, succinctly, its semantics. It would be, like Hume's sensations that are always unto themselves 'right' because they refer to nothing beyond themselves, a memory free-for-all, with no external constraint on memory rightness. (Here Wittgenstein might say, contrary to Hume, that thus here we can't talk about 'right'.)

Assessing the force of this last point, Davidson writes,

> The only object that would satisfy the twin requirements of being 'before the mind' and also such that it determines what the content of a thought must, like Hume's ideas and impressions, 'be what it seems and seem what it is'. There are no such objects, public or private, abstract or concrete. (Davidson, p. 63)

Taken together, these reflections give us growing reason to doubt that such mental objects, as alleged centers of inward-directed attention, are necessary in the way we initially pictured. Moreover, if they were to exist they would – if envisaged according to the underlying model or picture – either fail to correspond to the external relations that in part individuate the remembered event, or they would lose their semantic link to the world, thus severing any independent criterion of rightness in memory.[6]

Davidson emphasizes the conceptual rewards of freeing ourselves from the grip of the picture of thoughts-as-mysterious-mental-objects.[7] With this freedom, he suggests, we will be able to (1) see the natural linkages between the social nature of language, that is the external or relational determinants of thought and meaning and (2) secure the preservation of, rather than succumb to the behavioristic eradication of, first-person authority (see Davidson, pp. 63–4). Again, the parallel point would be true of the picture of memories-as-mysterious-mental-objects: with the image of object-storage and object-retrieval (another instance of dangerously modeling the inner on the outer) removed, we would indeed have our view opened to a multiplicity of aspects of memory presented within autobiographical writing – subtle particularities discernible only in context, which are otherwise crushed by the blunt force of the material-object model.

Wittgenstein labored both mightily and intricately against this falsifying, and conceptually blinding, model: he worked through the aforementioned pressures on our thinking propelling us toward the model in the first place. Wittgenstein, as we shall see, describes this picture with varying inflections in a number of philosophical contexts throughout his work. In *Philosophical Investigations* §604, he writes,

> It is easy to have a false picture of the processes called 'recognizing'; as if recognizing always consisted in comparing two impressions with one another. It is as if I carried a picture of an object with me and used it to perform an identification of an object as the one represented by the picture. Our memory seems to us to be the agent of such a comparison, by preserving a picture of what has been seen before, or by allowing us to look into the past (as if down a spy-glass).

Comparison, of course, requires that there be at least two objects or entities juxtaposed in such a way that we can discern the similarities and differences made evident through the back-and-forth scrutiny. Recognition, Wittgenstein also here claims, is too easily construed as comparison-conducted-inwardly, that is where, in the Lockeian or Humean model, an impression is compared with an idea (or a sensation with a reflection). Wittgenstein describes the process of recognition as one akin to comparing a picture we carry with us with an object in our visual field; if comparative scrutiny yields a match, the recognition is successful. Then turning this inward, that is into a wholly mental act, he adds that our memory, taken as the agent of the comparison, is pictured as a preserver of images of what has been seen before. And, making the link to our present concern perfectly explicit, he adds that this is what seems to allow us to look into the past.

Wittgenstein articulates a striking set of observations against this way of seeing memory and recognition in *The Blue and Brown Books*. There, identifying this picture as primitive – the picture, as he encapsulates it within that discussion, of 'comparing the man we see with a memory image in our mind and we find the two to agree' (Wittgenstein, 1958, p. 165)[8] – he offers the fairly blunt observation that in most cases of recognition no such comparison takes place (in contrast to the more rare contexts in which it does take place, for example when we recognize a criminal by his photograph in the post office). The temptation to picture the matter in this way, he there indicates, is fueled by the simple and accessible empirical fact that there are memory images. But the most powerful reminder of what we *actually* do comes next in his discussion: such an image, for example seeing in our mind's eye how the person looked when we last saw him a decade ago, comes into mind just *after* we have suddenly recognized him upon running into him in the street. The mental image, whatever role it may play, is not a precondition for recognition. Nor is it, *mutatis mutandis*, the precondition for memory. And in *Philosophical Investigations* §648, he very briefly describes a case, familiar enough, in which remembering clearly takes place but where mental images play no role whatsoever:

> 'I no longer remember the words I used, but I remember my intention precisely; I meant my words to quiet him.' What does my memory *shew* me; what does it bring before my mind? Suppose it did nothing but suggest those words to me! – and perhaps others which fill out the picture still more exactly. (Wittgenstein, 1953, §648)

It is the attention to particular cases that here again exposes the false sense of the obvious truth of the picture. And this kind of philosophical attention allows us to unearth and expose the presuppositions that would blind us to the intricate details of the rich weave of human memory-practices, a clear view of which is indispensable to our growing understanding of how autobiographical language actually works. In *Philosophical Investigations* §651, Wittgenstein presses the point further: ' "I remember that I should have been glad then to stay still longer." – What picture of this wish came before my mind? None at all.' This quite evidently reminds us that image-consultation is neither necessary nor sufficient as the essence of the concept 'memory'. And in the next line Wittgenstein both strengthens and extends the point to our memories of our feelings, in the case above of the precise emotional tone in which we experienced the wish to stay longer at the time: 'What I see in my memory allows no conclusion as to my feelings. And yet I remember quite clearly that they were there' (Wittgenstein, 1953, §651). Indeed, the image of the remembered scene, even if it were there and functioning (which in this particular case it is not – his words were 'None at all'), would still not be the right tool with which to recover the emotional content of the wish – and yet one clearly can remember the emotional tone of such remembered wishes.

At the outset of this chapter we saw that, if there is an intuitive distinction between biographical writing and autobiographical writing, it is the evident reliance on first-person memory in the latter that makes the difference.

But with both the Davidsonian and Wittgensteinian reflections behind us, how then should we think of the experiential content of a first-person memory? The answer – perhaps somewhat startling, given our intuitive expectations – Wittgenstein suggests, is that perhaps we should free ourselves of the very notion of *experiential content*, that is, as a uniform mental phenomenon that constitutes remembering, one that gives the word 'memory' its meaning. We think of memory as showing us the past, and of the autobiographer's memory as the instrument or device that shows him or her their own past; autobiographical truth will then be regarded as an accurate verbal description of what he or she sees therein. But Davidson suggested that the inner mysterious object would go the same way as the sense-data picture of experience, that is, as that which shows us the outer world, as soon as we escape the pernicious dualistic model behind these views. Wittgenstein saw very much the same point: in *Zettel* §663, he writes, 'But if memory shews us the past, how does it shew us that it is the past?' He replies to his own question, startlingly, as follows: 'It does *not* shew us the past. Any more than our senses shew us the present.' Our senses, conceived as data-collectors on the sense-data model, create the raw material for an inner picture of what we see before us. Similarly, the memory-experience would be the inner sense that collects the raw material for the inner picture of what we remember. Both, Wittgenstein and Davidson after him suggest, are deeply misled ways of construing our grasp of the present and our grasp of the past. In *Philosophical Investigations*, Wittgenstein makes this point in the most distilled form, reminding us that the very concept 'description' is out of place, and moreover deeply misleading when used in connection with the experience of memory. That concept, so used, requires that there be an object described.

Wittgenstein begins *Philosophical Investigations*, Part II, Section xiii with the sentence: 'When I say: "He was here half an hour ago" – that is, remembering it – this is not the description of a present experience' (Wittgenstein, 1953, p. 231). That is, the act of remembering that he was here as manifest in our saying someone was here half an hour ago is not a description of the present inner content, the present visual image. But of course it is difficult to suppress the powerful sense that there simply must be such an image that constitutes the inner content of the remembering. And one reason for this insistent picture is that we *can* have what Wittgenstein calls 'accompaniments' to remembering – and these, to confuse the issue, may well be visual images. Thus he continues the above discussion with 'Memory-*experiences* are accompaniments of remembering.' That is to say, a vivid memory image may well spring to mind when we find ourselves reminiscing about a person, say a beloved grandparent, now gone. But the image is not *itself*, here again, either a necessary or a sufficient condition for remembering – it comes as an adjunct of, or as an accompaniment to, the remembering. (To particularize the point, if this were the case, we would, in response to a sibling saying 'Remember how our grandfather always used to . . .', find ourselves unable to remember the grandfather *until* we called to mind the attendant visual image.)

It is also the case that many such images, as they may spring to mind in contexts of reminiscence, in truth are memory-images not of the persons themselves, but of photographs of those persons. And that is instructive for the easily observed reason that we here conflate the language-game of photograph-comparison (as in the criminal mug-shot case above) and remembering. The former is always visual, the latter not necessarily so. Compressing the conceptual genealogy of this philosophical picture, Wittgenstein remarks a few lines later in the above discussion in *Philosophical Investigations* that we get the *idea* of a memory-content only because we assimilate 'two psychological concepts', and then, quickly explaining that, adds, 'It is like assimilating two *games*. (Football has *goals*, tennis not)' (Wittgenstein, 1953, p. 231). Comparing a person to a photograph, like comparing one photograph with another, is obviously and inescapably visual. Remembering – for all the various and divergent things that that can mean as we explore (by reading autobiographical writing in a manner mindful of these philosophical issues) the nuances of particular cases – need not take that form, and thus need not have visual content. And where it does, that content may well enter the scene only *ex post facto* with regard to the act of remembering – it may be a subsequent accompaniment.

Breaking the spell of the visual picture is also aided by thinking of cases ranging through the other four senses: if we begin an invitation to recollect with the line 'Remember when . . .', the impulse to unify, and to reduce all variations to a common essence, can lead us directly to the visual-image picture. But we should consider as well invitations beginning with 'Remember how those cherries from the tree in our backyard tasted', or 'Remember the feel of that sea-island cotton . . .', or 'Remember the aroma of . . .', or 'Remember the melancholy voice of the oboe in . . .'. In each case, we may also recall a visual image of the cherry tree, the garment, the kitchen, and the oboist, but the remembering of the four non-visual experiences is not simultaneous with, nor identical with, nor reducible to, those images. It is also instructive to bear in mind that the word 'remembering' can itself impose, or strongly incline us toward, the visual picture, where the word 'reminiscing' does this to a perhaps lesser degree. Indeed, the idea of reminiscing seems to bring the verbal to the fore (in part because one usually reminisces socially, with another person; remembering may or may not have this social dimension.)

The very concept of description, once in place (in place, as Wittgenstein has shown, where it should not be, i.e. where it is placed in correspondence with the picture of memory here under review rather than in accordance with the facts, the human practices and experiences that picture is supposed to succinctly capture), leads to an ordering whereby the alleged memory-experience is first and the description of that inner experience follows. In *Remarks on the Philosophy of Psychology, Vol. I*, §1131, Wittgenstein articulates a densely compressed three-stage argument yielding a conclusion of considerable power vis-à-vis our understanding of memory-fuelled self-awareness. Announcing the subject with the word 'Memory', he gives, as the first stage, the example 'I still see us sitting at that table'. But then he asks '– But have I really the same visual picture – or one of those which I had then?' That is, if the view of memory presumed by Locke, Hume, and many others (including Augustine), were correct, that is if the reflection were cut, as a seal, from the sensation, or if the idea were an only-less-forceful-and-vivacious version of the sensory impression, then the memory image would of necessity so correspond. But we do often picture past events in our imaginations and as stimulated or occasioned by passing mentions of those events, in ways constructed or deriving from, but not necessarily in direct correspondence to, those past experiences. The striking and picture-unseating fact here is that language, in such cases, *precedes* the image. Then the second stage advances, 'Do I also certainly see the table and my friend from the same point of view as then, and so not see myself?' That is, the image called to mind in the course of our reminiscing conversation may well be an image that includes oneself in the scene – which evidently could not be the case were the empirical model correct. We do not see ourselves (except in mirrors, reflections, etc.) from our own distinctive perceptual vantage points, and it is of course only from those that we could have gotten the memory-originating sensations or impressions. To state the matter starkly, the linguistic is not (whatever else it may be) in a position of descriptive subservience to the visual. Then comes the third stage: ' – My memory image is not evidence of that past situation; as a photograph would be, which, having been taken then, now bears witness to me that this is how it was then.' The photograph is indeed the central component of a separate language-game; it is not only an externalized version of what we carry and what we call up inwardly as the content of the memory. This is because it exhibits evidential weight about the past in a way and with specificity that the memory image does not possess. Contra the empiricist picture, it is not the case that the memory image, like a lightly contrasted black-and-white photograph in comparison to a full color photographic print, is a lesser version of that prior visual sensation. Here is the conclusion following the three stages: 'The memory image and the memory words are on the *same* level.'[9] The linguistic dimension of memory is not, in the sense this picture would dictate, a description, and it thus is not secondary to the mental object it allegedly describes.

The empiricist picture (again, a conceptual model that is hardly restricted to the empiricists alone) leads us astray with false analogies, and it blocks our view of the multiform ways in which the words or phrases 'to remember', 'remembering', 'remembered', 'recollected', 'reminisced', and cognate terms are used. And a perspicuous overview of those uses is, as always, conceptually clarifying. These considerations show some of the thought – the analysis of the conceptual genealogies that lead to these powerfully influential and often submerged simplifying pictures of the acts of memory – that lead to Wittgenstein's exchange with his imagined interlocutor. That exchange was with the voice that does not remain vigilant about the grammatically concealed power of the misleading analogies we have heretofore excavated, in *Philosophical Investigations*, §305:

> 'But you surely cannot deny that, for example, in remembering, an inner process takes place.' – What gives the impression that we want to deny anything? When one says 'Still, an inner process does take place here' – one wants to go on: 'After all, you *see* it.' And it is this inner process that one means by the word 'remembering.' – The impression that we wanted to deny something arises from our setting our faces against the picture of the 'inner process.' What we deny is that the picture of the inner process gives us the correct idea of the use of the word 'to remember.' We say that this picture with its ramifications stands in the way of our seeing the use of the word as it is. (Wittgenstein, 1953)

If memory is not, after all, dependent upon an 'inner process' as here pictured, then the act of remembering as modeled according to this picture is not a source of knowledge *in the way we initially think*. We do not learn about the past by scrutinizing (and then, in autobiographical writing, describing) the inner process. The true nature of autobiographical reflection takes a different, far less unified course, and the meaning of 'to remember' is not reducible to a unitary inner process that provides the essence of the concept. We usually do not 'read off' the content of the memory from any inner entity, nor do we learn the concept of memory from inward-directed ostensive definition. Yet it would be wrong, as suggested in the preceding passage, to *deny* that remembering is a mental process (whatever, in varying particular contexts, might be meant by that phrase). Thus in *Remarks in the Philosophy of Psychology, Vol. I*, §105, Wittgenstein writes, as an analogy to the case of hearing or thinking of a word in some determinate meaning:

> And is it like that only with the experience of meaning? Isn't it so also with, e.g., that of remembering? If someone asks me what I have been doing in the last two hours, I answer him straight off and I don't read the answer off from an experience I am having. And yet one says that I *remembered*, and that this is a mental process.[10]

These points, again, once grasped in an expanded context sufficient to encompass the pressures on thought, the intellectual genealogies that Wittgenstein assiduously traces that led to the illusory pictures they are meant to dispel, are of the first importance to our understanding of autobiographical writing. Our relation to our past is no more passive than is our relation to what we presently visually perceive: we are not the containers of memory-images that a true narrative would accurately describe. Rather, we are in a continual process of reconsideration,[11] of reflective restructuring, and of repositioning the actions, events, occurrences, interactions, efforts, aspirations, achievements, intentions – in short, our words, deeds, and everything in between that, taken together, form the teleological trajectories of our selves. Such a developmental retrospective is never finally settled beyond the reach of re-juxtaposition with other related (and in some cases seemingly unrelated) life-events; such retrospective self-understanding is the result of an *active* labor of self-investigation, the content of which is dynamic, not static. And our relation to it is 'unfrozen'. Memories, understood in this way, are not inert visual images filed into storage by time and date. They are remembered experiences of all composite kinds, and, like works of art and like human selves, they take on and cast off relational properties, networks of interconnections to other experiences both similar and different.

Some of these emerging self-narratives will carry deep conviction; others will seem plausible; others possible but doubtable; and still others implausible. And then some will be, as fanciful whole-cloth revisionism, rejected outright. But their placement on this epistemological continuum, if the considerations we have reviewed of Davidson's and of Wittgenstein's are right, will – highly instructively – *not* be determined by the extent to which these narratives function as verified descriptions of inner objects or memory-images. The concept of memory is, as we have seen, not reducible to that, but rather is shown in its use throughout the vast body of autobiographical writing that our tradition has generated. And, most fundamentally, the language of that active process is not, against the picture of memory articulated by the empiricists and as operative at various levels of awareness in many other philosophical and literary-critical places, secondary to genuine memory content. In many cases, those verbal formulations, and re-contextualizing reformulations, just are the content of memory. And in turn, this language is not – as we also may well initially picture the matter – secondary to an inner process that allegedly precedes it. The traditional picture of memory prevents us from seeing – well, comprehending – the multiform employments of the word as it is used. But the response – a profound one made possible in and after Wittgenstein's work – is to proceed in a manner constantly mindful of the misleading power of conceptually embedded pictures or templates, and a vigilance with regard to the misdirecting influences of grammatical nuance and rhetorical phraseology in nourishing these illusions. This enables us to see the countless cases of autobiographical writing for what they in truth are – particularized literary 'reminders', as Wittgenstein uses the term, of the way we 'descend into ourselves'. [12]

Notes

1. See Malcolm, 1984.
2. See Monk, 1991.
3. I discuss the case of Augustine in 'Wittgenstein and the Question of True Self-Interpretation' (see Hagberg, 2002), and in 'The Self, Thinking: Wittgenstein, Augustine, and the Autobiographical Situation' (see Hagberg, 2004b).
4. I offer an examination of Dostoevsky's *Notes from Underground* in connection with problems of selfhood and self-examination in 'Wittgenstein Underground' (see Hagberg, 2004a).
5. See Davidson, p. 63 for a review of Putnam's argument.
6. It emerged during the investigations into the much-discussed false-memory syndrome of the 1980s and 1990s that one psychotherapeutic camp explicitly (and ruinously) did just this, declaring it a methodological principle that every memory voiced by a patient is to be accepted, and reinforced, unquestioningly.
7. I discuss this matter in much greater length in 'Autobiographical Consciousness: Wittgenstein, Private Experience, and the "Inner Picture"' (see Hagberg, 2004a).
8. For a set of very helpful references leading to various but interrelated texts of Wittgenstein's I am here indebted to Hans-Johann Glock, *A Wittgenstein Dictionary*; entry on 'Memory', pp. 241–243.
9. A variant of this remark (suggestive of the remark's wider significance) is found in *Zettel*, §650.
10. An illuminating discussion (to which I am indebted) of this passage can be found in Joachim Schulte, *Experience and Expression: Wittgenstein's Philosophy of Psychology* (Oxford: Oxford University Press, 1993), p. 98. (See also the fine full chapter on memory, pp. 95–119.)
11. I offer an elucidation of this idea, in connection with some remarks about this ongoing process of active reconsideration of one's past made by Iris Murdoch in her diary, and then in connection with Wittgenstein's remarks on 'seeing-as', in 'In a New Light: Wittgenstein, Aspect Perception, and Retrospective Change in Self-Understanding' (see Hagberg, 2005).
12. The deeply personal nature of this drive to escape linguistically motivated illusion is well described by Norman Malcolm. Malcolm writes, 'In a notebook of 1938 he wrote: "If anyone is unwilling to descend into himself, because this is too painful, he will remain superficial in his writing." In the following year he wrote: "The truth can be spoken only by one who rests in it; not by one who still rests in falsehood, and who reaches out from falsehood to truth just once."' In *Recollections of Wittgenstein*, ed. Rush Rhees (Oxford: Oxford University Press, 1984), p. xix. The kind of work undertaken by Wittgenstein as considered here – like a philosophically mindful reading of autobiography – is thus just such a 'descent into ourselves', and the intricate removal of misleading pictures, or 'disguises', thus earns the possibility of honest self-recognition.

Works cited

Davidson, Donald, 'Knowing One's Own Mind', pp. 43–64 in *Self-Knowledge*, ed. Quassim Cassam (Oxford: Oxford University Press, 1994).
Glock, Hans-Johann, *A Wittgenstein Dictionary* (Oxford: Blackwell, 1996).

Hagberg, Garry, 'Wittgenstein and the Question of True Self-Interpretation', pp. 381–406 in *Is There a Single Right Interpretation?* ed. Michael Krausz (University Park: Pennsylvania State University Press, 2002).

—— 'Autobiographical Consciousness: Wittgenstein, Private Experience, and the "Inner Picture" ', pp. 228–250 in *The Literary Wittgenstein* ed. John Gibson and Wolfgang Huemer (London: Routledge, 2004a).

—— 'The Self, Thinking: Wittgenstein, Augustine, and the Autobiographical Situation', pp. 215–233 in *Wittgenstein, Aesthetics, and Philosophy*, ed. Peter B. Lewis (Aldershot: Ashgate, 2004b).

—— 'Wittgenstein Underground', *Philosophy and Literature* 28, 2 (October 2004c), 379–392.

—— 'In a New Light: Wittgenstein, Aspect Perception, and Retrospective Change in Self-Understanding', in *Seeing Wittgenstein Anew*, ed. William Day and Victor Krebs (Cambridge: Cambridge University Press, 2005).

Malcolm, Norman, *Ludwig Wittgenstein: A Memoir, with a Biographical Sketch by G.H. von Wright* (Revised edition, Oxford: Oxford University Press, 1984).

Monk, Ray, *Ludwig Wittgenstein: The Duty of Genius* (London: Vintage, 1991).

Rhees, Rush (ed.), *Recollections of Wittgenstein* (Oxford: Oxford University Press, 1984).

Schulte, Joachim, *Experience and Expression: Wittgenstein's Philosophy of Psychology* (Oxford: Oxford University Press, 1993).

Wittgenstein, Ludwig, *Philosophical Investigations*, 2nd edition, trans. G.E.M. Anscombe (Oxford: Blackwell, 1953).

—— *The Blue and Brown Books* (Oxford: Basil Blackwell, 1958).

—— *Zettel*, 2nd edition, ed. G.E.M. Anscombe and G.H. von Wright, trans. G.E.M. Anscombe (Oxford: Basil Blackwell, 1981).

5
What Can My Nonsense Tell Me About You?

Brett Bourbon

Who would ask such a question? What could *my* nonsense tell me about *you*? If, as seems reasonable, the sense of a sentence is just the thought expressed, and if the logical form of that thought depends on a normative usage of words, then how can nonsense say anything? Why would anyone imagine that the deformation of the normative sense of words, with the resulting obfuscation of thought, could produce any further kind of sense that might matter? And yet such deformations are often attempted in modern poetry and literature. The writings of Gertrude Stein are exemplary of such aesthetically motivated nonsense, and thus offer a test case for the sense we can discover in nonsense.

If I try to imagine what kind of creature would write like Gertrude Stein, I don't doubt that it was a human being; but a human being trying to be what and trying to say what? I would write like Stein, I imagine, if I were trying to discover how I could write so that the words I write would find me, express me as if I were a *prophetes*, speaking the words of the god. And that just means asking how these words could be fully expressive and meaningful, and yet not be my words, be somehow lost to me.

Interpretation is a kind of re-description. The interpretation of nonsense sentences, of the facsimiles of thought mimicked by quasi-sentences (i.e. nonsensical strings of words), requires that we re-describe the ways in which they lack sense. The descriptions and interpretations of how Stein's sentences are nonsensical have been, by and large, inadequate and misleading, relying on incoherent theories of meaning. In this Chapter, I produce a more philosophically coherent descriptive typology of Steinian nonsense, and in so doing describe the interpretative possibilities this nonsense allows.

I

How is the following nonsensical? And how can we construe it as somehow meaningful?

The meaning of this is entirely and best to say the mark, best to say it best to show sudden places, best to make bitter, best to make the length tall and nothing broader, anything between the half. (*Tender Buttons*, 'A Drawing', Stein, 1997, p. 12)

I think one can reasonably have two opposing intuitions about this kind of Steinian sentence: (1) The words and phrases are not combined in conformity with semantic norms, syntactical constraints, and logical inferences such that they do not mean or constitute a thought. Such sentences, alone and in combinations, are not truth-preserving. Associations of some kind seem to organize the seemingly intelligible parts of the sentences. Thus such sentences are expressive in the way an expletive might be or as any set of sounds might be. I'll call this the *no-thought intuition*. (2) The second and competing intuition is that while there is no linguistic sense to such sentences, they express a specific kind of thought or sense of the world tied to and dependent on the person who says or writes them: a unique thought. I'll call this the *nothing-but-thought intuition*.

This last possibility is in many ways a desperate hope. Any such sentence expressing such a unique thought does not mean like ordinary, transparent sentences. Such a sentence must articulate some special code known to the person speaking – something like Humpty Dumpty and 'glory', by which he means 'there's a nice knock-down argument for you'. Can we, however, learn to speak Steinian, not just imitate the style of her writing, but use her words like we might use the re-defined 'glory'? If it were just a question of knowing the meaning of strange words or ordinary words with different but still determinate meaning, then the analogy with Humpty Dumpty might be apt (since the meaning of a word would be at issue). But Stein's words are normal English words, in fact simple ones for the most part, and so to learn the thoughts expressed through such sentences would mean learning the grammar of this way of speaking – learning the idiolect. Can we describe this grammar like we could Finnish, describe its transformations relative to English? Learn the norms so that we could be corrected when we repeated the wrong kind of noun? Since the answer to all of these questions is no, the content of Stein's sentences might be something we could guess at, but it would be difficult to use the words and their order to stabilize the content (her putative thought) into some inter-subjective form.

What has replaced thought in this case is just the person who pretends to speak these words, pretends to speak since she, herself, does not have any way of thinking through these words either, although she might think a lot of things as she said them. She might even think what she says constitutes a set of specific thoughts, but she would be wrong. If Stein read what she had just said, for example, she would probably not think the same thing, nor could she build other thoughts from bits of any other sentence, since all she could do would be to correlate some specific thought, expressed in some other language, with a specific set of words – like a code and not like a language.

The situation is the same for us. When reading Stein-like nonsense we can translate words into some allegory and justify the form of the sentences as expressive of this allegorical content. Or we can attempt to discover Stein's particular thoughts, associations, or intentions as a way of stabilizing interpretative options. This is either an impossible task or a trivial one. At best we might turn her writings into real codes for which we assume she had the key. We could on the other hand read what she writes as exemplifying a specific aesthetic, which we would articulate and justify. In any of these cases, it is not Stein's writings that mean, but our translations or descriptions of the code that mean, and these are articulated not in Steinian nonsense but in ordinary language.

Without a stable grammar what is said is not a sentence. If there is no sentence, then there is nothing to mean. If there is no stable syntax, then there are no normative criteria to use by which to determine the failure to mean, and thus no way to determine if something is meant. There are, however, degrees of nonsense. So in Stein's 'Composition as Explanation', itself an attempted description and justification of her aesthetic, Stein retains basic English syntax, and deforms sense, often through repetitions and transformations of words of one grammatical kind into words of another. Since, however, it is not clear how someone would say these things as a full and normal form of conversation (they would sound like a parody of some parody of a sage), it is hard to take seriously that this is Stein in any ordinary sense of her asking directions to the bookshop. Thus, it is the way this is written that makes its relation to Stein, and hence to us as readers, fictional. The meaning is not non-fictional in the sense of a description of what I did today, but in the metaphysical sense of a platonic dialogue: it is trying to show some obscure truth. Certainly what is said seems to be at the service of what seems to be first-person direct address in the voice that we take as the author's.

William Gass attempts to explain Stein's aesthetic nonsense. He asserts that Stein treats the 'elements of the sentence' as characters, 'as if they were people at a party, and begins a mental play with all of their possible relationships' (Gass, p. 29). This formulation, attractive as it may be, is not satisfactory. Gass's phrase 'all of their possible relationships' seems to suggest that Stein toys with all the possible meanings and all the possible arrangements of every possible word – which it is just not possible to do. It is impossible to play with all of a word's possible relationships, so the phrase 'possible relationships' is, in this context, empty. Gass's description of Stein's nonsense is, like her writing itself, a piece of nonsense.

We need a more precise description of Stein's writing. Reading Stein's aesthetic requires that we describe her nonsense in order to understand what it is she produces and how this nonsense pictures us, or seems to mean.

I want to provide a partial typology of her ways of losing sense in order to show what we can see of ourselves as linguistic creatures, as creatures involved and invested in language. I will divide her strategies into four kinds: (a) syntactical nonsense, (b) inferential nonsense (or the concatenation of sentences), (c) the concatenation of phrases, and (d) the appearance of randomness. (This last category overlaps with the others.)

Syntactical nonsense

It is common to claim that Stein's nonsense is syntactical, as opposed to the semantic punning nonsense of Joyce's *Finnegans Wake*: 'Toughtough, tootoological . . . Art, the imperfect subjunctive' (Joyce, p. 469.08–09). This misleads in both cases. Stein does produce syntactical nonsense, but only sometimes. The notion of syntax in this case is not very clear.

The following, while it still looks like a sentence, lacks the syntactic forms and constraints that would allow it to be a well-formed English sentence: '*Dog a the see they how sentence sleep.*' The sentence is not Stein's, but mine. I wrote it by trying to minimize the possible, normative syntactic fit of any particular word with the succeeding and preceding word. But it might strike one, if in the right mood, as a kind of poem (pronounced with a certain sage-like tone). Notice how if I change 'sentence' to 'sentences' or 'sleep' into 'sleeps' I can turn this last bit into a phrase, with the effect of making it seem like a description of nonsense in general or this sentence in particular: 'Dog a the see they how sentences sleep' (or 'sentence sleeps').

One might take Stein to be approaching something like this degree of syntactic nonsense in the following lines from *Tender Buttons*:

IT WAS BLACK, BLACK TOOK
   Black ink best wheel bale brown. (p. 17)

If the first line is a kind of title, then the second line lacks a verb, and hence predicates nothing of anything. One can make a kind of sentence from 'Black took black ink, best wheel, bale brown', although with what meaning seems too much trouble to discover. The second line, as it stands, is just a list, a concatenation of words, or if we take them in pairs, then of adjective–noun phrases (black ink, best wheel) with the final 'bale brown' inverting the pattern. In any case, disorders of this sort produce nonsense at the level of syntax. If one wanted to increase the disorder of writing to include phonology, as Stein does not, then one would lose words and syntax: ghav bloqbb.

The concatenation of sentences: inferential nonsense

If the word-syntax relation is the most basic unit of meaning Stein disorders, the largest unit – barring the work as a whole – is the inferential and narrative relations between and among sentences. Inferential nonsense either looks random relative to normal modes of inference or narrative, or we can assume the only relevant relation is not in what is said or in the world described *per se*, but in the mind seeing and saying. Stein writes,

> Oh grammar is so fine.
> Think of duplicate as mine.
> It stops because you stop. Think of that. . . .
> (*How to Write*, 'A Grammarian', Stein, 1975, p. 111)

How can we evaluate the sense and validity of these even to answer what is meant by 'grammar'? The diminishment of the logical or narrative resources in these lines means their force comes from the mind that seems to speak them, or through our attempts to show that these sentences are about grammar. By confusing inferences and diminishing the inferential connections between sentences, any semblance of sense in any particular sentence will evoke the idea, the memory of those absent inferential norms. The only thing that can satisfy the ordering power of those norms so evoked would be the mind of the author or our own role as interpreter: the loss of the coherence of thought marked by inferences encourages the unique, *nothing-but-thought* interpretation. The oracle feel of the lines implies the distorting 'intelligence' as a stand-in for the lost inferential norms.

The lack or confusion of inferential connections between sentences can distort the sense and logic of words within sentences. The quasi-claim 'sugar is not a vegetable' could be true or false depending on how one understands 'vegetable'; our confusion rests on wondering why anyone would think sugar would be a vegetable. If the logic or semantic relations to sentences before and after the sentence 'sugar is not a vegetable' (*Tender Buttons*, 'A Substance in a Cushion', Stein, 1997, p. 3) are unclear, missing, or indeterminate, except as an expression of a meta-interpretation, then the mind displayed is not in the text, but is the writer's. Since the sugar-vegetable phrase does not mean here, it can only mean when it was written. The nonsensical sentence therefore points to the mind that wrote it, and describes this mind as alien to ours. Describing the nonsense, then, I find myself back at seeing *nothing-but-thought*, which, however, I do not recognize as thought.

The concatenation of phrases

The above non-inferentially constrained kinds of parataxis can invade a sentence. A putative sentence would then read like a concatenation of phrases, often, in Stein's case, seemingly consisting of two phrases whose semantic implications and syntax conflict, but not enough to turn the quasi-sentence into a random string of words.

There is a difference between the syntax of what we call a sentence and the syntax we might analogically use to describe how these sentences fit together with each other. The paratactic relation between sentences is not the same as using a paratactic like logic to pressure a single sentence into nonsense, into a non-sentence: a list of sentences is, for example, less indeterminate than a list of words.

'I love my love with a b because she is precious' (*How to Write*, 'A Grammarian', Stein, 1975, p. 105) is amusing. The phrase 'with a b' could mean anything, nothing, or something very specific. If I imagined anything rested on knowing what 'b' means I could try to find some evidence internal to the text that associates this 'b' with some kind of meaning. Or I could try to find extra-textual evidence for a particular meaning, which, in some way, would be an attempt to identify with the mind that made it (as the only site of intentional meaning left). Or one could pursue one's own associative interpretation through reading the text. More extreme forms of nonsense would make internal evidence increasingly senseless and in need of similar interpretation. The more syntactically nonsensical a string of words is, the more one either identifies with the author's mind or relies on one's own associations, given whatever linguistic limits the text seems to retain. If a generative algorithm replaces the mind of the author, then reliance on the reader's interpretative creativity is only further increased.

If, therefore, we understand such sentences to express Stein's associative 'thinking', or if we understand these sentences as random, we give them meaning by justifying their form relative to how they were produced. In other words, to make sense of such a sentence requires that one speculate about how it was produced, to make explicit possible associative links that would have resulted in these words in this order.

The appearance of randomness: A metaphor for mind

There are two ways of producing paratactic nonsense: (1) by procedure or (2) by association. In the first case, the production of nonsense is effected through some specified procedure that randomizes the order of words relative to our normal usage. The procedure is arbitrary or justified aesthetically but not semantically, and thus the order of words is arbitrary relative to a meaningful use of words. What is arbitrary can seem random. A procedure, if empty, is a formalized association, without the possibility of making explicit the content of these associations. If the association is not generated procedurally, then it is an expression of Stein's psychology, or maybe an effect of the seemingly random play of her mind, without explicit recoverable content. Even if we knew the reason why a word was chosen, that would not help us understand what it means within the sentence in which it is used. The words chosen might form a surface trace of someone's attention, associations, stimuli, and forgetfulness, none of which would determine the content of the sentence. These traces all lack the inter-subjective constraints that are required for a sentence to mean something (there are a number of competing ways of accounting for these constraints). The particular meanings and associations of that mind will remain trivial and outside of the normative constraints and inferential structures of thought; this becomes a way of seeing Stein's mind distended in this nonsense.

A randomizing procedure can mimic a mind seemingly gone awry. When faced with writing produced through authorial associations, reading becomes an impossible pursuit of the author's psychology: the patterns of association in relation to the various stimuli, beliefs, memories, ideas, emotions, and so on which produced the text. This is an impossible pursuit because the sheer contingency of the relation between words and motive makes the causes and associations organizing the words irrecoverable. We know a mind chose these words, but we cannot know why. All we can offer are justifications of this order. We cannot read the work of art. We can only do aesthetics.

Similarly, this associative logic does not give the words meaning, but rather it offers the promise of an interpretation of the words through the justification of their inclusion – where what is left of meaning is the mental operation that produced these particular words. Further objectification is possible. One can generate words, in the spirit of Oulipo, by procedure: why not write down every third word of every third sentence in every third page of every third volume of the 3rd edition of the *Encyclopaedia Britannica*? Such poetry cannot mean anything separate from its interpretation or its justification. It might intimate something, or it might mean within an interpretation offered either as a justification of the nonsense (something Stein does herself) or as an example of some something given by the interpretation. An interpretation can make sense, at least we can understand it enough to dismiss it, but meaning has ceased to be a possibility for such poetry (thus any interpretation that pretends to offer the meaning of the poetry is confused; one could, of course, always read it as a code).

The difference between random (relative to some norm) and associational (having psychological content) may not be apparent in the words themselves (what is associational to the writer can seem random to the reader). In this case the differences between having a particular symptomatic or psychological sense or not depend on understanding how the writing was produced. Reading for associations would center on Stein's thought, intentions, and feelings, or on the act of writing, where sense is deformed relative to our normative expectations. If the target shown by these putative associations or random generation is Stein or our expectations, then in both cases the lack of meaning is compensated by our attention, as readers, to an underlying and justifying psychology (the content of Stein's or our associations attached to the words or phrases).

One might want to argue that Stein is replacing the usual norms describing our usage in English of a set of words with some other counter set of norms, partially parasitic on the usual norms. If so, then we should be able to explicitly articulate what these new norms are. I think in general we cannot because words are used or mean, when they do mean, just what they normally do, and when they do not they simply lack a semantic sense separate from some further interpretation of them, in which case they have the sense they have in that interpretation. The consequence is that the possibilities of meaning, the possible norms, are too many to settle down into anything like the stability apparent in our usual linguistic practices. What replaces semantic norms, in this case, are associations that are expressive to the degree that those associations can be re-described as analogous with some other domain governed by the norms of ordinary language.

II

In all of these cases, there is no meaning to recover separate from the justifying associational logic or from the procedure by which the work was produced, which, once recovered, can then be evaluated or justified. Recovering some sense from this kind of poetry or writing requires the invention of a mind that could mean what is said, or else the acceptance that the poetry means nothing. Stein, consciously or not, is fighting against these two conclusions. She often fights, as do her defenders, using metaphysics, as in 'Composition as Explanation'. These metaphysical theories or pictures often come down to various versions of 'all is flux' or 'all is interpretation'. I think all of these metaphysical pictures incoherent and inconclusive, but they are not my concern here.

My concern is rather what can we conclude from Stein's kind of writing that seems so unnaturally inconclusive? Stein uses ordinary words with few lexicographic distortions. Her sentences are often semantically confused and seemingly fragmented into two syntactical patterns. In much of Stein's writing she performs a kind of semantic shifting, in which various senses of complex phrases and philosophically significant words collect on the surface of the text or of her attention as if with symbolic import. In *The Geographical History of America*, she repeatedly deforms or empties the sense of philosophical terms like 'human nature', 'human mind', 'interesting', 'autobiography', 'dead', 'habit', 'it is so', and others through a complex and gestural set of private associations instantiated through repetitive uses and re-definitions of these words. While these associations organize the vocabulary, the words are used to describe inter-subjective aspects of our psychology, anthropology, and art. The particularity of her statements, and of these deformations, seem to generalize the portrait of her own mind as exemplary of our being human, of how the world is, and of how words and art might mean. If we take the import expressed in these associations to be uniquely someone's thought, then any particular word, implying all of the others in a non-obvious way, can mark a kind of quasi-first person 'I': the first-person Stein pronoun. These words are pronoun-like because they are uniquely expressive of the person who uses them (reads them) and yet they are formally available for any person willing to use them seriously.

The terms sifted together are black boxes, whose sense and extension remain obscure, vague, and non-intuitive. In effect, this makes the force and content of these distinctions dependent on Stein's missing mind: her associations, beliefs, and intentions. If we take them as fully expressive of her thought, we can only show the content of these unique thoughts by translating them into ordinary language, and thus they would no longer be unique in the way purported. If we simply stipulate or read the sense into these distinctions, we are simply playing with allegories and codes: at best displays of cleverness. If what is said is nothing more than Stein's particular thinking, associations, and intentions, then Stein's thinking is fully expressed in this network of black boxes. Or if the sentences are taken as empty, then these black box terms are empty nodes around which associations collect in the same way as they would seem to for Stein as she wrote. Thus, the quasi-universal or exemplary standpoint she offers (the Stein pronoun) is not formal as in Kant, since it is only the subjectivism of association itself that she offers as that standpoint, and thus she has no ground to appeal to any humanness in this, unlike in the third *Critique*, where the cognitive model allows, in our disinterested stance, the faculties to produce a harmony and pleasure that is a function of our common human endowment. The nonsense that acts as the universal standpoint for Stein presumes such a common endowment; it does not show it except as the way we make sense of her words.

Stein is attempting to universalize herself by subjectivizing (denormalizing) her language to show it as singular, and thus as the one thing that anyone is. This singularity, shown by the way she writes, is modelled on her own particularity, exemplified in her writing. This is intimated in the ending chant of *The Making of Americans*: 'Any one has come to be a dead one. Any one has not come to be such a one to be a dead one.... Many who were living have come to be a dead one. Any one has come not to be a dead one. Any one has come to be a dead one' (Stein, 1995, p. 907). What is asserted here is the particularity of any one being anyone. But what does it mean to assert that? Humans are live and dead ones. To be a one might just mean that we are particular things. The repetitions and funny grammar are just tricks to give the appearance of depth, and are easily translated away. If the content of Stein's sentences is something we can state in a natural language, for example 'the particularity of any one being anyone', then we do not need the initial nonsense sentence. The nonsense would be simply rhetorical. If we cannot state the content of a sentence in a natural language, then it has no content. If her sentences were uniquely expressive, then she would be fully blank to us. Neither of these options would constitute reading the sentence. That can only be achieved by offering a justification of the form of Stein's sentences relative to the way they produce the ideas of content we imagine we read. Any such account would be question-begging. The problem here is that the idea of content oscillates between the *no-thought intuition* (nonsense is nonsense) and the *nothing-but-thought-intuition* (unique thought). There is no way to resolve this oscillation without simply translating our interpretations into an ordinary, sensible set of sentences.

Interpretation would thus be a process of standing in for the mind, for the collector of associations and beliefs. Stein's semantic and quasi-syntactical distortions force us to question if these statements can count as thoughts. Her writing primarily consists of assertions, and thus implies at least something like intent. It would be the task of interpretation to translate the form of her sentences into what we imagine she meant. In so doing we attempt to reconnect the meaning of a sentence to what is said, as if we were interpreting an oracle.

Because what we read, therefore, is a fiction about Stein's mind as a stand-in for the human mind, there is little at issue in reading what the writings might mean. We can read to justify Stein's aesthetic or we can reconstitute aspects of the mind that created it (various associations, for example). We can trace internal patterns within the work or *oeuvre*. This would include phonological similarities, visual cues, word repetitions, or associational patterns ascribed to or assumed by Stein. We can then allegorize the text relative to a limited set of patterns, associations, and possible meanings of words and phrases (reading 'Tender Buttons' as a sexual reference and so on). The specific associations we posit, the meanings and references we stipulate and which Stein might have stipulated, however, are all facsimiles of thought. The putative contents of her sentences (what would be the thoughts expressed) are not expressed by her words. The words and phrases are targets for our invention or her association, more like prompts for private memory or imagination. The identification of an association between a phrase and an idea or physical thing does not constitute a thought. Together, these prompts and targets logically express her particularity, the quasi-thoughts forming a picture of a mind absent from the text. The sentences are justified only relative to the particularity of that mind, but that mind, even for Stein, is only something remembered, invented, and imagined.

The problem of how to interpret Stein's text, therefore, is less a question of exegesis than a way of justifying the mode of writing relative to whatever sense we imagine we discover in it. The discovery of meaning in Stein's texts, however, seems hardly necessary for two reasons:

(1) The words and phrases often mean just what they say, 'I do not know where I am going but I am on my way and then suddenly well not perhaps suddenly but perhaps yes I do know where I am going and I do not like that' (Stein, 1995, p. 391). Such writing descends from the project she describes in *The Gradual Making of the Making of Americans*: 'the complete description of something, with ultimately the complete description of anything with ultimately the complete description of everything' (Stein, 1990, p. 255). The detailed, obsessive insistence of this kind of description and its quasi-phenomenological stream of consciousness form distorts normal sense, but in a naïve Grandma Moses kind of way.

(2) Her associations and deformations can only be taken as thought if they are normalized into ordinary English. If we take her writing as a code, then one can do this, but then it hardly seems interesting. If it is not a code, then there is no way to normalize the words into thoughts without inventing a theory to do so. We are left with no way to decide between the dual intuitions with which I began. Her sentences do not mean or they mean one unique thing. I often have the impression that she means something, but she is not sure what. (Some people might think this describes the ineffable, but I think it rather describes the empty.)

We read the words of Steinian nonsense relative to what we imagine could be the thought justifying the disorder. If we do not do that, then the words mean nothing. Stein's nonsense depends, therefore, on a mind to justify it – a mind making associations, a posited person whose mind is these associations. The sense and justification of this nonsense is displaced back into the mind of the writer or the mind of the reader (who would then try to match it: think these thoughts, whatever they are). The mind of the author is not recoverable, even for her. Maybe some readers enjoy being deranged occasionally. Stein justifies this type of writing as an expression of the moment that includes the entire world (a form of radical holism), and as such cannot be articulated nor represented. Thus, her mind frames the text but the mind is itself unframed (and maybe unhinged), unlimited except as the world that is gone and is in itself not knowable.

Reading Stein can become a way of describing how deforming language can show someone as a kind of blankness, which at the same time becomes a picture of human beings. Stein attempts to make language hyper-expressive by deforming it into certain kinds of nonsense. She tries to pry herself out of language in order to pry language into being her or being a thing, and thus to show it to us all. Stein's offering herself, however, as a human pronoun fails except as an invitation to mimic her. If I try to pry myself from language, I end up only prying myself from one end of a phrase to another.

The Stein oracle, like the Stein pronoun, is factitious. A failed oracle is a pied piper. If we squint we can hear the music.

Works cited

Gass, William, Preface to *The Geographical History of America or the Relation between Human Nature and the Human Mind* (Baltimore: Johns Hopkins University Press, 1995).

Joyce, James, *Finnegans Wake* (Harmondsworth: Penguin, 1999).

Stein, Gertrude, *How to Write* (New York: Dover, 1975).

—— *Selected Writings of Gertrude Stein*, ed. F.W. Dupee and Carl Van Vechten (New York: Vintage, 1990).

—— *Making of Americans, Being a History of a Family's Progress* (New York: Dalkey Archives, 1995).

—— *The Geographical History of America or the Relation between Human Nature and the Human Mind* (Baltimore: Johns Hopkins University Press, 1995).

—— *Tender Buttons: Objects, Food, Rooms* (New York: Dover, 1997).

Part III
Encounters with Literature in German Philosophy

Introduction

The relationship between literature and philosophy has been a particularly close one throughout the history of German thought, owing largely to the importance of Romanticism in the intellectual development of that tradition. Philosophers such as Fichte (1762–1814) and Schelling (1775–1854) are as central to German Romanticism as writers like Goethe (1749–1832) and Schiller (1759–1805), and disciplinary distinctions between literature, philosophy, and criticism or theory are frequently questionable, or even inappropriate, when discussing this movement. It would, for example, be hard to categorize the writings of the Schlegel brothers August (1767–1845) and Friedrich (1772–1829) within such a scheme, and the latter's claim that 'philosophy poeticises and poetry philosophises' sums up the difficulty. The legacy of German Romanticism – in particular this close association of literature and philosophy – and its importance throughout the evolution of literary theory is traced by Andrew Bowie in his study *From Romanticism to Critical Theory: The Philosophy of German Literary Theory* (London: Routledge, 1997), which provides an excellent orientation to the historical origins of the philosophy/literature interface in German thought.

Relatedly, another significant development anticipated by nineteenth-century German thought is the tendency, associated with much contemporary critical theory, to blur the boundaries between literary and philosophical discourse. Probably the most radical innovator in this regard would be Friedrich Nietzsche (1844–1900), whose texts such as *Thus Spake Zarathustra* and *The Gay Science* make abundant use of such devices as narrative, symbolism, allegory, and metaphor, in a style that is, if anything, more 'literary' than 'philosophical' (in the traditional senses of these terms). Indeed, Nietzsche asserted that truth itself is a fictional construct, sustained by metaphors – an argument that puts in question any straightforward distinction between modes of philosophical and literary expression (this view is most clearly articulated in his essay 'On Truth and Lying in an Extra-Moral Sense'). Jacques Derrida paid tribute to the importance of these aspects of Nietzsche's writings. (See especially his *Spurs: Nietzsche's Styles* [trans. Barbara Harlow. Chicago: University of Chicago Press, 1979]). Other illuminating discussions include Henry Staten's *Nietzsche's Voice* (Ithaca: Cornell University Press, 1990); John Carson Pettey's *Nietzsche's Philosophical and Narrative Styles* (New York: Peter Lang, 1992); and Bernd Magnus, Stanley Stewart and Jean-Pierre Mileur's *Nietzsche's Case: Philosophy As/And Literature* (London: Routledge, 1993).

In the twentieth century, German philosophy encompassed the widest possible diversity of positions and schools, and it would not be possible to do justice to them all within the confines of this section. The first major breakthrough of this period, and perhaps the most important, was the thought of Edmund Husserl (1859–1938), which inaugurated modern phenomenology – the analysis of the structures through which we experience and 'intend' the phenomena of the world around us. Given that, for Husserl, the study of perception, decoding, and projection of meaning is central to philosophical inquiry, one might expect his work to have exerted a formative influence over the field of literary theory. Yet, in the main, Husserl has been less directly influential to literary study than his importance in philosophy might suggest, and the mainstream of literary criticism and theory has been more directly influenced by philosophical offshoots from Husserl's thought than by Husserl himself (though there have been exceptions to this, notably Derrida's *Speech and Phenomena and Other Essays on Husserl's Theory of Signs*, trans. David B Allison. Evanston: Northwestern University Press, 1973). Ralph Strehle's essay attempts to redress this imbalance by reading Husserl's work alongside the fiction of Virginia Woolf, and demonstrating a close similarity of concern in the way Husserl and Woolf engage with issues of intersubjectivity, time, and narrative.

In terms of the relationship between philosophy and literature, the most influential development from Husserlian phenomenology has been the existentialist thought of Martin Heidegger (1889–1976), which conceives of poetry as fundamental to man's relation to, and communion with, the world. Heidegger's notion that, as he puts it, 'poetically man dwells', has drawn comment from many philosophers, and from literary critics and theorists of numerous persuasions. Veronique Foti's *Heidegger and the Poets: Poiesis, Sophia, Techne* (New Jersey: Humanities Press International, 1991) considers Heidegger's views alongside readings of a wide variety of German poets. For an excellent introduction to the literary aspects of Heidegger's thought, see Timothy Clark's *Martin Heidegger* (London: Routledge Critical Thinkers, 2002). A more general discussion is given by Marc Froment-Meurice in his *That Is To Say: Heidegger's Poetics* (trans. Jan Plug. Stanford: Stanford University Press, 1998). In this section, Jennifer Anna Gosetti-Ferencei's essay discusses Heidegger's view of the centrality of poetry, and explores some of the political implications that might be salvaged from the ideas of a thinker tainted by his association with Nazism.

Another offshoot of Husserl's phenomenology is the movement known as hermeneutic philosophy, derived largely from the thought of Hans-Georg Gadamer (1900–2002), in particular his *Truth and Method* (Second, revised edition – trans. Joel Weinsheimer and Donald G. Marshall. New York: Cross-road, 1989). Drawing on the earlier ideas of Schleiermacher (1768–1834) and Dilthey (1833–1911), Gadamer's work describes a 'hermeneutic circle', wherein our interpretations of the world are constantly being updated and modified as the expectations and hypotheses on which they are based (them-selves interpretations of sorts) prove to be valid or invalid. This model, applied to the way we read texts rather than the way we read the world, has been a formative influence on the reader-response criticism and reception theory associated with the so-called Constance School, the most widely read members of which include Wolfgang Iser and Hans-Robert Jauss. Their work attempted to translate phenomenological and hermeneutic philosophy's ideas about the structure of interpretation into a way of describing the process of reading, and indeed literary study itself. A concise account of this is Iser's 'The Reading Process: A Phenomenological Approach' in his *The Implied Reader: Patterns of Communication in Prose from Bunyan to Beckett* (Baltimore: Johns Hopkins University Press, 1974). Jauss's more historical approach is outlined in his *Toward an Aesthetic of Reception* (trans. Timothy Bahti. Minneapolis: University of Minnesota Press, 1982). Gadamer's own reflections on literary themes are available in his *Literature and Philosophy in Dialogue: Essays in German Literary Theory* (trans. Robert H. Paslick. Albany: Suny Press, 1994).

Husserl, Heidegger, and Gadamer form one of the two principal axes of twentieth-century German thought. The other, quite distinct from these positions, is derived from Marx and Hegel, and its proponents such as Theodor Adorno (1903–69) and Herbert Marcuse (1898–1979) came to be known as the Frankfurt School. Philosophy, for the Frankfurt School, was intimately wedded to social theory, but entailed a self-interrogating self-consciousness that averted stagnation into mere theoretism or positivism: it provided an approach its practitioners called Critical Theory. The Frankfurt School emphasized the centrality of aesthetics to philosophy, and their writ-ings (especially Adorno's) on literature, music, art, and the 'culture industry' have been widely influential to literary critics and theorists. Adorno's thought is discussed in Simon Malpas's essay 'Form, Reflection, Disclosure: Literary Aesthetics and Contemporary Criticism', in the concluding section of this book.

One of the most complex and interesting figures associated with the Frank-furt School, Walter Benjamin (1892–1940), is the focus of the last of the essays in this section. Literature is arguably even more central to Benjamin's work than to Adorno's, and he carries to extremes the self-critical methods of the Frankfurt School in readings that perform 'immanent critique' of artworks and literary texts. Richard Lane's essay examines the opposition towards 'theory' in Benjamin's work, and the philosophical alternatives to it he practises instead.

Finally, a provocative and entertaining book of essays by one of the most skilful readers of both literary and philosophical texts in the German tradition is Werner Hamacher's *Premises: Essays on Philosophy and Literature from Kant to Celan* (trans. Peter Fenves. Cambridge: Harvard University Press, 1996). Hamacher's work covers the broadest variety of writers and thinkers, and exemplifies the complex but rewarding nature of the best interdisciplinary work in the contemporary 'literature and philosophy' dialogue.

David Rudrum

6
A Risky Business: Internal Time and Objective Time in Husserl and Woolf
Ralph Strehle

The discussion that follows aims to chart a series of relationships, encapsulated in the broader relationship between the philosophy of Edmund Husserl and the novels of Virginia Woolf. The crucial relationship under scrutiny here is that between the self and the other, and the question of intersubjectivity that this relationship raises. But this relationship is itself related to another – the relationship between the self and time. And in scrutinizing this latter relationship, a further distinction emerges between two temporalities: a subjective, internal time, and an objective, external time. The relationship between these two temporalities is of central importance in understanding the relationship between the self and the other, as I hope to demonstrate in readings of Husserl and Woolf.

In his transcendental phenomenology, Husserl differentiates between the 'natural attitude' and the 'transcendental attitude'. The 'natural attitude' comprises worldly reality in its broadest sense. As such, the natural attitude is a product or objectification of internal time. Having 'one spatiotemporal actuality' shared by subjects and objects alike, it is an intersubjective space (Husserl, 1989a, §30, p. 57). 'The existence-sense [*Seinssinn*] of the world', Husserl asserts, is its 'thereness-for-everyone' (Husserl, 1988, §43, p. 92). It is a place where subjects are related 'to one another in love and aversion, in disposition and action, in discourse and discussion' (Husserl, 1989b, §49, p. 192). Discussing empathy in *Experience and Judgement*, Husserl explains that the natural attitude relies on the constitution of an 'intersubjectively common time' which, crucially, is related to secondary and not primary memory, that is, to actual recollections and expectations rather than the more classically phenomenological processes of retention and protention. 'In empathy', says Husserl,

> an objective, intersubjectively common time, in which everything individual in lived experiences and temporal objectivities must be capable of being ordered, is constituted. This constitution can be reduced to the fact

that for every ego empathy is nothing other than a special group of posi-
tional presentifications in relation to memories and expectations.(Husserl,
1973a, §38, p. 165)

So for Husserl, the 'natural attitude' and, with it, empathy and intersubjectivity, are bound up with the construction of an objective, ordered time
in which 'each point presents an objective time-point that can be identified
again and again' (Husserl, 1991, p. 113).

This notion of time that underpins the natural attitude is also the condition for dialogue or communication:

> In this unique world... everything that I have perceived and which I
> can now remember or about which others can report to me as what they
> have perceived or remembered, has its place. Everything has its unity in
> that it has its fixed temporal position in this objective world, its place in
> objective time. (Husserl, 1973a, §38, p. 163)

What is important here is Husserl's awareness that intersubjectivity requires
not only the constitution of an objective time but also language as a means
of objectifying and communicating one's experiences. The natural attitude is thus also the domain of storytelling: stories, ultimately, of selfhood
confirmed or questioned by an other in this intersubjective space.

In Virginia Woolf's writing, this link between the constitution of an
objective and intersubjective space and the necessity of storytelling receives
great importance. As Bernard says in *The Waves*,

> [I]n order to make you understand, to give you my life, I must tell you a
> story – and there are so many, and so many – stories of childhood, stories
> of school, love, marriage, death, and so on; and none of them are true.
> Yet like children we tell each other stories, and to decorate them we make
> up these ridiculous, flamboyant, beautiful phrases. (Woolf, *The Waves*,
> p. 199)

Of course, for Husserl, at least in his later writings, the question of truth
lacks relevance. The more interesting question (for him, at least) was to find
the transcendental conditions for selfhood, which would lead him to interrogate internal time consciousness – I shall attempt this in due course. First,
however, I want to identify a common point of emphasis: sequence seems
to be a fundamental characteristic of selfhood in Husserl and Woolf. In *The
Waves*, Neville demands that Bernard 'describe what we have all seen so that
it becomes a sequence. Bernard says there is always a story. I am a story. Louis
is a story' (Woolf, *The Waves*, p. 28). The sequentiality mentioned by Neville
here is a linear continuum engendered out of lived experience ('what we have
seen'). Its prerequisite is the constitution of objective time. 'Every past', says

Husserl, 'is unilaterally coordinated with an original now and its content; all are separated in linear continua of endless pasts and are joined together in a two-dimensional system in which these linear continua continuously blend into one another and constitute a *single* linear continuum' (Husserl, 1973a, Appendix I, p. 385).

But this form of temporality – a single, linear, continuous time with a shared, objective existence that can be communicated – is not the only way of conceptualizing time, or indeed of experiencing it. Even the most casual readings of Woolf or Husserl reveal another, more obvious common point of emphasis: a fascination with the very different experience of time that takes place subjectively or internally. Woolf's experiments in stream of consciousness are clear examples of this. The difference between subjective and objective time is the central theme of *Mrs Dalloway*, where interior monologues are regularly punctuated by clocks chiming the hours (*The Hours* was, of course, the novel's working title). Indeed, few novelists have explored the interrelation between selfhood and temporality in as much complexity as Woolf. And few philosophers have explored this same interrelation in as much complexity as Husserl.

For Husserl, internal time, as opposed to objective time, is character-ized as the 'continuous production of modifications of modifications' of temporal fields which comprise primal impressions, retentions, and proten-tions (Husserl, 1991, Appendix I, p. 106). For example, with the occurrence of a new temporal field, the original temporal field becomes a retention of the present temporal field, whilst the former retention of the original temporal field is pushed further into the past and becomes a second-degree retention of the present temporal field. According to Husserl, every 'now' that sinks into the past retains its identity although it is exposed to the constant flux of modification (Husserl, 1991, §30, p. 64). To be more precise, every 'now' retains its identical temporal position (Husserl, 1991, §31, pp. 70–71). This identical temporal position or objective time-point is linked to the primal impression of a 'now-phase'. The primal impression is not only the point from which retentions and protentions emerge, thereby constituting a 'now-phase', but also the point of absolute presence: 'Primal impression has as its content that which the word "now" signifies, insofar as it is taken in the strictest sense. Each new now is the content of a new primal impression' (Husserl, 1991, §31, p. 70). Yet Husserl immediately admits that

> the now is precisely only an ideal limit, something abstract, which can be nothing by itself. Moreover, it remains to be said that even this ideal now is not something *toto coelo* different from the not-now but is continuously mediated with it. And to this corresponds the continuous transition of perception into primary memory. (Husserl, 1991, p. 42)

Crucially then, the 'now' of a primal impression, as opposed to the 'now-phase', cannot be experienced. 'We are', says Husserl, 'conscious of what has just concluded only in the form of retention, or in the form of backwards-glancing remembrance' (Husserl, 1989a, §44). The pure 'now' with its content is an *'Atopon'* (Sommer, p. 162). (Incidentally, the deconstructive claim that there is a metaphysics of presence in Husserl's phenomenology is founded on the confusion of the 'now' of the primal impression with the retentional 'now' of the 'now-phase').

Husserl's examination of internal time takes place within his analysis of the 'transcendental attitude', which differs from the objective time of the natural attitude. He calls the shift of emphasis from the communal, intersubjective world to the subject in its transcendental, world-constituting function the 'transcendental-phenomenological reduction' (Held, 1966, p. 17). The main characteristic of transcendental subjectivity is its intentionality. In *Cartesian Meditations* Husserl outlines its basic features: 'the word intentionality signifies nothing else than this universal fundamental property of consciousness: to be consciousness *of* something; as a *cogito*, to bear within itself its *cogitatum'* (Husserl, 1988, §14, p. 33)[1]. However, this assertion that intentionality means 'consciousness of something' is qualified in a later paragraph, where Husserl characterizes intentional acts as 'sense-fashionings' in that they ascribe a certain sense of being to objects.

Husserl's description of intentionality has seemed problematic to some. According to Emmanuel Levinas, for example, it enables the possession of objects via its incorporating movement towards exteriority, and is thus a form of violence: 'The notion of act involves a violence essentially: the violence of transitivity' (Levinas, p. 27). But Levinas's remark should be received with caution. First, because Husserl talks about inanimate bodies (*Körper*) and not human bodies (*Leiber*); and secondly, because a close analysis of internal time reveals that neither animate nor inanimate objects can be adequately objectified in the natural attitude. This is because all bodies – even inanimate objects and mere 'things' – transcend the constituted 'cogitatum' or 'alter ego'. For Husserl, transcendence pertains to inanimate bodies because they can only be recognized within a 'presentive-appresentive' perception. In other words, even inanimate bodies or things are not subject (or, as Levinas might say, *subjected*) to what Husserl calls 'fulfilling presentation'.

Consider, for example, what happens in the act of perception that takes place when one sees an object, say a house. Although one perceives a house as a three-dimensional object of a certain shape, strictly speaking one only sees one aspect of the house, that is the front, the roof, or the rear side. There remain aspects which are there, yet without presentational content. Husserl calls these 'appresentations', and the correlating perceptual act 'appresentive perception'. The perception of the house 'in the flesh' is 'presentive-appresentive' perception, and for Husserl this is a transcending form of perception:

[I]n the object of such a presentive-appresentive perception . . . we must distinguish noematically between that part which is genuinely perceived and the rest, which is not strictly perceived and yet is indeed there too. Thus every perception of this type is transcending: it posits more as itself-there than it makes 'actually' present at a time. Every external perception belongs here – for example, perception of a house (front-rear). (Husserl, 1988, §55, p. 122)[2]

Since each perceived object includes aspects which are only appresented, there is always an 'aiming-beyond [*Hinausmeinen*]' to possible determinations. As Elizabeth Ströker expresses it, noetically speaking, there is a horizon of 'possibilities and "presumabilities" [*Vermutlichkeiten*] of new experiences' (Ströker, p. 88).[3] Depending on whether further experiences are directed toward the object itself or its surrounding, Husserl speaks of the explication of a thing's inner or its outer horizons (Husserl, 1966, §1, p. 7). The transcendence of an inanimate body does not so much lie in its having infinite horizons but in the fact that direct intention is not possible. In Husserl, then, intentionality is, strictly speaking, retentional.

If internal time itself is something which can only provide identity retrospectively, the task of understanding another human being with its own inner time (as opposed to a mere inanimate body like a house) proves doubly difficult. Within his discussion of intersubjectivity in his *Cartesian Meditations*, Husserl outlines the appresentation of the other as follows:

I am *here* somatically, the center of a primordial 'world' oriented around me . . . the other body there enters into a pairing association with my body here and, being given perceptually, becomes the core of an appresentation, the core of my experience of a coexisting ego, that ego, according to the whole sense-giving course of the association, must be appresented *as an ego now coexisting in the mode There*, 'such as I should be if I were there'. My own ego, however . . . is actual now with the content belonging to his Here. Therefore an ego is *appresented*, as *other* than mine. That which is primordially incompatible, in simultaneous coexistence, becomes compatible: because my primordial ego constitutes the ego who is other for him by an appresentative apperception, which, according to its intrinsic nature, never demands and never is open to fulfilment by presentation. (Husserl, 1988, §54, p. 119)

Fundamentally, then, the process of a pairing association 'never demands and never is open to fulfilment by presentation'. This primordial incompatibility is not only constitutive of intersubjectivity, but of subjectivity in general, comprising the subject's primordial sphere, where it fashions the '*Seins-Sinn*' of objects.

A clear illustration of this is provided in Woolf's *To the Lighthouse*, where Husserl's pairing association constantly and consistently fails. The moment, for example, when Mr Ramsay broods over the inevitable fate of all human activity and achievement – 'how we know nothing and the sea eats away the ground we stand on' (Woolf, *Lighthouse*, p. 50) – is precisely the moment when Mrs Ramsay looks up to Mr Ramsay as he stands on the edge of the lawn, thinking of him 'as a stake driven into the bed of a channel upon which the gulls perch and the waves beat' (Woolf, *Lighthouse*, p. 50). Clearly, Mr Ramsay's perception of himself and Mrs Ramsay's perception of her husband could not be more contradictory. The inability to, as it were, pair one's own inner time with somebody else's in an act of empathy is also experienced by Lily Briscoe. She imagines sitting at Mrs Ramsay's knees whilst actually painting an abstract painting of her at a distance. '[T]he picture was not of them, she said. Or, not in his sense [Mr. Bankes' sense of resemblance]. There were other senses, too, in which one might reverence them. By a shadow here and a light there' (Woolf, *Lighthouse*, p. 59). At this point, Lily is standing on the edge of the lawn, while Mrs Ramsay sits in the window with her son James:

> Sitting on the floor with her arms round Mrs. Ramsay's knees, close as she could get, smiling to think that Mrs. Ramsay would never know the reason of that pressure, she imagined how in the chambers of the mind and heart of the woman who was, physically, touching her, were stood, like the treasures in the tombs of kings, tablets bearing sacred inscriptions, which if one could spell them out would teach one everything, but they would never be offered openly, never made public. What art was there, known to love or cunning, by which one pressed through those secret chambers? What device for becoming, like waters poured into one jar, inextricably the same, one with the object one adored? Could the body achieve it, or the mind . . . Nothing happened. Nothing! Nothing! as she leant her head against Mrs. Ramsay's knees. (Woolf, *Lighthouse*, p. 57)

Standing on the lawn, Lily imagines being there at the window with Mrs Ramsay, more specifically, inside her mind. Her inability 'to become inextricably the same, one with the object one adored', rests precisely on her possessing a different temporal and spatial location.

In *Phänomenology der Intersubjectivität* Husserl clearly addresses the unbridgeable chasm between the temporal lives of different egos:

> Die Zeit meines strömenden Lebens und die meines Nachbarn ist . . . abgrundtief geschieden, und selbst dieses Wort sagt noch in seiner Bildlichkeit zu wenig. Sowie sie als diese Zeit . . . einig würde mit der nachbarlichen, wären wir beide ein Ich. (Husserl, 1973b, Text no. 20, p. 339)[4]

Toward the end of *To the Lighthouse*, Lily stands again on the lawn painting a picture 'she had never finished' (Woolf, *Lighthouse*, p. 161). It is a picture involving a tree which she remembers wanting to move to the middle of the painting. Since she painted such a picture at the Ramsay's, and since the only picture she painted there appears to be that which includes Mrs Ramsay, it can be assumed that Lily is finishing that very picture. Although Mrs Ramsay is long dead, Lily sees Mrs Ramsay as she 'sat there quite simply, in the chair, flicked her needles to and fro, knitted her reddish-brown stocking, cast her shadow on the step. There she sat' (Woolf, *Lighthouse*, p. 219). This time, Lily will finish the painting, and Woolf implies that she will do so precisely because Mrs Ramsay is no longer a being with her own spatial and temporal situatedness and thus difference.

Such, according to Husserl, are the inevitable limitations of internal, subjective time: by definition, it cannot be intersubjective. However, before drawing to conclusions that lament the shortcomings of an isolated, internal temporality, we would do well to consider that objective time is not without its problems either. A shared, intersubjective notion of time is probably at its clearest in our notions of history and tradition. Tradition is sedimented, culturally sanctioned, objective time. Husserl is well aware of the fact that subjects in the natural attitude are historically situated. (With his genetic analysis, he clearly anticipated much of Heidegger and the recent concern with historicity). '[M]en belonging to one and the same world live in a loose cultural community', argues Husserl,

> and accordingly constitute different surrounding worlds of culture, as concrete life-worlds in which the relatively or absolutely separate communities live their passive and active lives. Each man understands first of all . . . *his* concrete surrounding world or *his* culture; and he does so precisely as a man who belongs to the community fashioning it historically. (Husserl, 1988, §58, p. 133)

In Woolf, too, tradition is fundamentally exclusive. Rather than a sense-fashioning, providing its subjects with stories of selfhood, it is a sense-imposition. Walking through the corridors of his school, Louis muses that '[a]bove all, we have inherited traditions. These stone flags have been worn for six hundred years. On these walls are inscribed the names of men of war, of statesmen, of some unhappy poets' (Woolf, *The Waves*, p. 45). In *The Waves*, tradition literally comes to speak in the person of Dr Crane, whose sermons are experienced by Bernard and Neville as oppressive and violent. ' "The brute menaces my liberty," said Neville, "when he prays. Unwarmed by imagination, his words fall cold on my head like paving-stones, while the gilt cross heaves on his waistcoat." ' (Woolf, *The Waves*, p. 26). By maintaining order, tradition forecloses the possibility of change and revision and becomes an exclusionary repetition of the same. When Crane's sermon ends, Bernard comments that 'He [Crane] has minced the dance of the white butterflies at the door to powder' (Woolf, *The Waves*,

p. 27). The white butterflies here refer not only to language 'unwarmed by imagination', but also to the butterflies that Bernard, Neville, Jinny, and Susan collect in the garden-scene at the beginning of the novel and which, as Louis imagines things, will be laid on a 'pocket-handkerchief on the gravel' (Woolf, *The Waves*, p. 8). Tradition neither allows for butterfly-language – a language that, in Bernard's phrase, cannot 'foretell the flight of a word' and is thus open to change (Woolf, *The Waves*, p. 96) – nor for the idiosyncratic particularity, a handkerchief spread out on the ground. The violence of tradition is most obvious in the symbolic function of the handkerchief. In the garden-scene, the reader learns that 'Susan has spread her anguish out. Her pocket-handkerchief is laid on the roots of the beech trees and she sobs, sitting crumpled where she has fallen' (Woolf, *The Waves*, pp. 9–10). Susan's crumpled posture is recalled at a later stage when, during her school days, she explains that each night she 'tear[s] off the old day from the calendar, and screw[s] it tight into a ball' (Woolf, *The Waves*, p. 30). Ultimately, it is in the description of the boys marching in troops and throwing 'dirty pocket-handkerchiefs clotted with blood screwed up into corners' (Woolf, *The Waves*, p. 36) that the violence against women within tradition and the patriarchal order is revealed: here, the natural attitude, insofar as it can be identified with sedimented lived cultural time, simply upholds an existing patriarchal order.

The natural attitude then, as historically sedimented objective time, can be a place of prejudice and exclusionary practices. Husserl, after all, asserts that

> [a] deeper understanding, one that opens up the horizon of the past (which is co-determinant for an understanding of the present itself), is essentially possible to all members of [a] community, with a certain originality possible to them alone and barred to anyone from another community who enters into relation with theirs. (Husserl, 1988, §58, p. 133)

This emphasizes the incommensurabilty of interpretive communities. But a closer analysis of the constitution of the natural attitude reveals that any cultural community is a loose and fragile construct because, for Husserl, the natural attitude and its objective time are constituted out of internal time. In other words, harmony and accord between the members of a respective community are not firmly anchored features of the natural attitude. Rather, they are post-hoc achievements which are constitutionally unsound. As a consequence, no cultural community can resort to a legitimizing arche-discourse, and instead must rely on its own performative re-enactments based on the tautological principle that 'we are what we are because we are what we are'. This, I take it, is what is so insidious about the concept of 'tradition'.

It cannot be denied that most of the time communication in the natural attitude takes place successfully, and that understanding can be achieved.

Neither the natural attitude nor the transcendental attitude is unproblematic, but the achievement of a shared intersubjectivity is by no means an impossible task. According to Husserl, this is so because the world we live in, that is, our cultural world, is always already known in general:

> In the continuous validation of its being, the world, present to consciousness as horizon, has the subjective general character of trustworthiness as a horizon of existents known in general but, on that account, still not known as regards individual particularities. This indeterminate general trustworthiness is allotted to all things which attain separate validity as existent. (Husserl, 1973a, §8, p. 37)

Husserl's 'indeterminate general trustworthiness' is, strictly speaking, an ethical attitude in which the existent is allowed to reveal itself. It is important to understand that this 'trustworthiness' pre-exists the crucial moment in which the phenomenological subject intends his/her world: as such, our sharing our world with others is based on trust and, in a sense, ethics. This is a result of the subject being affected by the existent before the existent can be intended by the subject as cogitatum. '[B]efore every moment of cognition', argues Husserl,

> the object of cognition is already present as a *dynamis* which is to turn into an *entelecheia*. This 'preliminary presence' [*Voranliegen*] means that the object affects us as entering into the background of our field of consciousness, or even that it is already in the foreground, possibly already grasped, but only afterward awakens 'the interest in cognition'... But always preliminary to this grasping is affection, which is not the affecting of an isolated, particular object. 'To affect' means to stand out from the environment, which is always copresent, to attract interest to oneself, possibly interest in cognition. (Husserl, 1973a, §7, pp. 29–30)

This 'preliminary presence' in which the subject is being affected clearly recalls Husserl's 'primal impression'. Although Husserl refers to objects rather than animate bodies, strictly speaking, it cannot be ascertained which one has entered the subject's primordial sphere. In Levinas's terms, it is unclear whether what is taking place is a transdescendence into the realm of the material or a transascendence into the realm of the other. Husserl's notion of 'indeterminate general trustworthiness' thus anticipates Jacques Derrida's notion of hospitality which 'requires that I open up my home and that I give not only to the foreigner... but to the absolute, unknown, anonymous other' (Derrida, p. 25). 'Indeterminate general trustworthiness' consequently also contains the risk that whoever or whatever I invite and welcome might turn out to be an adversary. Fundamentally, within Husserl's phenomenology this risk is not an accident that might occur in the natural attitude as a result of bad politics, but is the transcendental condition for there to be a natural attitude and politics in the first place. However much we might want to seal off our cultural community from others, it will always, as Husserl says, remain a 'loose cultural community' (Husserl, 1988, §58, p. 133).

Naturally, Husserl's phenomenology does not provide us with an ethics of how we ought to conduct our lives with others in the natural attitude – it is a phenomenology, after all. What he does, however, is make us aware of the fact that whatever we do in our daily affairs with others, be they from the same or a different community, is a risky business. This risk carries initially neither good nor bad connotations, for the outcome of an action cannot be predicted (even if it has traditionally worked in one's favor). And once again, Woolf illustrates this clearly: Lily Briscoe is aware of this risk involved in daily affairs, yet she embraces this risk rather than falling into apathy. 'One line placed on the canvas committed her to innumerable risks, to frequent and irrevocable decisions... Still the risk must be run; the mark made' (Woolf, *Lighthouse*, p. 172).

Notes

1. For a good discussion of Husserl's and Brentano's concept of intentionality, see Schutz, pp. 23–39.
2. See also Husserl, 1997, §16, p. 43.
3. See also Held, 1998, p. 14.
4. 'The time of my passing life and that of my neighbour are separated by an abyss and even the metaphoricity of this word is insufficient to express this. If this time as such... were to fuse with that of my neighbour, we would both become one "I" with one life'. [my trans.]

Works cited

Derrida, Jacques, *Of Hospitality*, trans. Rachel Bowlby (Stanford: Stanford University Press, 2000).
Held, Klaus *Lebendige Gegenwart: Die Frage Nach Der Seinsweise Des Transzendentalen Ich Bei Edmund Husserl Entwickelt Am Leitfaden Der Zeitproblematik* (Den Haag: Martinus Nijhoff, 1966).
——'Einleitung', in *Edmund Husserl. Phänomenologie der Lebenswelt. Ausgewählte Texte II*, ed. Klaus Held (Stuttgart: Reclam, 1998).
Husserl, Edmund, *Analysen zur Passiven Synthesis. Aus Vorlesungs- und Forschungsmanuskripten 1918–1926*, ed. Margot Fleischer (Den Haag: Martinus Nijhoff, 1966).
——*Experience and Judgment: Investigations in a Genealogy of Logic*, ed. Ludwig Landgrebe, trans. James S. Churchill and Karl Ameriks (London: Routledge, 1973a).
——*Zur Phänomenologie der Intersubjektivität. Texte aus dem Nachlass. Dritter Teil: 1929–1935*, 3 vols, ed. Iso Kern (Den Haag: Martinus Nijhoff, 1973b).
——*Cartesian Meditations: An Introduction to Phenomenology*, trans. Dorion Cairns (2nd ed. Dordrecht: Nijhoff, 1988).
——*Ideas Pertaining to a Pure Phenomenology and to a Phenomenological Philosophy. First Book: General Introduction to a Pure Phenomenology*, trans. Richard Rojcewicz and André Schuwer (Dordrecht: Kluwer, 1989a).

——*Ideas Pertaining To A Pure Phenomenology And To A Phenomenological Philosophy. Second Book: Studies In The Phenomenology of Constitution*, trans. Richard Rojcewicz and André Schuwer (Dordrecht: Kluwer, 1989b).

——*On the Phenomenology of the Consciousness of Internal Time (1893–1917)*, trans. John Barnett Brough (Dordrecht: Kluwer, 1991).

——*Thing and Space: Lectures of 1907*, trans. Richard Rojcewicz (Dordrecht: Kluwer, 1997).

Levinas, Emmanuel, *Totality and Infinity: An Essay on Exteriority*, trans. Alphonso Lingis (Pittsburgh: Duquesne University Press, 1969).

Schutz, Alfred, 'Some Leading Concepts of Phenomenology', in *Essays in Phenomenology*, ed. Maurice Natanson (Den Haag: Martinus Nijhoff, 1966).

Sommer, Manfred, *Lebenswelt und Zeitbewußtsein* (Frankfurt am Main: Suhrkamp, 1990).

Ströker, Elizabeth, *Husserl's Transcendental Phenomenology*, trans. Lee Hardy (Stanford: Stanford University Press, 1993).

Virginia Woolf, *The Waves*, ed. Gillian Beer (Oxford: Oxford University Press, 1992).

——*To The Lighthouse,* ed. Stella McNichol, Introduction by Hermione Lee (Harmondsworth: Penguin, 1992).

7
The Poetics of Thinking

Jennifer Anna Gosetti-Ferencei

The poeticization of thinking

Concerning Heidegger's involvement with German fascism in the early 1930s, when Heidegger joined the Nazi party and, as Rector of the University of Freiburg, embraced a National Socialist vision of the 'self-assertion of the German university', Hans Jonas, his bitterly disappointed student, stated that not only Heidegger's politics but philosophy itself 'had declared bankruptcy'. Heidegger, the 'most profound thinker' of that time, had erred not only politically, but had brought philosophy astray from its service of the good. Furthermore, Heidegger had invoked poetry, specifically Hölderlin's, as the primordial resource for his thinking of strife, struggle, and historical decisionism for the German people as a *Volk*, and their exclusive destiny. Though Heidegger later finds poetry also a source for extricating himself from his errors, and indeed for a very promising notion of non-violent, poetic dwelling, nevertheless at a certain juncture the poetic is implicated in a profound failure. To Heidegger's failure Jonas poses a counterexample, the 'strict and uncompromising Kantian' professor of philosophy Julius Ebbinghaus, who 'passed the test admirably' and resisted succumbing to the Nazi fervor – Ebbinghaus claimed later that without Kant 'I wouldn't have been able to do it.'[1]

This account by Heidegger's student has a number of implications: that a straightforward, unpoetic faith in rational thinking, attended by an explicit ethics, though perhaps lackluster in comparison with Heidegger's creative and daring ontology, is capable of sustaining the uprightness of philosophy and preventing the philosopher from a breach of faith with the good. It has been suggested that the 'nobility of philosophical life; has been challenged not only by Heidegger's moral failings but perhaps also by his aestheticism, or poeticization of philosophy'.[2] A co-implication – and what concerns me in this essay – is that the poetic, especially in the form of what Jonas calls Heidegger's 'mythopoetics', drawn from Hölderlin, ought to generate suspicion, recalling those reasons Plato gave for suppressing poetry: poets lack knowledge of the good; while perhaps divinely inspired, they succumb to excesses incompatible with 'a rightly and nobly ordered soul' (*Republic*, Book X). Add these (poetical) excesses – not to mention a poetic theory that embraces strife and struggle – to political missteps and the fanaticism of a surrounding ideology, and a thinker might be drawn to the point where, as Heidegger said at the end of the war, 'only a god can save us'.

Heidegger claims in 'Origin of the Work of Art' that the work of art involves the setting-up and setting-forth (*das Aufstellen* and *das Herstellen*) of truth, and that poetry is capable of 'founding' history – a term (*das Stiften*) echoed in Hölderlin's poem '*Andenken*' which Heidegger discussed at the University of Freiburg in his *Vorlesungen Wintersemester 1941–1942*. These claims demand critical scrutiny when read, as he meant them to be, in a (albeit not exclusively) political context (see Heidegger, 1960 and 1992). The nature of poetry and the thinking that attends it, and the relationship of poetic thinking to truth, is what I would like to examine here, in light of such scrutiny.

My aim is not primarily to assess the poetic from a political standpoint, but to argue that Heidegger, in his claims about the poet's role in founding the events of truth and history, underestimates some important characteristics of the poetic which, if given their due, undermine the more politically disturbing aspects of his notion of poetic founding. The poetic to which I refer involves the uniquely self-referential and plurisignificant nature of poetic language, such that poetry, by resisting eidetic closure, destabilizes the very truths it evokes. Moreover, poetry's truths – insofar as we retain that term – are of the order of the imagination, which is not to suggest that they are as such less powerful or less relevant for actuality, but rather that poetic language and its imagery withhold settling in univocal designations of Being. An acceptance of this withholding tallies with Heidegger's later, and more convincing, *Gelassenheit* theory of poetic language. To Heidegger's theory of founding, I propose not simply Heidegger's own later alternative, but rather a poetics which, diverging from Heidegger's later theory, includes a post-representational account of imagination and the poetic image. This reconsideration could also rethink the poetic in usurpation of an aestheticization, or poeticization of history (Lacoue-Labarthe, 1990, Chapter 7).

Before outlining an alternative to Heideggerian founding, the context of Heidegger's poetics needs recapitulating. First, why did Heidegger turn to the poetic as the primordial resource for thinking? Of course, when Heidegger describes poetry as the essence of thought, he self-consciously disputes a long tradition of philosophical rejection of the poetic. Not only classical Greek, but modern German philosophers, too, chastised the poetic thinkers among them for reasons similar to Plato's. References to the literature of Shakespeare, Sophocles, and Goethe notwithstanding, Hegel's *Phenomenology of Spirit* warns against poetic inspiration. Hegel saw philosophy's laborious progress toward the Absolute as endangered by the claims Romanticism (and he himself once) had made for the poetic. As in classical thought, Hegel regarded the task and methods of philosophy as radically different from those of poetry; the Romantics' highly aestheticized ambitions had hindered philosophy. The claim that the Absolute, the unity of life, the holy, the divine, Being, the thing itself, could be grasped best in poetic intuition, or in art, was incompatible with a genuine science or knowledge (*Wissenschaft*) of truth. More pertinently, Hegel criticizes 'intuitive and poetic thinking', a thinking marked by 'the arbitrary combinations of an imagination that has only been disorganized by its thoughts, an imagery that is neither fish nor flesh, neither poetry nor philosophy' (Hegel, p. 42). Philosophy should not be snagged by particulars, caught up in mere 'animal' feeling, or left to the vagaries of individual genius (Hegel, p. 43). There are to be no 'direct revelations from heaven' (Hegel, p. 42); and so the poetic impulse, insofar as it had infected philosophy, was to be overcome.

More than a century after the *Phenomenology of Spirit*, Heidegger embarks upon a radically different engagement with poetry, which seems to be, at first glance, a return to its Romantic heritage – distressing in light of 1930s politics, with which it engaged. Against neo-Kantianism, which had relegated aesthetics to a tertiary discipline of philosophy, Heidegger argues that poetic language is thought's very essence, and in order for philosophy to become real thinking it must become more poetic. Put more strongly, only with poetry is a rigorous thinking possible, because a poetic understanding of language reveals the very conditions of thought. Even in *Being and Time* Heidegger introduces a philosophical justification for addressing our encounter with the world in poetic terms.[3] Heidegger further argues that a deconstructive 'confrontation', an *Auseinandersetzung*, with the history of philosophical concepts is needed in order to understand our relationship to Being, and that a productive confrontation with poetry must be enlisted as its alternative.[4]

The aforementioned political entanglements of Heidegger's first direct engagements with language (1935–42) also need brief elaboration. In *An Introduction to Metaphysics* (1935), Heidegger links poetry or the poetic with violence and strife in the setting-forth of truth, the 'shattering' of Being also linked to political strife, and in the same text makes vague reference to the 'inner greatness' of the National Socialist movement (Heidegger, 1953). In 'The Origin of the Work of Art', Heidegger claims that art, especially the poetry of Hölderlin, instructs Germans in the self-revealing setting-up of truth, as does the founding of a political state, and he addresses specifically the German *Volk* and the 'decision' which the work of art and Hölderlin puts to them. Heidegger interprets Hölderlin's poem '*Der Ister*' as a meditation on German destiny, as an encounter with the foreign 'for the sake of the national or the proper' and decidedly rejects any influence of Enlightenment thinkers, such as Goethe, in his view of Hölderlin's as yet not fully recognized contribution to German destiny. Whatever the subtleties and complications of Heidegger's approach to poetry in these texts – which clearly demand a more nuanced political interpretation than can be given here – they are implicated in the failure Hans Jonas articulated, if only because they invoke nationalist terms even when recognizing the necessity of confrontation with what is other, and because of the extreme violence this nationalism was provoking and legitimating in Germany and in Europe during these years, almost literally under Heidegger's window. At this point Heidegger had not yet admitted his 'error' in participating, however directly or indirectly, in the promotion of certain features of National Socialism.[5]

Some have attempted to sever Heidegger's 'mythopoetics' from his existential phenomenology, and so salvage the latter's immeasurable contribution on Continental philosophy to come. Yet one cannot simply dismiss Heidegger's investment in poetry if he is right that metaphysics had reached an impasse; and furthermore, one cannot get far with Heidegger's poetics without accepting the priority of his ontological concerns.[6] In claiming that the poetic – with, in Hölderlin, its references to the gods, the divine or the holy, and, as Heidegger interprets it, the nearly apocalyptic oblivion of Being into which metaphysical thought (and modern technology) has led us – is the idiomatic resource for thinking, is Heidegger not destroying the long evolution of philosophy which had sought to liberate itself from the ungroundedness of mystical reverie? Is he not sacrificing philosophy's objectivity and autonomy, and thus its legitimacy, to 'mythological' notions? (Jonas, pp. 49, 150). Was Heidegger's 'indulgence' in the poetic responsible for his aestheticization of politics and, conversely, his distressing politicization of poetry? (Hatab, pp. 203–6).

These questions have emerged as Heidegger's involvement in politics, and its relation to his philosophy, has been better understood. But the poetic, or Heidegger's turn to poetic thinking, also affords him extrication from his errors of the 1930s–1940s. The later *Gelassenheit* theory of non-violent, peaceful dwelling, bewonderment, and shelter of the self-unfolding of Being in, for instance, manifestations of nature is also indebted to his reading of Hölderlin and poetic language in general; and so it is impossible to see the poetic as solely initiating a thinking of violence, strife, or excess. If poetry is revolutionary, it also engenders a nurturing acceptance of what is,[7] if not directly, a positive social vision: poetry later instructs Heidegger on a new path of thinking that gently shelters, rather than violently instigates, Being's *Ereignis* or happening.

Moreover, the strategy of severing Heidegger's investment in poetry from his theory of language in order to avoid the dangers of aestheticism, as in a recent study of Heidegger, is problematic (Hatab, Chapter 2 and epilogue). For the trajectory of Heidegger's thinking, and certainly his theory of language, is unreadable without taking seriously his profound investment in poetry. Heidegger in *Being and Time* already saw the need for a radical liberation of language and of his own methodology; this liberation develops through his interpretations of Hölderlin, George, Trakl, Rilke, and other poets. To understand why poetry is a central element of his thought, we might contrast poetic receptivity to what Heidegger sees as modern philosophy's failure to think Being.

Poetic thinking and the turn to Hölderlin

Heidegger's productive confrontation with poetry is a method of interpretation that draws from 'essential' poems insights into Being which are obscured by other kinds of linguistic assertions, by what he considers an inauthentic metaphysics. Heidegger had shown in *Being and Time* 'how the possibility of an inauthentic and partial relationship toward things inheres in the very nature of the human makeup, along with the intent to overcome it' (de Man, p. 104). Heidegger finds this inauthentic relationship reflected in modern philosophy, in its valorization of rational subjectivity to the strict exclusion of other forms of knowing, and in its reduction, for instance, of Being to logical constructs. Heidegger performs a deconstruction (*Abbau*) of the metaphysical concepts which, as a philosophical reflection of this tendency, had obscured Being. In the wake of such, he must find a new access to Being through contemplating an 'authentic', that is, poetic, language, receptive to Being on its own terms, rather than through traditional kinds of argument which fix Being in logical constructs. Poetry essentially differs from other kinds of language in rendering apparent its role in revealing Being, and so Heidegger points to poems by Hölderlin in which the poet's task is explicitly addressed.

Heidegger understands an engagement with – and the thinker's reception of – the 'essence' of poetry as crucial to our survival as thoughtful beings, as beings capable of ontological questioning. With this as his leitmotif, Heidegger develops a poetic theory of unique philosophical implications, for it is an account not only of creative language but of language *per se*. Heidegger did not argue, along the lines of Romantics like Schlegel, that philosophy itself should be transformed into poetry. Rather, philosophy is to give way to 'thinking' (*Denken*), and thinking is possible as a rigorous meditation upon poetry (*Dichten*). Heidegger claims that 'the two kinds of utterance *par excellence*, poetry and thinking, have not yet been sought out in their proper habitat', their nearness to each other (Heidegger, 1959, p. 81). Gadamer summarizes, 'The path of the West, which is also the path leading to science, has forced upon us the separation and a never completely achievable unity of poetizing and thinking', but in Heidegger it is precisely the distance between them 'that establishes at the same time a certain nearness' (Gadamer, p. 145). As if against Hegel's worry about the confusion inherent in 'poetic thinking', Heidegger specifies that 'Poetry and thinking meet each other in one and the same only when, and only as long as, they remain distinctly in the distinctness of their nature' (Heidegger, 1971b, p. 218).

The nearness of poetizing and thinking has to do with the nature of language, of what Heidegger calls 'saying' (*das Sagen*). Heidegger examines language not as a structure of communication, but in relation to the coming-into-presence of what is, of what is revealed or appears; a relation inherently phenomenological. In his essay 'The Way to Language', Heidegger associates saying with *Ereignis*, an appropriating event. (In German, the word *Ereignis* is homophonous with *eigen*, one's own or proper, and denotes an *event*). In saying, in 'the sounding of the word', one does not appropriate in the sense of coming-to-own the object of speech; rather, the human being is released to his/her ownmost nature, to what is proper to the essence of being human: the initiative relation to presence. This is for Heidegger a listening: 'every spoken word is already an answer' because saying is an encountering response to beings, and, by 'listening' through language, bringing them to presence (to appear) in light of Being itself. (Heidegger, 1959, p. 129).

'Thinking', for Heidegger, involves a privileged relationship to the poetic and its idiom, and can uniquely interpret this revelation, which is coupled with a mysterious concealment. The play between revealing and concealment that occurs in poetic language is regarded as a primordial strife or struggle – '*der Urstreit von Lichtung und Verbergung*' (Heidegger, 1960, p. 54). Making a connection between the 1935 'Origin of the Work of Art' essay and the 1941–42 lectures on Hölderlin, we can say that poetry, through this struggle, 'founds' (*stiftet*) truth; and thinking 'grounds' (*grundet*) what is there instituted. Heidegger does not call upon the thinker to decide the meaning or mediate the effect of poetic assertions, as did Plato. Rather, thinking yields to its service of the poetic in order to discover the latter's silent or 'unsaid' essence which pertains to Being itself. Nevertheless, 'priority is given to thinking, from which in some "open" sense poetizing finds its realization' (White, p. 146).

What Heidegger calls 'thinking' requires breaking down the metaphysics of subjectivity and objectivity. For Heidegger, the self-disclosure of Being, its coming-to-disclosure in phenomena, and primarily through language, is the condition or 'ground' of 'thinking'. Heidegger could not fully analyze this ground in *Being and Time*, which deferred to the human being's existential structures as the site of ontological happening, and retained a still 'logical' mode of analysis. It took what some call a 'turn' in Heidegger's thinking to raise the question of Being from the perspective not of the human subject but of Being as such, insofar as it gives itself specifically to us. Being had to be grasped in the way it discloses itself through language, at once giving and withholding itself in giving. Truth is to be grasped not primarily in linguistic assertion (when language is said to function as the externalization of a subject's intentions), but as the intermittent reversals of a state of concealment, conceptualized by Heidegger, using creative etymology of the Greek term, as *a-letheia* or 'unconcealment'. Poetry is in essence a site for these reversals; *and* a site for what he called 'founding' or establishment of truth, rendered necessary especially by (compared with classical Greece) modernity's extreme ontological penury or 'fallenness'.

Hölderlin is certainly the inspiration here, considering his Romantic condemnation of modern Germany. Drawing from Hölderlin's poem *'Brod und Wein'*, Heidegger presents his poetic ontology as necessitated by the hard times – the 'spiritual decline' (Heidegger, 1953, p. 38) into which philosophy, and Western culture at large, had fallen: a time of crisis, from which the gods have fled and the world has lost its holiness. In Hölderlin Heidegger finds an historicization of Dasein's severe fallenness – which *Being and Time* had analyzed as Dasein's ontically primary condition, existentially inevitable, but not irrevocable. Heidegger's conception of (and responses to) our fallenness is a notion to which his errors of the 1930s might be traced, believing, as he did, that Nazism provided a counter-thrust against the instrumentalization of the dominant Western cultures – American capitalism and Bolshevist socialism. Technical rationality, Heidegger felt, left the human being homeless and uprooted, alienated from Being in an obsessively materialist technicity which 'enframes' the world as a resource to be manipulated. This buries an original access to Being, and obscures an essential relation of the human being to history. Heidegger thought that great works, such as the founding of a new political state or the creation of an artwork, asserted Being anew by confronting a 'people' (*Volk*), specifically the German people, with a decision to be made. This recalls the 'resoluteness' (*Entschlossenheit*) required for Dasein's turning-away from inauthenticity (Heidegger, 1979). The work of art had to be wrested from the 'aesthetic alienation' of modernity, wherein it was relegated to the arcane realm of art criticism, far from its 'original' role of founding a culture and a people.[8] Heidegger sees the lack of relevance of modern works of art, and poetry's relegation to the mere imaginary, as symptomatic of a more primary problem of thinking long reflected in philosophical self-conceptions in the West – a 'forgetting of Being', whereas 'founding', through the poetic work and its grounding in thoughtful interpretation, is the reception of Being's own event.

Why does Hölderlin, in particular, become emblematic of Heideggerian poetics? Uniquely, Hölderlin is self-consciously faithful to the 'strangeness' of language. *Das Fremde* – the strange or foreign – is an explicit Hölderlinian motif; Heidegger, in his lecture course on the poem *'Der Ister'*, transforms this motif into a meditation upon *Unheimlichkeit* (translated as 'uncanniness'), which in German suggests being 'not at home'. An experience of language such as had in poetry is an uncanny one because it illuminates that we are both 'at home' in Being and, linguistically, separated off or alienated from it. (Hölderlin also explores this theme in his novel *Hyperion*, in poems such as *'Der Mensch'*, in the philosophical essay-fragment 'Judgment and Being', and in his reflections on Greek tragedy.) Language can bring us into intimacy with others – set them into a 'world' – just as it sets us apart from them, and from Being as such. This setting-apart or alienation (*Entfremdung*) is especially prominent in modernity (Heidegger, 1992, p. 10), but the poetry of Hölderlin was to bring-into-being a 'future which could usher in an overcoming of the present forgetfulness of Being', prevailing over the godlessness of the technological age (Gadamer, p. 152). Heidegger thinks this in nearly 'mythological'[9] terms: the poet must endure an extremely difficult time of interstice, between the departed gods and those to come – a recurrent theme in Hölderlin's poetry – in order to found a new possibility of dwelling.[10] In later decades this dwelling involves a non-violent, non-appropriative 'letting-be' (*Gelassenheit*), but in the 1930s and early 1940s it concerns a specifically German destiny and prescribes the necessity of violence, sacrifice, and danger in its founding.

Another reason for Hölderlin's preeminence in Heidegger's poetics, some-what underemphasized in the scholarly literature, lies in Hölderlin's complex relationship to philosophy. Despite his Kantian influences, intense rela-tionship with Hegel, and views on poetry articulated in largely idealist terms, Hölderlin as poet provides for Heidegger a reversal of the metaphys-ical thinking dominant in German idealism. Heidegger's view of language, I have argued elsewhere, stands in tension with Hölderlin's own theorizing;[11] Hölderlin's philosophy, though remaining incipient in essays, letters, and fragmentary writings, and overshadowed by his more prominent classmates, Hegel and Schelling, challenges, but does not abandon, the terminology of the aesthetics Heidegger seeks to overcome. Yet Heidegger follows the tenor of Hölderlin's great hymns, in having 'to see Hölderlin not as a person belonging to the age of idealism' (Gadamer, p. 152) but belonging to a time between the fled gods of old – a disenchanted, technological time – and a new, tentative time of relating anew to (calling forth) the divine. This in-between time, this interstice, is a time of ontological destiny, and poetry serves as its vessel. This destiny links language to history (Heidegger, 1959, p. 133).[12]

Hölderlin's work, and Hölderlin as a poetical figure, become for Heidegger a model of the 'essence of poetry', a notion which has drawn criticism, for it suggests a univocal, though unsaid (Heidegger, 1959, p. 135), meaning at the heart of poetry, a meaning, moreover, which only the thinker can access and articulate. A few questions arise here: Is the thinker uniquely capable of comprehending the singular essence of the poem and determining its relevance for a people? (After all, Hölderlin's poetry has also attracted many leftist readings[13]). Moreover, Heidegger's interpretation of poetry, in its near-exclusive devotion to Hölderlin, 'has struck many as idiosyncratic to the extreme' (Fried, p. 29)[14] and has been criticized by scholars unwilling to grant poetry an exclusively ontological function.[15] What would be the form of these 'truths' founded by the poetic?

Before addressing these questions, we must clarify Heidegger's meaning here: this 'essence' is not an ordinary generalization, a category or standard for all poems. It is not the universal or general, but the inner source of poetry's ontological significance. 'Essence' (*das Wesen*) here is linked to

Heidegger's notion of the 'origin' (*der Ursprung*); essential poetry is poetry which shelters Being's original self-concealing manifestation. The essence of poetry in Hölderlin is not necessarily that of other poets, nor that of any given canon. Heidegger articulates the notion of the essence of poetry in a meditation on Hölderlin's specific and explicit insights into language. This meditation also rejects philological fidelity and biographical reference as irrelevant, and the methods of ordinary *Literaturwissenschaft* as philosophically inadequate.

Heidegger is right that in Hölderlin something more is happening than literary critical readings of poetical devices can account for, and that a biographical interpretation of his poems would not discover their philosophical meaning. The thinker approaches the poem with a primary, extra-*wissenschaftliche* access. Thinking discovers in Hölderlin that language is not merely a means to identify or express something; it is not primarily understood as a relationship between a subject and objects that subject is said to cognize, or the artist and his intended meanings. In Hölderlin's view, language is a calling (*Ruf*), an occupation (*Beruf*), a both dangerous and innocent one; language draws the human being toward the 'origin' of what is. Language is dangerous because it situates human beings as uniquely capable of articulating – and losing – a grasp of Being itself, a loss leading to alienation from poetic mediation, which, ironically, precludes the experience of 'uncanniness'. Because Hölderlin's poems thematize the poet as one endowed with a special, dangerous task of founding truths in a godless time, Heidegger calls him the 'poet of poets'. Hölderlin poetizes the very task of poetry when he writes, '. . . *was bleibet aber/ stiften die Dichter*'.

In contrast to technical and practical discourse, poetry, in its 'simplicity and intensity', provides 'means to arouse a sense of original wonder' that a grasp of Being requires (Corngold, p. 199). This sense of wonder issues from our linguistic relation to the world, a relation which, though engaged constantly, generally escapes our notice. According to Heidegger, the human being 'finds the proper abode of his [*sic*] existence in language – whether he is aware of it or not' (Heidegger, 1959, p. 57). Yet in everyday speaking 'language does *not* bring itself to language but holds back' – a withholding essential to our ability to 'deal with something and negotiate something by speaking' (Heidegger, 1959, p. 59). Heidegger's account conceptualizes the essential differences between everyday language and the special use of language in poetry.

One of the principal ontological features of poetic language according to Heidegger is its capability, following Hölderlin's poem, of 'founding' truth, which Heidegger likens to founding a political state. In 'The Origin of the Work of Art', the work of art is granted a role in truth as setting-up and setting-forth; the work of art is conceived as the interstice between poeisis and praxis. The political act is another mode of this same ontological founding. Indeed, 'to neglect the political dimension of Heidegger's text is to risk restricting "The Origin of the Work of Art" to the realm of aesthetic alienation, instead of recognizing it as a response to aesthetic alienation' (Bernasconi in Risser, p. 99). Heidegger wanted poetry's founding of truth to have an explicitly historical relevance, even if we interpret this not in the narrow sense of localized (Nazi) politics but in the broader context of the historicity of a people.

A critique of poetic founding

Yet further reflection on certain features of language even in Heidegger's own terms invites speculation about the nature of 'founding' (*das Stiften*), and the 'grounding' (*die Gründung*) Heidegger associates with poetry and creative making in 'Origin of the Work of Art' (Heidegger, 1960, p. 80). It is unclear whether Heidegger, in this earlier text, derives the notion of 'founding' from Hölderlin; but in 1941–42 he gives a lengthy interpretation of the poem '*Andenken*', wherein Hölderlin writes, '*was bleibet aber/ stiften die Dichter*'. There, Heidegger meditates explicitly upon the founding-capacity of poetic language as a Hölderlinian truth.

Heidegger's specification about the meaning of 'founding' employs exactly the same terminology in both texts: both involve a tripartite *Schenkung*, *Gründung*, and *Anfang* – a sending granting (Heidegger refers to the homology between *schicken*, to give, and *schenken*, to send); grounding; and original beginning; and in both texts founding is defined with reference to Hölderlin (Heidegger, 1960, p. 80; 1992, p. 193). But what does it mean to say, as Hölderlin declares in '*Andenken*', that poets found what remains? In what sense? And what is it that does or can 'remain', given the finitude of human life and memory which, Hölderlin's speaker says in his poem, is both given and taken by the sea?

In both 'Origin of the Work of Art' and the '*Andenken*' lectures, Heidegger links 'founding' with the arrival of the historical and with '*das Kommende*' (Heidegger, 1960, pp. 77–8; 1992, p. 193). Poetic language both reaches back to and prepares for an understanding of origin, which is both historical in the usual sense – a reaching back to the past – and a preparatory founding of the future. The historical remains in essence past, but occurs or happens as the opening out of an arriving destiny. Heidegger's sense of the 'historical people' to whom Hölderlin's poetry is apparently addressed is a people capable of taking up their essential origin – their Germanness – in an incipient future yet (in 1935) to be fully realized. The Germans must, according to Heidegger, face the 'either/or' decision about their authentic fate, which will involve strife, struggle, and sacrifice. For readers of *Being and Time* this recalls the unity of lived temporality achieved by authentic resoluteness in the present, an *Augenblick* which takes up one's past within a fearless encounter with the most extreme future (death). In Heidegger's reading, the poem prepares the between-time, the 'whiling' (*die Weile*) for the coming of fate (*des Schicksals*); the poet prepares a people for the already-sent arrival of a coming destiny (Heidegger, 1992, p. 194). In both texts, two features of founding seem to be unified by a third: what is granted and the beginning or origin are given form by the nature of 'grounding' – the way a political state, with its reference to both a people (and their past) and a destiny (the future), is given form in the 'grounding act'.

The self-referentiality of poetic language

In considering Hölderlin's poem '*Andenken*' further and Heidegger's inter-pretation thereof, let us note certain features of poetic language as opposed to that of ordinary prosaic communication, all of which in my view trouble Heidegger's notion of poetic founding. To begin with, the special character of poetic language is its self-referentiality, and this introduces my first objec-tion against Heidegger's theory. As Heidegger admits, the 'strangeness' of language in poetry is related to the fact that the poetic word and its truth are independent of an external state of affairs. Poetry does not refer to a truth outside of itself, it is responsible for 'founding' (*stiften*) or establishing a truth. In his essay 'The Way to Language', Heidegger quotes Novalis's claim about 'the peculiar property of language, namely that language is concerned exclusively with itself' (Heidegger, 1959, p. 133). While a poem, by virtue of images, refers to the world, and is understood through this reference, poetry is constituted by 'the fact that the word in some cases makes itself believable from itself and does not require a fulfillment from somewhere else – indeed, it does not even permit it' (Gadamer, p. 146). Heidegger does not concede a reading of poetic language according to the power of the image, which he understands as external reference by way of the symbol, wherein, for instance, the sun, moon, and wind mentioned in Hölderlin's poem would evoke some world behind or beyond it, some netherworld (*irgendwelche Hinterwelt*) (Heidegger, 1992, pp. 39–40). In restricting the role of the image *(Bild)* to the literary devices of symbol and metaphor, however, Heidegger leaves untouched the image as the anchor of its own self-referentiality; in other words, he overlooks the image as phenomenon. I will return to the problem of the image shortly.

How does Heidegger describe the self-referentiality of poetic language? The power of the poetic word is that it brings about independent truth; it founds itself as truth but with only indirect and partial access to non-imaginary, literal reality. In poetry, words have a 'trustworthiness and self-evidence of their own, which brings it about that they call something forth, just as names do' (Gadamer, p. 147). But this trustworthiness is due to the chasm that separates poetic language from the literal, for its truth is guar-anteed only by not being subject to empirical cognition and the demands of praxis. In everyday language, signs necessarily recede from notice and illuminate exclusively an external reference. If as speakers or listeners we become conscious about our words, their sounds and ordering, as we enunciate or hear them, the function of language is interrupted, and the flow of meaning – what language accomplishes – tends to be lost. The experience of learning a foreign language provides a useful example: one submits to fluency only when syntactical features, the unfamiliar sounds and awkward grammatical demands of a language, become secondary and cease to stand out, recede behind semantic meaning. Only when it goes unnoticed does the foreign language take on the character of ordinary, everyday language. But poetry – with its devices and imaginative leaps, its challenges to grammar, its 'liberation from logic' (to quote again from *Being and Time*) – requires just this troubling of everyday uses of speech: the experience one 'undergoes' with language comes to the surface in poetic language. Such experience is, to quote Heidegger, 'given voice' in poetic expression (Heidegger, 1959, p. 59). Signs do not recede from notice but rather penetrate one's awareness, as when the rhythm of a poetic line, as it were, envelops what is meant in an atmosphere which informs, enriches, or refracts its meaning.

In the context of the self-referentiality of language, it is worth pondering the seeming transition from language to history and to the event of Being (*Ereignis*) when Heidegger grants poetry a founding role. If poetic language is historical and history is nothing other than the self-unconcealment of Being, then Heidegger makes no real transition, since Being, which language reveals, is history. Yet Heidegger complicates matters by identifying various means by which the happening of truth can occur. Focusing specifically on the act of founding (grounding) a political state, we approach the relationship between founding and praxis. The grounding of a political state is a praxical act with an accusative object. That an event of Being, at least in Heidegger's 1935 account, could occur in the act of founding of a political state (*die staatgründende Tat*) (Heidegger, 1960, p. 82) according to the same ontological structure of founding as in a work of art – in both cases, a form is determined for the happening of truth (Heidegger, 1960, p. 73) – implies more than an analogous connection between two modes of the happening of truth. The two modes of founding share the same ontological form. This justifies Heidegger's employment of Hölderlin in his political orientation – an address to the Germans to embrace their destiny – even though Heidegger considered this employment beyond politics in the ordinary sense. Of course Heidegger does not suggest that the content of Hölderlin's poems should give empirical direction to the political state Heidegger himself might have envisioned. Rather, it is the way in which poetry addresses a people ontologically that its relationship to a political founding act is made.

Yet I would argue that the founding of poetic language, in its self-referentiality, stands out in juxtaposition to praxis, of acts in which political views become manifest as political order by rendering a form (*Gestalt*) to the historical given. Contrary to the political founding act, poetry's self-reference maintains a withholding from, rather than initiation of, the hold upon and transformation of the historical given. Transformation occurs not in praxis but rather at the level of the imagination, which is external to Heidegger's post-aesthetic lexicon. The relationship of (poetical) truth to poetic language is not an accusative case: it is not that poetry (in the nominative subject position) sets forth or engenders truth (in the accusative object position), the way one can say that a political act (such as voting a leader into office or writing a constitution or waging a war) can found a political state. Rather, poetic language is a form of truth or, better said, poetic language 'truths', if use of the noun as a verb be permitted, only with reference to itself. That is why, as Heidegger also observes, a poem cannot be said to be correct or incorrect according to the correspondence theory of truth.

That poetry 'truths' is, I think, the meaning of poetry as the 'event' of Being. When Hölderlin writes, '*was bleibet aber, stiften die Dichter*', Hölderlin identifies what remains with the poem itself, or with (and here is my ultimate point of divergence from Heidegger's philosophy) the poetic image.[16] The poet founds not history as such but the poetic image by giving it form. 'What remains' is juxtaposed to the finitude of ordinary memory (mentioned in the poem as given and taken by the sea), to which the poetic image forges a resistance. While Heidegger does not want *Andenken* (remembrance) to be reduced to *Erinnerung* (memory), it is the latter that occasions the need for the former in Hölderlin's poem: that the sea gives and takes memory is what renders necessary the kind of remembrance of which the poetical image is capable. Thus the poetic image resists not just ontological *Verborgenheit* or self-concealment but certain aspects of human finitude.

The plurisignificance of poetic language

My second point regarding Heidegger's theory of the founding of truth regards poetry's plurisignificance. While Heidegger wants Hölderlin's poetry to force a decision and a decisiveness about the essence of the German people and its destiny, I contend that the meaning of poetic language cannot be reduced to a single essential 'saying' that could instigate what Heidegger calls an historical 'either/or'. Poetry's calling something forth is a bringing-into-being, a kind of *poeisis* that Heidegger analyzed in terms of unconceal-ment. Given the concealment that remains in any disclosive articulation, poetry, through the lens of the poetic, is plurisignificant, for it exposes that no one saying is a total revelation of what is. Being, while disclosable, remains elusive even for the thinker and the poet, and its elusiveness is partly due to the indeterminate horizon that subtends every revelation. Yet while exquisitely sensitive to the self-concealing nature of Being, Heidegger's granting of a common form to the poetic and the founding political act is justified by their sharing a common origin. The notion of founding in both cases involves the singular origin of what is founded, which in both cases involves the dwelling of an historical people (Heidegger, 1960, p. 43).

Heidegger aims to 'gather' the poem to an essential destiny – to bring about the destiny of Being that 'decides what remains fateful within [Hölderlin's] poetry' (Heidegger, 1971b, p. 142).

This fate or destiny is outside the economy of the poetic self and any biographical reference: it is as a messenger or vessel of (onto-)history that the poet is described in terms of heroism and courage.[17] Yet the heroism is coupled with a peculiar receptivity, since the poet 'effaces himself before the poem, which alone remains . . . in its abrupt presence' (Froment-Meurice, p. 81). This abrupt presence is, however, glossed over by the thinker who brings to 'decision' its singular essence, as when Heidegger reduces the inherent plurisignificance (*Mehrdeutigkeit*) of poetic language (as he does, for instance, in a reading of Trakl) to 'one side of a greater issue, whose other side is determined by poetry's innermost site'. In essential poetry there is no 'scatter[ing] in vague equivocations' but only a rigorously precise vision. In stark contrast to Keats's negative capability, Heidegger rejects the 'vagueness of groping poetic uncertainty' (Heidegger, 1959, p. 192). Perhaps this restraint imposed upon meaning assuages Heidegger's anxiety about 'unholy fragmentation' in an increasingly global, technical world (Heidegger, 1959, p. 179) to which poetry is said to offer an alternative. Yet this restriction of poetry's meaning to a univocal essence is called into question by phenomenological attention to the poetic image.

The poem's plurisignificance in part arises from reverberations of poetical images in contrast to, for instance, eidetic concepts. While the latter (for instance the idea of a triangle) localizes a fixed universal, the poetical image involves an open reverberation which does not settle upon a necessarily closed and singular determination. The complexity and texture of the poem is rendered by the incompatible layers of significance brought about by images. The wedding of illogically but poetically related images gives the poem both its atmospheric tone and a compound significance. In Hölderlin's 'In Lovely Blue', for instance, a beautiful brook rolling through the landscape 'like the eye of God' through the milky way creates a metaphoric connection between the brook, which is after all minute, finite, and a part of creation, and the eye of God, who is, despite the specification of a part, infinite and whole. This connection is to be read, at first glance, on the level of aesthetic-symbolic perception of the landscape – the romantic and Platonic association of beauty as divine. To stop here would be to render the image univocal by virtue of its function as symbol: beautiful brook = presence of the divine in the world. But the very juxtaposition between the (mere) earthly brook and the divine eye gives the poem another level of significance: the insufficiency of worldly things to render the wholeness of God. The necessity of imagining God as having an eye is then troubling. The metaphor resists its own potential symbolic closure, as does the poem as a whole. The image refers, on the one hand, to the hubris of human attempts to imitate or present in 'images' the divine and, on the other, to their incapacity.

Nonetheless the poem itself asserts this hubristic act as necessary, as that fate to which the human being is doomed; the third stanza of the poem refers to the suffering of having to 'quarrel with God'. 'Images', Hölderlin writes in the first stanza, are 'so very holy, that truly one is often fearful of describing them'. But in the third and last stanza, after comparing the brook to God's eye, Hölderlin's speaker presents a critical and contrary image of eyes: 'The image of the man has eyes; the moon, on the other hand, light.' Having eyes to see is one thing, but giving light is quite another. While giving light is in harmony with the universe, seeing is not necessarily so. And so we read in the concluding stanza, 'King Oedipus had one eye too many perhaps', and find the speaker connecting the sufferings of Oedipus with his own: 'I am pulled as streams are by the ending of something – something that spreads like Asia. Suffering of the source that Oedipus had, of course.' While eyes see, they see as if in a mirror; only light itself is at one with the visible. Thus the metaphoric connection between the beautiful brook and the eye of God is troublingly ambiguous, suggesting both the capacity and the incapacity of the poetic vision to render the divine.[18]

The poetic image and the poetic imagination

While what Heidegger calls the time-space of poetry (*der Zeit-Raum der Dichtung*) is set up and set forth by images – in '*Andenken*' by the northeast wind which ensures the voyage of sailors, which Heidegger calls the secret of the entire poem (*das Geheimnis des ganzen Gedichtes*) (Heidegger, 1992, p. 32) – he repeatedly refuses to grant the image a part in his interpretation. In addition to rejecting the notion of symbol associated with images, he also rejects their indeterminacy. We cannot take the poeticized of the poem to be a description of something experienced (for instance, an image of the gardens of Bordeaux, which Hölderlin had doubtless seen on his journey to France before composing this poem); for as description the image is '*zu unbestimmt*'. Heidegger does not see this indeterminateness as facility, harboring poetry's essential indirectness, and its alternative to the language of determinate judgements; this 'free play', to use Kant's terminology, could be described as a reverberation of the phenomena beyond what, strictly speaking, is intuited, into the indeterminately apperceived or co-intuited horizon. Heidegger overlooks the fact that the indeterminacy of poetic images involves unsaid associations conjured alongside what is specifically localizable. This is the kind of reverberation that happens in 'remembrance' itself: memory of the friends and the landscape the speaker in Hölderlin's '*Andenken*' misses is recalled not by exhaustive description or positive accounting, and certainly not by closed conceptual determination, but by partial and open-ended reference. Heidegger takes pains to defend Hölderlin's poem from a criticism of just this open-endedness, seeing the latter not as a capacity but rather as an 'incapacity to compose a unified and complete picture in its fullness and orderliness' ('*das Unvermögen, ein einheitlich vollständiges Bild in seiner Fülle und Gesetzlichkeit durchzukomponieren*'). The poem, according to Heidegger, is not description, a compilation of bits and pieces of images and memory, but about a far deeper essential (and also singular) origin – the object of the poet's 'founding' (Heidegger, 1992, p. 52).

Correlate to Heidegger's refusal of the image is the absence of the imagination: rejecting the latter is intrinsic to Heidegger's alternative to traditional aesthetics. Heidegger rejects poetry's subscription to the 'mere' imaginary in 'Origin of the Work of Art', and in the later '. . . *Dichterisch wohnet der Mensch . . .*'. For Heidegger the poetic is truthful by specifically not being imaginary, by presencing a world for its praxical concretization in a potential mode of dwelling, be that violent struggle or, later, non-violent *Gelassenheit*. The imagination, moreover, subscribes to the subjectivistic aesthetics which Heidegger rejects, and to the phenomenology of artistic creation centered upon the artist – who, Heidegger emphatically explains, is not the origin of the work of art. To secure the ontological relevance of art, Heidegger has to remove it from this kind of language of consciousness. The latter, however, continually reappears as Heidegger takes pains to interpret what Hölderlin must have meant by reference to the 'me' (*mir*) and the first-person experience in his poems, and to the memory the sea in '*Andenken*' is said to grant and give (Heidegger, 1992, pp. 36, 38). In short, Heidegger rejects the poetic consciousness (experience, memory, feeling) in favor of poetical reception – and founding – of '*das Kommende*'.

Before his turn to poetry, however, Heidegger gave a significant role to the imagination in an interpretation of Kant's *Critique of Pure Reason*. There he regards the transcendental imagination as 'the ground of the intrinsic possibility of the ontological synthesis' (Heidegger, 1962, p. 141). When turning a few years later to art and poetic language, however, Heidegger distances his theory completely from the radical potential he had unlocked in his Kant interpretation. Nor does Heidegger return to Kant's notion of reflective judgment from the *Critique of Judgment*, wherein the imagination and understanding participate in a non-legislative 'free play'. Heidegger views Kant's aesthetics as determined by the symbolic relationship between the sensuous and the supersensuous; in rejecting the symbolism inherent in Kant's account, Heidegger throws the baby out with the bathwater, and so does not investigate the freedom accorded to the imagination in aesthetic experience. The aesthetic imagination, however, could have helped Heidegger, for in its exceptional non-subservience to the understanding, it might be a site of receptivity for the play of Being in its self-withdrawing unfolding. In accepting the imagination as a part of a genuinely phenomenological poetics, however, I would conceive of the imagination not exclusively as a faculty of intuitive presentation, but also as a source of both controlled spontaneity and critical negativity. It is unbound to the discourse of stable essences and the 'metaphysics of presence' that characterizes the telos of rational understanding. In juxtaposition, non-imaginative truths would be troubled in their finality and totality because they lack the kind of open reverberation described above; and so from a poetical point of view it is the latter, ironically, which appear horizonally incomplete (see Gosetti, 2001).

Heidegger follows traditional aesthetics in conceiving the imagination as what he, like Hegel, called mere 'picture' thinking (Hegel, p. 37), or as the reverie of dreams, or as tarrying with mere illusions (Heidegger, 1983). Thus Heidegger's interpretations of poems often center on specific words and their creative etymology, but rarely on images – or rather Heidegger does not ponder the nature of the image as such even when it is essential to his interpretation. It is as if Heidegger is avoiding the surface of the poem in favor of its essential depths. Heidegger's refusal of the image hampers an acceptance of the full implications of the self-referentiality and plurisignificance of language. If the poets, according to Hölderlin's poem, found what lasts, could this not be accomplished by virtue of poetical images, through which what is otherwise ineffable, plurisignificant, evanescent, or missed is brought to remembrance? This seems to me to be the meaning of Hölderlin's discussion of the gardens of Bordeaux, the stream dropping into the river and the oaks and white poplars and other missed effects of life there, the brown women walking on holidays, the breezes passing, heavy with dreams, over the leisurely paths.[19] Memory is given and taken by the sea, Hölderlin writes, but the poets, who call up the atmospheric reality of these things, and of the friends who are gone, can give life to 'what remains' in images carefully intuited and composed. It is in the poem that the remaining is accomplished, and so the poem is not a symbol of something other to itself, but rather refers to itself as this remaining. Moreover, Hölderlin's reference not to what absolutely or permanently is, but rather to what remains or withstands falling away, is an indication of finitude that does not figure in Heidegger's interpretation. That poets found what remains, in the wake of all that does not remain, is a tentative stance of resistance against finitude, not its annihilation. The accomplishments of poetry, too, are provisional, even if they are able to 'found what lasts'. Moreover, it is not concealment which is Hölderlin's concern, but actual loss – of friends and memories and moments of happiness. Poetic images cannot give back what is lost, but they can provide a grounding for 'what remains' – namely, remembrance of such.

In short, poetical remembrance is inherently of the order of the imagination. Heidegger's reconception of truth as ontological unconcealment can be seen as troubling the distinction between the imaginary and the true, particularly from Heidegger's phenomenological viewpoint. The imaginative need not be relegated to the unreal; for the preservation of meaning in images – the imaginary – is phenomenologically distinguishable from empirical reality but not thereby to be disregarded as *necessarily* false. In neglecting the imagination in favor of the historical form of thoughtful-practical founding, does Heidegger rule out poetry's autonomy from both the world it reflects and the thinker who interprets it? This autonomy is the source of poetry's creative power; but as self-referential and plurisignificant, the truths it is said to found are subject to the same instability and indeterminateness as are the images which ground them.

Poetic language and letting-be

My alternative view of the nature of poetic language – taking into account its self-referentiality, its plurisignificance, and its imaginary nature – need not preclude Heidegger's more promising theory of poetic dwelling described, not in terms of strife and decision, but of *Gelassenheit*, a gentle self-forgetting in a letting-be and shelter of what is. Moreover, my references to the phenomenological subject need not entail a return to the ego-centered metaphysics and Cartesian rationalism Heidegger rejected. In my view it is precisely the self-reference of poetic language, translated as non-possession and non-manipulation of the real; its plurisignificant reverberation, or irre-ducibility to determinate or legislative cognition; and the imaginative quality of language (since what is withheld in the giving is 'retained' via the imagin-ation) which can best engender the *Gelassenheit* stance Heidegger articulates after abandoning his involvement with nationalism.

It has been suggested that, given his emphasis on unconcealment, Heidegger's notion of truth need not be incompatible with the public, unbiased, or real, despite that his view of language necessarily 'disrupts certain conceptions of "objective reality" '.[20] Yet the reversal that is uncon-cealment must be thought in its self-reference and plurisignificance. This plurisignificance is broached in Heidegger's notion that untruth is essen-tial to truth (Heidegger, 1960, p. 53; 1962, p. 146). Heidegger's thinking indeed profits from the plurisignificant nature of poetic language, for he wants an account of Being that is incompatible with any singular proposi-tional formulation. Heidegger's notion of *Ereignis* allows us to speak of Being in a way that precludes arbitrary or wholly groundless disclosure, and yet one which is irreducible to a single phenomenon; if poetic language and its attendant thinking are associated with an *Ereignis*, they necessarily evade any definitive or singularly narrative conception of the 'destinal'. If I am right here, poetic language, even as Heidegger describes it in 'The Origin of the Work of Art', would be incompatible with the founding Heidegger attributes to poetry and the political act alike. For it would be incompatible with any given standpoint of history from which the 'parting' (*Scheidung*) of a decision (*Entscheidung*) could be made. The event of poetic language as a self-referential bringing-into-being would not be the kind of event that 'answers to the coming world era', as if that destiny were already decided (Heidegger, 1971b, p. 142), and the human being (the German) need only heed its own nature in order to follow that historical trajectory. Perhaps the *Ereignis* of poetic language is more radically elusive – more radically imaginative – than even Heidegger had suspected.

My suggestions pertain to the troubling tone of closure in Heidegger's account of Hölderlin, involving an always-already 'sent' history of Being (*Seinsgeschichte*) and a decisionism which totalizes an essence – of the human being, of language, of history – to be seized. Poetic language founds or establishes truth only in a very qualified sense, for its self-referentiality exceeds, though not evading, the logic of play between groundedness and unconcealment; and so it exceeds – by failing to achieve – the nature of a definitively ascertainable (however elusive) event. This is not to deny the relation between poetry and truth, but to deny poetry's – and thus the thinker's – access to truth *as such*, truth in what Heidegger calls its 'pure arrival' (Heidegger, 1971b, p. 142).

It is important to note Heidegger's admission that this 'truth' is not opposed to the possibility of error, given Heidegger's emphasis on the mystery and concealment that always remains. In 'The Origin of the Work of Art', the work (of art, of political founding) marks the struggle between the disclosive nature of 'world' and the concealing nature of 'earth'. Heidegger here sees truth as having to be wrested out of concealment, a wresting with violent overtones: battle, struggle, strife. Yet poetic revelation, like any other, is always partial revelation; and while its self-configuration reflects this partiality, and so reflects the essence of language, this does not cancel its own finitude, its own limits. The possibility of error, indeed, its inevitability, consists in that in the encounter with Being, beings come to be understood or seen in a certain light, whereas other aspects remain hidden or 'unsaid', outside those limits. Is this not an admission of the radical finitude of the poetic, even if we afford poetic language the 'essence' Heidegger ascribes it? The notion of *Gelassenheit* poetic dwelling, drawn from a poem by Hölderlin, has been claimed in scholarship as the ground of a late-emerging ethics,[21] despite – or perhaps, as Fred Dallmayr argues, as a 'radical change of political course' away from – Heidegger's involvement with fascist politics (Dallmayr, p. 143). Do the self-reference, plurisignificance, and imaginative features of poetic language I have mentioned not collaborate with a *Gelassenheit* stance toward truth?

Several possibilities arise for a reader, if invested in Heidegger's granting of ontological relevance to poetry, yet deeply concerned, as Hans Jonas suggests, that Heidegger misused Hölderlin, and the notion of the poetic in general, in his involvement with nationalism. One might guide Heidegger's later works, his notion of the event (*Ereignis*) and its unfolding, toward a self-deconstruction, so that the play of revealing and concealing of Being resists univocal destiny.[22] One might point to the formal characteristics of poetry, as I have done here, which trouble the historical founding Heidegger aligns with political acts. One might investigate Heidegger's notion of poetic *Ereignis*, and any attendant prescriptions for dwelling, in light of the finitude to which in my reading Hölderlin continually pays tribute. If we follow Heidegger's (Hölderlinian) suggestion that poetry and art necessarily involve some kind of danger, some inevitable entanglement in error precisely because of its relation to truth, the danger resides not only for the thinker who interprets them, but in the realm of poetic language itself, by virtue of the destabilization from which its own truths are not immune.

Philippe Lacoue-Labarthe argues there is a 'responsibility' of thinking toward poetry and toward the responsibility 'with which poetry believes itself to be authorized'. In my view, the responsibility of poetry is not directly an ethical responsibility – for poetry is not necessarily subservient to an idea of the good – and yet 'it is a matter . . . of that to which poetry testifies in attesting as such, that is to say, in attesting in its relation to the true, in its *telling truth*' (Lacoue-Labarthe, 1999, pp. 93, 92). The truth-telling of poetry is a fragile business from which one can never extract certainties or destinies, and which will never yield to a standard of truth other than that subject to the kinds of qualifications I have outlined here. Moreover, if Heidegger's formulation of poetic truth in 'The Origin of the Work of Art' is implicated in the political and moral failure described by Jonas, it is not Heidegger's turn to poetry – his poetics of thinking – as such that is to be faulted. For there is, as I have suggested, an alternative to the founding Heidegger attributes to poetry, and to poetic language itself. And it is, again, poetic language – and a poetics of thinking – which afforded Heidegger's extrication, if not absolution, from his errors.

Notes

1. See Dallmayr for an account of the promising possibilities in Heidegger's later thought. For my account of a 'dual' philosophy in Heidegger see also the introductory chapter of *Heidegger, Hölderlin, and the Subject of Poetic Language*. The account to which I refer is given in Jonas, p. 49.
2. In reference to the 'nobility of the philosophical life', see the helpful posing of this problem in Bernasconi, pp. 56–8. I use the term 'aestheticism' as Gérard Genette employs it, as treating from an aesthetic (or here, poetical) point of view what ought to be regarded as a moral issue. See Genette, p. 26.
3. See Agamben, and also Corngold, wherein it is argued that *Being and Time* provides a poetics and, moreover, a 'stubborn penetration . . . into the modern poetic consciousness', p. 200.
4. An interpretation of the notion of *Auseinandersetzung* is given in Fried, p. 16.
5. By 'directly' I refer to his short tenure as the Rector of the University of Freiburg and his views expressed in the university newspaper promoting some of Hitler's policies; see Heidegger's address, 'Self-Assertion of the German University'. I say 'certain features' of this ideology because it is well regarded that Heidegger did not accept the biologism or overt racism of the Nazi viewpoint, for example, against which Heidegger makes statements in some of his lectures.
6. This is in contrast to such treatments as given by Froment-Meurice, p. 13.
7. This duality of revolutionary and nurturing aspects can be found, for instance, in Kristeva's poetic theory.

8. See Robert Bernasconi's discussion of the notion of aesthetic alienation in 'The Greatness of the Work of Art', in Risser, pp. 98–99.
9. This term is used for Heidegger's language by Jonas (p. 150).
10. Heidegger's discussion of dwelling is found primarily in later works, but in 'Origin of the Work of Art' it is an essential concept: it belongs to the notion of the 'world' which the work of art opens up in tension with the earth. Thus *'[a]uf die Erde und in sie gruendet der geschichtliche Mensch sein wohnen in der Welt'* (Heidegger, 1960, p. 43).
11. Cf. Julian Young, who claims that Heidegger's early readings of Hölderlin treat him as a thinker rather than as a poet (Young, 2002).
12. Linking poetry to destiny in the context of Hölderlin, Heidegger asserts, *'. . . dass es allein schicksalhaft uns angeht, weil es uns selbst, das Geschick dichtet, in dem wir stehen, ob wir es wissen oder nicht, ob wir bereit sind, uns darein zu schicken oder nicht'* (Heidegger, 1971a, pp. 182–3).
13. See Fehervary, 1977.
14. Critics of Heidegger's interpretation include Theodor Adorno, Paul de Man, Dieter Henrich, Jacques Derrida, Verónique Foti, and John D. Caputo, to name only a few.
15. See, for instance, Froment-Meurice, p. 11.
16. Occasionally I employ 'poetic image' as a composite noun, denoting the imagistic whole created in the poem; other times I refer specifically to a singular image or compilation of several images.
17. Philippe Lacoue-Labarthe considers Heidegger's heroic reading of the poet-figure in juxtaposition to the courage in Walter Benjamin's reading. Whereas Heidegger sees the Hölderlinian poet courageous in calling to the absent gods and bringing about history, Benjamin's reading involves the courage of atheism. The political implications of this difference are substantial. See Lacoue-Labarthe, 1999, pp. 81–2.
18. I have used David Constantine's translation of Hölderlin's poem *'In lieblicher Blaue'*. See Hölderlin, pp. 103–4.
19. My summary here is indebted to David Constantine's translation, p. 60.
20. Hatab makes this point (p. 40). The citation is from p. 41.
21. See also Young, Chapter 7; Jacques Taminiaux, 'Heidegger on Values', in Risser; and Dallmayr.
22. See a reading of Heidegger through Derrida in Roth, Chapter 5.

Works cited

Agamben, Giorgio, 'The Passion of Facticity', in *Potentialities: Collected Essays in Philosophy*, ed. and trans. Daniel Heller-Roazen (Stanford: Stanford University Press, 1999).

Bernasconi, Robert, *Heidegger In Question* (New Jersey: Humanities Press, 1993).

Corngold, Stanley, 'Heidegger's *Being and Time*: Implications for Poetics', in *The Fate of the Self: German Writers and French Theory* (Durham: Duke University Press, 1994).

Dallmayr, Fred, *The Other Heidegger* (Ithaca: Cornell University Press, 1993).

de Man, Paul, 'Heidegger Reconsidered', in *Critical Writings 1953–1978*, ed. Lindsay Waters (Minneapolis: University of Minnesota Press, 1989).

Fehervary, Helen, *Hölderlin and the Left: The Search for a Dialectic of Art and Life* (Heidelberg: Carl Winter Universitätsverlag, 1977).

Fried,Gregory, *Heidegger's Polemos: From Being to Politics* (New Haven: Yale University Press, 2000).

Froment-Meurice, Marc, *That Is To Say: Heidegger's Poetics*, trans. Jan Plug (Stanford: Stanford University Press, 1996).

Gadamer, Hans-Georg, 'Thinking and Poetizing in Heidegger and in Hölderlin's "Andenken"', in *Heidegger Toward the Turn: Essays on the Work of the 1930's*, ed. James Risser (Albany: State University of New York Press, 1999).

Genette, Gérard, *The Aesthetic Relation*, trans. G.M. Goshgarian (Ithaca: Cornell University Press, 1999).

Gosetti, Jennifer Anna, 'Phenomenological Literature: From the Natural Attitude to "Recognition"', *Philosophy Today* 45, 5 (2001).

Gosetti-Ferencei, Jennifer Anna, *Heidegger, Hölderlin, and the Subject of Poetic Language* (Ashland: Fordham University Press, 2004).

Hatab, Lawrence J., *Ethics and Finitude: Heideggerian Contributions to Moral Philosophy* (Oxford: Rowman & Littlefield, 2002).

Hegel, Georg Wilhelm Friedrich, *Phenomenology of Spirit*, trans. A.V. Miller (Oxford: Oxford University Press, 1977).

Heidegger, Martin, *Einführung in die Metaphysik* (Tübingen: Niemeyer Verlag, 1953). *An Introduction to Metaphysics,* trans. Ralph Manheim (New York: Anchor Books, 1959).

—— *Unterwegs zur Sprache* (Pfullingen: Verlag Günter Neske, 1959). *On the Way to Language* (New York: Harper & Row, 1971).

—— *Der Ursprung des Kunstwerkes* (Stuttgart: Reclam, 1960).

—— *Kant and the Problem of Metaphysics*, trans. James S. Churchill (Bloomington: Indiana University Press, 1962).

—— *Erläuterungen zu Hölderlins Dichtung, 5. Auflage* (Frankfurt am Main: Vittorio Klostermann, 1971a).

—— *Poetry, Language, and Thought*, trans. Albert Hofstadter (New York: Harper & Row, 1971b).

—— *Sein und Zeit, 15. Auflage* (Tübingen: Niemeyer, 1979). Translation: *Being and Time*, trans. John Macquarrie and Edward Robinson (Oxford: Blackwell, 1962).

—— *Aus der Erfahrung des Denkens, Gesamtausgabe 13*, ed. Hermann Heidegger (Frankfurt am Main: Vittorio Klostermann, 1983).

—— *Hölderlins Hymne 'Andenken', Gesamtausgabe Band 52* (Frankfurt am Main: Vittorio Klostermann, 1992).

Hölderlin, Friedrich, *Selected Poems*, trans. David Constantine (Bloodaxe Books: Newcastle upon Tyne, 1996).

Jonas, Hans, *Mortality and Morality: A Search for the Good After Auschwitz*, ed. Lawrence Vogel (Evanston: Northwestern University Press, 1996).

Lacoue-Labarthe, Philippe, *Heidegger, Art, and Politics,* trans. Chris Turner (Oxford: Basil Blackwell, 1990).

—— 'Poetry's Courage', in *The Solid Letter: Readings of Friedrich Hölderlin*, ed. Aris Fioretos (Stanford University Press: Stanford, 1999).

Risser, James (ed.), *Heidegger Toward the Turn: Essays on the Work of the 1930's* (Albany: State University of New York Press, 1999).

Roth, Michael, *The Poetics of Resistance: Heidegger's Line* (Evanston: Northwestern University Press, 1996).

White, David A., *Heidegger and the Language of Poetry* (Lincoln: University of Nebraska Press, 1978).

Young, Julian, *Heidegger's Later Philosophy* (Cambridge: Cambridge University Press, 2002).

8
Construction without Theory: Oblique Reflections on Walter Benjamin's Goethe

Richard J. Lane

In Benjamin's First Sketches of his monumental work *The Arcades Project* (Paris Arcades <I>, 1927–1930), there is an ambiguous reference to the methodology of the project: 'Formula: construction out of facts. Construction with the complete elimination of theory. What only Goethe in his morphological writings has attempted' (Benjamin, 1999a, p. 864, <O°, 73>). Benjamin's reference to *morphology* is regarded in what follows here as a guide to the complex interplay of literature and philosophy in his work, where 'philosophy' is another word for 'metaphysics' in this case as mapped out by Jacobson:

> it [metaphysics] is a highly speculative philosophy of fundamental questions regarding politics and theology, drawing on a near scholastic aptitude for categorical analysis and Talmudic rigor within a conception of divine continuity of meaning. In this way it is in fact a philosophy of divine as well as profane questions. 'Metaphysics,' Scholem once remarks [*sic*] in his Swiss notebook, 'is a legitimate theory in the subjunctive form'. (Jacobson, p. 5)

Just as we can ask of Goethe 'is this (morphological method) scientific?' we can also ask of Benjamin's project 'is this philosophy?' (Buck-Morss, p. 216). Oswald Spengler regarded Goethe's morphological writing as not only highly efficacious but also a model approach for the revealing of 'destiny': 'The two concepts, Goethe's form-fulfilment and Darwin's evolution, are in as complete opposition as destiny to causality...' (Spengler, Vol. II, p. 32), and: 'If the reader examines Goethe's writings in natural science, he will be astounded to find how "living nature" can be set forth without formulae, without laws, almost without a trace of the causal' (Spengler, Vol. I, p. 154). Of course Spengler's main target here is Kant, whose concept of a reduced or restricted 'experience' was also a serious problem for Benjamin. The potentially confusing constellation here of proper names inside and outside of parentheses – Benjamin, Buck-Morss, Darwin, Goethe, Kant, Spengler – is indicative and mimetic of the critical mass of intertexts (sacred and profane), allusions, objects, and proper names that are found across Benjamin's work as a whole.

Adding another proper name to the above list – in relation to the morphological approach and the desire for 'Construction with the complete elimination of theory' – brings Wittgenstein into the constellation. As Monk asserts, 'Again and again in his lectures Wittgenstein tried to explain that he was not offering any philosophical *theory*; he was offering only the means to escape any *need* of such a theory' (Monk, p. 301). In literary-critical terms, Wittgenstein shifts in his own project from *telling* to *showing*, a narrational transition that Wayne C. Booth found in general disturbing because of the concomitant destabilizing of the reliable narrator (in many respects, Booth's classic *The Rhetoric of Fiction* is a defence of authorial 'telling'). Wittgenstein's shift or turn was decisive: '. . . the really decisive moment came when he began to take literally the idea of the *Tractatus* that the philosopher has nothing to *say*, but only something to *show*, and applied that idea with complete rigour, abandoning altogether the attempt to say something with "pseudo-propositions" ' (Monk, p. 302). The shift or turn here reveals further links throughout the constellation of proper names and interrelated concepts:

> This emphasis on *seeing* connections links Wittgenstein's later philosophy with Spengler's *Decline of the West*, and at the same time provides the key to understanding the connection between his cultural pessimism and the themes of his later work. In *The Decline of the West* Spengler distinguishes between the Principle of Form (*Gestalt*) and the Principle of Law: with the former went history, poetry and life; with the latter went physics, mathematics and death. [. . .] [Spengler] argued for a conception of history that saw the historian's job, not as gathering facts and providing explanations, but as perceiving the significance of events by seeing the morphological (or, as Spengler preferred to say, physiognomic) relations between them.
>
> Spengler's notion of a physiognomic method of history was, as he acknowledges, inspired by Goethe's notion of a morphological study of nature, as exemplified in Goethe's poem *Die Metamorphose der Pflanze*, which follows the development of the plant-form from the leaf through a series of intermediate forms. (Monk, pp. 302–303)

Philosophy (with the shift from telling to showing) becomes an activity that is performed, as with a Beckett play, such as *Quad*, the players completing their courses, producing patterns, or meanings as events and shapes. But even the 'showing', stripped of the unnecessary supplement of metanarrative or commentary (Wittgenstein's dreaded 'logical analysis' of a proposition or statement of fact), can construct an interiority, which is precisely what happened with *Quad*, and the 'supposed danger zone' 'E' (Beckett, p. 453), the central intersecting point which needs the 'deviation' of a mimetically reproduced square, to avoid the collision of the players.

Wittgenstein pictures the lack of metanarrative or commentary in another way: no 'fundamental' explanation (of an activity, a rule, etc.) is necessary (Monk, p. 302). In fact the logical conclusion for this anti-theory line is Wittgenstein's infamous 'silence'. But in making a comparison with Goethe, the simplicity and beauty of silence is disturbed by F. Waismann's wider claim (in collaboration with Wittgenstein): 'That [Goethe's morphology] is precisely what we are doing here. We are collating one form of language with its environment, or transforming it in imagination so as to gain a view of the whole of space in which the structure of language has its being' (Monk, p. 304). Language, which simply functions within its context, or environment, can be examined as such (*revealed* would perhaps be a better word); there is a sequence of words, they function in a particular way, and that is the end of it. Or, that would be the end of it without Waismann's phrase 'transforming it in imagination so as to gain a view of the whole of space in which the structure of language has its being'. The collation is, in this supplementary phrase, a gathering or assemblage which enables an overarching perspective, transcending the specific instance of language-use (the event) not to see some separate 'grammar' at work, but rather, the architectonics of the space in which language exists. Is this overarching perspective always attained? Not necessarily, since thought can be a torment, disordered, and a squandering of energy: 'I *squander* [*verschwende*] an unspeakable amount of effort making an arrangement of my thoughts which may have no value at all' (Wittgenstein, 1980, p. 28). Interestingly, in the preceding statement, Wittgenstein separates thoughts and writing; in thought, the natural sequence is one which is disordered, whereas rearrangement into the ordered sequence (writing) is a torment. The collation does not engage with the extravagant waste of energy that occurs in the process of creating a particular sequence of words.

How tenuous are the connections here between Benjamin and Wittgenstein? Are there really strong 'signals and affinities' as Stanley Cavell puts it? The family resemblances *are* reasonably strong, especially Cavell's brief exploration of 'The conjunction of melancholy with . . . ennui or boredom' (Cavell, p. 238):

The conjunction of melancholy with, let me call it, ennui or boredom, speaks to one of the guiding forces of Wittgenstein's thoughts in the *Investigations*, the recognition that his mode of philosophizing seems to 'destroy everything interesting (all that is great and important)' (*PI*, §118). Wittgenstein voices this recognition explicitly just once (and once more can be taken to imply it [see *PI*, §570]), but it is invoked each time he follows the method of language-games, that is to say, punctually through the bulk of the *Investigations*. That this destruction, as Wittgenstein notes, leaves behind as it were no scene of devastation, no place that has become 'only bits of stone and rubble' (*PI*, §118) . . . suggests that the imaginary destruction of what we called great and important reveals our investments to have been imaginary, with the terribly real implication that so far as philosophy was and is our life (and there is no surveying the extent) our life has been trained as a rescue from boredom, delivered to an anxious twilight of interest. (Cavell, p. 238)

Cavell goes on to explore connections between certain 'preoccupations' found in Benjamin's *Trauerspiel* book and Wittgenstein's *Philosophical Invest-igations*, namely the 'emblems of melancholy', here 'the dog, the stone, and the sphere' (Cavell, p. 239). This raises another question, perhaps the most important one for this essay, as to whether these emblems as found in Wittgenstein have anything to do with philosophy: '. . . such considerations would, at best, be responded to as curiosities by more representative members of my field, and at worst, not without proper impatience, as an avoidance or betrayal of philosophy (as if I perversely emphasize the aspect of the *Investigations* that is itself a betrayal of philosophy)' (Cavell, p. 239). Cavell's amusing 'negative dialectic' that follows this statement should be read in full, especially the tracing of animals, stones, and angels to Hansenn's book *Walter Benjamin's Other History*, and Heidegger's 'articulation of Dasein's historicity' (Cavell, p. 240). In tracing, also, the ways in which analytical philosophers might wish to strip Wittgenstein of 'the occasional animals and the odd flarings of pathos, perverseness, suffocation, lostness' (Cavell, p. 241), Cavell suggests that a core uncontaminated 'doctrine' is presumably felt to survive. While Cavell – by this point in his essay – has already provided a number of methodological models that argue the complete opposite, it is also possible that such a central 'doctrine' would in itself be incredibly boring. The melancholic philosopher, waking up to such a core doctrine stripped of all its asides, labyrinthine byways, animals, stones, and even angels, would, like the splenetic Englishman waking up to the rain, shoot himself (Benjamin, 1999a, p. 102, D1,3).

In *The Arcades Project*, Benjamin speaks of boredom as 'the external surface of unconscious events' (Benjamin, 1999a, p. 106, D2a,2) or as 'a warm gray fabric lined on the inside with the most lustrous and colorful of silks' with which 'we wrap ourselves when we dream' (Benjamin, 1999a, p. 105, D2a,1). He extends the analogy even further in a brief meditation on the Paris arcades:

the sleeper looks bored and gray within his sheath. And when he later wakes and wants to tell of what he dreamed, he communicates by and large only this boredom. For who would be able at one stroke to turn the lining of time to the outside? Yet to narrate dreams signifies nothing else. And in no other way can one deal with the arcades – structures in which we relive, as in a dream, the life of our parents and grandparents, as the embryo in the womb relives the life of animals. Existence in these spaces flows then without accent, like the events in dreams. (Benjamin, 1999a, p. 106, D2a,1)

Is Benjamin proffering a theory here? Or is he eliminating theory? Turning 'the lining of time to the outside' may be another description of the expected or longed-for result of the dialectical images that Benjamin constructs throughout the *Arcades Project*, the 'image flashing up in the now of its recognizability' (Benjamin, 1999a, p. 473, N9,7). This messianic hope is also a radical switching, forging otherwise less well explored links in Benjamin's work, such as that between his concept of origin and Franz Rosenzweig's concept of revelation ('Notes (IV)', Benjamin, 1999b, Vol. II, p. 687). Are such linkages created via stylistic manipulation?

Elsewhere, I have discussed some analogies between *The Arcades Project* and the British experimental writer B.S. Johnson (Lane, 2005), in particular Johnson's book-in-a-box called *The Unfortunates*. *The Unfortunates* has unnumbered chapters (except for the first and last), and the chapters are not bound together, so that they can be shuffled into different orders. Reshuffling the chapters creates new and striking juxtapositions between blocks of text, memories, and descriptions; memories are produced in a pseudo-random order that mimics human frailty and subjectivity. Of most interest here is the way in which a 'morphological' reading of the text is not only possible, but necessary; stylistic manipulation of the binding also creates a process that can be thought of, via catachresis, as a theological concept (which may also bind Benjamin and Kierkegaard [Sussman, p. 175]), or, in the secular realm, as analogous to the Duchampian transparent 'bindings' or boxes: Duchamp's showcases 'with sliding glass panes' (Duchamp, p. 7; Lane, 2005, p. 231). What I have avoided saying here so far is that this potential elimination of theory is a stylistic choice or fashion statement that reveals the language-games or actions of the modern philosopher:

Familiar words [in *The Arcades Project*] such as *boredom, collector,* and *panorama* replace technical terms such as *subjectivity, transcendental,* and *speculative . . .* Presenting oneself as something other than a philosopher is a fashion 'must,' in other words, for anyone who wishes to be a philosopher. Not to be one at all, to be other than one – this is considerably more difficult, especially if, as the transcendental philosophy of the scholastics proposes, *unum* and *ens,* 'one' and 'being,' are convertible terms. Not to be one is the same as not being at all. Being so would be possible – if it is possible – only for a constitutively inconsistent plurality, which, by virtue of its inconsistency, cannot be made into a unit of ordered elements. The fashion of the philosopher is, for this reason, the de-fashioning fashion *kat exochen*: It consists in forever going out of fashion. (Fenves, p. 81)

Does the *morphological* function or work here 'better' than the *theoretical*? The presentation of 'facts' about, say, boredom, the collector, and the panorama approaches the ideal of Goethe or the later Wittgenstein. Morphology can be thought of here as theory or philosophy 'in a different key', just as literature can be perceived as doing philosophy 'better than philosophy does' (see Eaglestone, pp. 43–4).

A strange thing occurs in *The Arcades Project*, as Fenves points out, whereby the avoidance of '. . . the technical terms of philosophical discourse, comes to revolve around the word *monad*' (Fenves, p. 83). In other words, the plain style of description, the collation of objects, words, images found in the Paris arcades, all intersect or are bound together by this most technical and unusual word 'monad'. And the monad is the remainder, the residuum, par excellence, after the dialectical upheavals have taken place:

> What remains of the word *monad*, for its part, is the original spin from which it sprang: It names that which remains unaffected. The image of this paradisal condition, as Leibniz famously notes, is the absence of windows – an absence that materializes itself in nineteenth-century Paris in panoramas, theatres, and arcades, the windows of which, as Benjamin notes, look upward but not outward. (Fenves, p. 86)

How does the plain style, the absence of theory, the descriptive showing rather than philosophical telling, find itself in *The Arcades Project* in confluence with a monadology? Is there a folding at work here, of the sort identified by Deleuze? Or should the key phrase be – given that this essay is commenting obliquely on Benjamin's readings of Goethe – 'elective affinity' (*Wahlverwandtschaft*)? It is important here to be wary of the various English translations of this term, as Löwy warns, 'The concept [*Wahlverwandtschaft*] allows us to understand processes of interaction which arise neither from direct causality nor from the "expressive" relationship between form and content (where, for example, the religious form is the "expression" of a political or social content)' (Löwy, p. 12). Löwy goes on to situate Benjamin historically in a force-field of correspondences:

> there had to appear a certain *constellation* of historical, social and cultural factors. Only then could a process of *attractio electiva* or 'cultural symbi-osis' develop between messianism and revolutionary utopia within the *Weltanschauung* of a large group of German-speaking Jewish intellectuals, involving mutual stimulation and nourishment and, in certain cases, even combination or fusion of the two spiritual figures. (Löwy, p. 21)

Waismann's statement, addressed earlier – 'That [Goethe's morphology] is precisely what we are doing here. We are collating one form of language with its environment, or transforming it in imagination so as to gain a view of the whole of space in which the structure of language has its being' (Monk, p. 304) – can be reworked via the cultural *Wahlverwandtschaft* recognized by Löwy and others, where 'the whole space' is viewed not in some neutral fashion, but in the light of anticipation. Thus every moment must be prepared to assume or accept the plenitude of utopia or eternity, to loosely paraphrase Rosenzweig in light of the *Wahlverwandtschaft* (Rosenzweig, p. 228). The question asked of Benjamin's highly creative texts, 'is this philosophy?' now becomes: is this elective affinity, between messianism and revolutionary utopianism, a theological mode? The latter question has long been debated among Benjamin scholars, but what is of immediate concern here is the way in which a *contrapuntal mode* of thinking, and writing (rather than selecting one particular approach), can be said to be at work across Benjamin's entire *oeuvre*. Any convolute, draft, or fragment from *The Arcades Project* bears this latter statement out, and a cursory paraphrase and analysis of two sections from the 'Materials for the Exposé of 1935' – Sections 8 and 9 (Benjamin, 1999a, pp. 907–8) – will suffice.

Sections 8 and 9 of the 'Materials' provide a schematic draft for the completed Exposé, an architectonic blueprint that begins with 'dialectical stages', and proceeds through definitions of awakening, collecting, and dreaming with reference to Freud and Aragon (No. 8), then exploring notions of 'dream-variation-image', false redemption (*Jugendstil*), and theories of awakening and perspective (No. 9). Comments on the dialectical stages (in the Paris arcades) – of splendour transmuted into decay, and unconscious experience transmuted into a force-field consciously penetrated – are followed in Section 8 by a framing of 'the collective' as possessing 'Not-yet-conscious knowledge'; awakening is a schema whereby insight brings into consciousness this knowledge. It is not the case that 'the collective' needs to be told something, guided, educated, and so on; rather 'they' need to be woken up from a state of ongoing dreaming. The schema of awakening, however, is also a recognition of the messianic relationship of present and future; again, it is not the case that some supplementary (or 'progressive') force, group, or cause will awaken 'the collective', rather 'they' wake to the explosive possibilities of Today (Rosenzweig, p. 234). The contrapuntal mode here is foregrounded by Benjamin's remark that 'what Proust intends with the experimental rearrangement of furniture is no different from what Bloch tries to grasp as darkness of the lived moment' (Benjamin, 1999a, p. 907). Rearrangement is awakening: it is also the rearrangement that becomes or recovers the configuration of the 'moment' (that overdetermined philosophical and theological term in Kierkegaard, Nietzsche, Bloch, etc.) via imitation 'in the realm of language' (Benjamin, 1999a, p. 907). Benjamin charts here the physiological triggering of remembrance via the linguistic construction of a 'theoretical' awakening – this, of course, is analogous to Scholem's notion of a 'legitimate theory in the subjunctive form'. Remembrance is a mode of resistance here, in the sense that 'the collective' needs to shed the notion that it has always been 'created' in the sense of worked upon, leading to a permanently passive, somnambulistic being. The 'lived moment' of awakening is thus a 'momentariness', to use Rosenzweig's word, whereby 'existence as such challenges the constant renewal of becoming created' (Rosenzweig, p. 121). The constant renewal – surely what the subject strives for – is a vacuity, a hyperreality, that can only be perceived as such via the awareness of dialectical transformation (for Benjamin, an awareness triggered by the Paris arcades). Benjamin completes his contrapuntal schema by asking what sort of 'comportment . . . is adequate to true waking being?' (Benjamin, 1999a, p. 907). The 'Materials' continue in relation to this question in the following section where Benjamin shifts from linguistic imitation to the 'dream-variation-image'; partly a repetition of the 'moment' reached in Section 8, partly its amplification and intensification, the shift to a particular description of a dialectical image opens up the vista of the 'dream vision' *that penetrates the waking world*. This apparently opposing force (i.e., instead of the unconscious 'consciously penetrated') is a dialectical reversal, a mechanism that Benjamin sets to work across multiple realms in his monumental text. Benjamin crosses out a marginal aside, a reminder to himself of Aragon's cryptic remark that 'the arcades are what they are for us here through the fact that they no longer are (in themselves)' (Benjamin, 1999a, p. 909). This slightly ridiculous comment – no doubt better removed or placed under erasure – nonetheless adds one final component to the 'stationary' moment of the dream-variation-image: that it is not a sequential accumulation of historical events or forces, rather it engenders a radical reversal through a 're-commencement' (Rosenzweig, p. 290).

In conclusion, this sequence from *The Arcades Project*, that makes up one small part of the 'Materials for the Exposé of 1935', reveals the anticipatory space of the morphological method, as adapted and (partially) adopted by Benjamin, a space where anarchic and messianic configurations (conceptual, linguistic, imaged) are deployed not just to awaken 'the collective' but also as a cognition of immediate experience. The latter is no longer the nineteenth-century world of 'adventure' but the far more unstable comportment towards 'fate'; the gathering storm in Benjamin's time, and the chaotic conditions of post First World War Europe, pointed towards war as its 'unsurpassed prefiguration' (Benjamin, 1999a, p. 801, m1a,5). Fate, for Benjamin, conceals the concept of 'total experience' which humanity is qualified for via a new found 'empathy with exchange value' (Benjamin, 1999a, p. 801, m1a,5 and m1a,6). The monadology of *The Arcades Project*, that rock upon which founders any purely perspectival or postmodernist reading of the text, is given architectonic form with the study of those nineteenth-century houses and passages that, like a dream, have no outside (Benjamin, 1999a,

'First Sketches', p. 839, <F°, 9>). Thus Benjamin writes, 'The true has no windows. Nowhere does the true look out to the universe. And the interest of the panorama is in seeing the true city'. (Benjamin, 1999a, 'First Sketches', p. 840, <F°, 24>). Benjamin's 'construction out of facts' disrupts the fate that not only awaits the subject but becomes essential to his or her perceptual training; intermittence is now the tempo of the new that 'never alters' (Benjamin, 1999a, 'First Sketches', p. 843, <G°, 17> and <G°, 19>), yet the monadology is a residuum that still forces the question, 'is this philosophy?'.

Works cited

Beckett, Samuel, *The Complete Dramatic Works* (London: Faber & Faber, 1990).

Benjamin, Walter, *The Arcades Project*, trans. Howard Eiland and Kevin McLaughlin (Cambridge, Massachusetts and London, England: Belknap Press of Harvard University Press, 1999a).

——*Selected Writings: Volume 2, 1927–1934*, trans. Rodney Livingstone *et al.* (Cambridge, Massachusetts and London, England: Belknap Press of Harvard University Press, 1999b).

Buck-Morss, Susan, *The Dialectics of Seeing: Walter Benjamin and The Arcades Project* (Cambridge, Massachusetts: MIT Press, 1999).

Cavell, Stanley, 'Benjamin and Wittgenstein: Signals and Affinities', *Critical Inquiry, Angelus Novus: Perspectives on Walter Benjamin*, 25, 2 (Winter 1999), 235–46.

Deleuze, Gilles, *The Fold: Leibniz and the Baroque*, trans. Tom Conley (London: Athlone, 2001).

Duchamp, Marcel, *À l'infinitif/in the infinitive*, a typotranslation by Richard Hamilton and Ecke Bonk of Marcel Duchamp's White Box (Over Wallop, UK: The Typosophic Society, 1999).

Eaglestone, Robert, 'Beckett in the Wilderness: Writing about (Not) Writing about Beckett', pp. 40–52 in ed. Richard J. Lane, *Beckett and Philosophy* (Basingstoke: Palgrave, 2002).

Fenves, Peter, 'Of Philosophical Style – from Leibniz to Benjamin', *Boundary 2, Benjamin Now: Critical Encounters with The Arcades Project*, ed. Kevin McLaughlin and Philip Rosen, 30, 1 (Spring 2003), 67–87.

Jacobson, Eric, *Metaphysics of The Profane: The Political Theology of Walter Benjamin and Gershom Scholem* (New York: Columbia University Press, 2003).

Johnson, B.S., *The Unfortunates*, intro. by Jonathan Coe (London: Picador, 1999).

Lane, Richard J. (ed.), *Beckett and Philosophy* (Basingstoke: Palgrave, 2002).

——*Reading Walter Benjamin: Writing Through the Catastrophe* (Manchester: Manchester University Press, 2005).

Löwy, Michael, *Redemption & Utopia: Jewish Libertarian Thought in Central Europe, A Study in Elective Affinity*, trans. Hope Heaney (London: Athlone, 1992).

Monk, Ray, *Ludwig Wittgenstein: The Duty of Genius* (London: Vintage, 1991).

Rosenzweig, Franz, *The Star of Redemption*, trans. William W. Hallo (Notre Dame: University of Notre Dame Press, 1985).

Spengler, Oswald, *The Decline of the West* (volumes one and two), trans. Charles Francis Atkinson (London: George Allen & Unwin, 1926).

Sussman, Henry 'Between the Registers: The Allegory of Space in Walter Benjamin's *Arcades Project*', *Boundary 2, Benjamin Now: Critical Encounters with* The Arcades Project, ed. Kevin McLaughlin and Philip Rosen, 30, 1 (Spring 2003), 169–90.

Waismann, F., *The Principles of Linguistic Philosophy*, ed. R. Harré (London: Macmillan and New York: St Martin's, 1965).
Williams, John R., *The Life of Goethe* (Oxford: Blackwell, 2001).
Wittgenstein, Ludwig, *Philosophical Investigations*, 2nd ed., trans. G.E.M. Anscombe (Oxford: Blackwell, 1953).
——*Culture And Value*, trans. Peter Winch, ed. G.H. Von Wright in collaboration with Heikki Nyman (Chicago: University of Chicago Press, 1980).

Part IV
Literature and Philosophy: The Question of Ethics

Introduction

Philosophical reflection on literature has historically been dominated by controversies surrounding its ethical significance. Indeed, in the Classical tradition, such debates about the moral value of poetry go back further than the study of poetry in its own right, at least insofar as Plato's *Republic* predates Aristotle's *Poetics*. And, from eighteenth-century disputes as to whether the newly emergent form of the novel corrupted the virtues of the young ladies that read it to the contemporary debates about the effects of violence on television, arguments about the moral consequences of literature have been more numerous and more vociferous than arguments about the study of literature itself. Ethical reflection on literature is, then, a more established way – or at least a more pervasive way – of engaging with the subject than literary criticism.

In tracing the origins of these debates, it is easy to simplify the ambivalence of Plato's stance regarding literature, and all too common to overlook the praise he gives to poetry. Yet, nevertheless, his work is the principal source of the ideas that literature tells lies, and that it has a malign and corrupting effect on the morals of those who read it. As regards the first of these charges, distrust of literature has indeed been common throughout the subsequent philosophical tradition, and despite Sir Philip Sidney's contention as far back as 1580 that 'the poet, he nothing affirmeth, and therefore never lieth', the equating of fiction with lies remained commonplace until, with the advent of Romanticism, the notion of 'poetic truth' gained some currency in philosophical circles. Indeed, several twentieth-century speech act philosophers (such as J.L. Austin or John Searle) have reasserted the position that literary discourse cannot be thought of as 'truthful' in the sense that ordinary language can.

The second of Plato's ideas – that literature exerts a corrupting moral influence – is the more familiar, and is of more relevance here. Interestingly, it was precisely in repudiation of claims like these that literary criticism in England established itself. F.R. Leavis in particular sought to justify the study of literary texts in terms of the moral vision that great works of literature strove to communicate, and for the first generations of literary academics in Britain, the moral importance of reading was thus imperative. Rather than a source of moral corruption, then, literature came to be viewed as a means of moral regeneration. Such a claim obviously bolstered the prestige of the new discipline of English studies, yet – perhaps to preserve the disciplinary 'purity' of English as a new subject – it lacked any serious philosophical engagement with the nature of the ethical or moral judgments behind it. Indeed, Leavis himself often voiced his impatience with philosophy, and, citing the 'concreteness' of literature against the abstract nature of theorizing, his readings of texts conceived their ethical aspects in a relatively straightforward fashion, which, in its refusal to engage with philosophy, took for granted an unproblematic moral consensus.

Against the background of a Leavisite emphasis on the moral mission of literary criticism, the advent of theory came as a timely but controversial intervention. Marxism in particular sought to reappraise the humanist emphasis on moral agency by focusing on political readings instead. The next generation of theorists, mostly structuralists, viewed texts in a scientist light that was strikingly indifferent to questions of the moral and ethical, whilst theorists after structuralism tended to emphasize multiple readings of texts. For traditional critics, such readings were tantamount to relativism, whilst deconstructive readings that seemed to highlight how texts problematize, refuse, or withhold moral comment seemed to have no ethics whatsoever, and even to undermine, from a philosophical point of view, the very terms and grounds on which we might try to make ethical evaluations. From the standpoint of both the traditional literary critic and the traditional philosopher, then, theory appeared either uncritically disinterested in the ethical, or dangerously subversive of the basis for moral judgments in literature – or, indeed, both.

Thus, by the end of the 1980s, an unlikely alliance of literary critics and philosophers emerged, united against the (perceived) moral indifference of Continental theory, and championing literature as a source of humanist values instead. The clearest articulation of this reaction in literary criticism is Wayne C. Booth's *The Company We Keep: An Ethics of Fiction* (Berkeley and LA: University of California Press, 1988). However, most of the credit for the interdisciplinary bridgebuilding belongs to philosophy, perhaps because of traditional criticism's residual Leavisite suspicion of the abstract. Martha C. Nussbaum, a moral philosopher whose work draws frequently on literature, is foremost amongst those who practise philosophy as an alternative to the indifference of theory towards humanism. She argues that literature places us in positions that encourage us to identify with the other, thereby cultivating sympathy in the reader, and enhancing our capacity for moral judgment.

See her *Love's Knowledge: Essays on Philosophy and Literature* (Oxford: Oxford University Press, 1990) for a collection of her interdisciplinary work.

If theory's alleged lack of concern with the ethical had achieved the unforeseen side effect of bringing moral philosophy and literary criticism closer together, then it was precisely against the allegations of this lack that many exponents of theory began to challenge this picture by turning towards ethics. Deconstruction in particular had been criticized for its allegedly immoral undermining of traditional reading practices. So, from the late 1980s, deconstruction began to defend itself. J. Hillis Miller's *The Ethics of Reading* (New York: Columbia University Press, 1987) maintained that the act of reading carried an almost performative ethical force, which was all the more potent for not being containable within any given reading. To an extent, Miller's is an ethics of unreadability, arguing that the irreducibility of the act of reading, as embraced by decontruction's mode of reading, is an ethical imperative. Tellingly, his study is exemplified by readings of both philosophical and novelistic texts. Simon Critchley's *The Ethics of Deconstruction* (first published Oxford: Blackwell, 1992, 2nd ed. Edinburgh: Edinburgh University Press, 1999) approaches the issue from a more philosophical standpoint. Critchley demonstrates the ethical insights of a deconstructive refusal of closure, arguing that the ethical moment is prior to and resistant to the normative and systematic strictures of traditional moral philosophy. Critchley's text is particularly noteworthy for its engagement with the thought of Emmanuel Levinas.

Levinas has been the central figure of a recent 'Ethical Turn' (or, perhaps, 'Ethical Return') of contemporary literary theory, which has embraced philosophical consideration of the nature of the ethical. Despite Levinas's professed distrust of the sphere of art, and occasionally of some aspects of language itself, his radical assertion that 'ethics is first philosophy' and his claim that subjectivity entails a responsibility towards the other have been hugely influential for theorists and critics seeking to re-evaluate the basis from which literature might be considered ethical. Illuminating discussions of this include Robert Eaglestone's *Ethical Criticism: Reading After Levinas* (Edinburgh: Edinburgh University Press, 1997) and Jill Robbins's *Altered Reading: Levinas and Literature* (Chicago: University of Chicago Press, 1999). Roland A. Champagne's *The Ethics of Reading According to Emmanuel Levinas* (Chiasma: 7, Amsterdam: Rodopi, 1998) gives a range of Levinasian readings of a wide variety of (principally French) literary texts, whilst Michael Eskin's *Ethics and Dialogue in the Works of Levinas, Bakhtin, Mandelshtam, and Celan* (Oxford: Oxford University Press, 2000) focuses more on poetry and translation. *The Cambridge Companion to Levinas*, ed. Simon Critchley and Robert Bernasconi (Cambridge: Cambridge University Press, 2002) is also a helpful resource.

However, there is more to the return to ethical criticism than this upsurge of interest in the thought of Levinas. The broader co-ordinates of this tendency are set out in *Mapping the Ethical Turn: A Reader in Ethics, Culture and*

Literary Theory, eds Todd F. Davis and Kenneth Womack (Charlottesville: University Press of Virginia, 2001), with essays from crucial figures such as Nussbaum, Booth, and Miller. For a useful outline of the origins of recent ethical criticism, see Andrew Gibson's *Postmodernity, Ethics, and the Novel: From Leavis to Levinas* (London: Routledge, 1999). Perhaps the theorist who encompasses the broadest spectrum of philosophical, literary, and theoretical insights in his discussions of ethics would be Geoffrey Galt Harpham, whose *Getting it Right: Language, Literature, and Ethics* (Chicago: University of Chicago Press, 1992) and *Shadows of Ethics: Criticism and the Just Society* (Durham, NC: Duke University Press, 1999) constitute valuable interventions in the debate over the ethical aspects of literature and criticism.

All the chapters in this part engage in the discussion of moral and ethical dimensions of literature in original and innovative ways. Taking issue with the position of Nussbaum, Mary C. Rawlinson argues that our ethical considerations of literature involve identification with situations that are ambiguous and that lack universality, making literature a serious challenge to the frameworks on which moral philosophies are founded, while Rupert Read formulates an analysis of the nature and ethics of forgiveness by questioning how and whether acts of forgiveness can be said to take place at all.

David Rudrum

9
Liminal Agencies: Literature as Moral Philosophy

Mary C. Rawlinson

The 'quarrel' between philosophy and poetry over truth was already an 'ancient enmity' in Plato's time (Plato, *Republic*, line 607b). In considering the idea of Justice, Plato's Socrates insists that literature has no power to 'teach the truth adequately to others', nor 'to educate men and make them better' (Plato, *Republic*, line 599d). Literature is inimical to justice because it is an 'illusionism', 'an imitation of a phantasm... far removed from the truth' (Plato, *Republic*, line 598b).[1] Instead of evoking, even to the degree that perceptual objects do, the one true world of the Forms, the images of art and literature capture only the distorting illusion of the artist's own way of seeing or style, by which the unity of reality seems to be fractured into a multiplicity of perspectives and worlds. It thus undermines the central philosophical idea of the universality, the univocity, of truth. Moreover, literature is dangerously open to interpretation. It cannot choose its interlocutor. It cannot 'defend itself', nor determine 'when to speak and when to be silent'. It is 'parentless' and 'not lawfully begotten' (Plato, *Phaedrus*, line 275d). It is at best the bastard, orphaned remainder of living speech.[2] Thus, the philosopher 'will not seriously incline to "write" his thoughts "in water" with pen and ink, sowing words which can neither speak for themselves nor teach the truth adequately to others' (Plato, *Phaedrus*, line 276c).

The philosopher concerned with Justice and the Good commits himself to educating others, and only his 'living word', sown like a seed in the ripe soil of a 'congenial soul', can bring forth the 'vision of Truth' (Plato, *Republic*, line 607b). To think that the illusionism of art and literature has a place in this project is to 'disgrace' oneself, to reveal that one cannot even 'distinguish dream from reality'.

Post-Platonic philosophers from Aristotle to Hegel do accord to art and literature a heuristic role in the education of the soul and the achievement of justice. If properly regulated, both in its production and in its dissemination, literature serves to supplement the more adequate theoretical analyses

129

of philosophy. For those souls incapable of the systematic thinking of philosophy, it provides a nonconceptual access to ideas of justice and universality. Thus, as for Aristotle, the properly controlled catharsis evoked by literature can be useful in shaping a soul that is unmoved by philosophical argument.[3] Or, the images of literature can provide a sensuous presentation of the universal as in Kant's analysis of Beauty as 'symbol of morality' (Kant, 1987, §59, pp. 225–30). Or, while incapable of 'thoughts' and 'concepts', as Hegel argues, literature can yield knowledge of formal features of experience that contribute to the philosopher's systematic account of the universe of mind (Hegel, 1975, pp. 1035–6). In each case, literature is valued because it evokes *feelings* that either substitute images for philosophy's discursive knowledge or supply helpful clues in the process of attaining that knowledge.

Recent efforts to defend literature against philosophical critique repeat these evaluations. In her beautiful book *On Beauty and Being Just* Elaine Scarry argues that 'a set of political complaints' has made it impossible to address the beauty of literature and art. In the 1980s and 1990s, she asserts, 'conversation about the beauty of these things has been banished' from the humanities, because beauty stands condemned of 'damaging our capacity to attend to problems of injustice' (Scarry, p. 57). Either it distracts us from attending to unjust social arrangements or it leads us to attend to the object in a way that 'reifies' it and is, thus, harmful to it. Her argument, to the contrary, is that beauty serves the moral good and social justice because it 'intensifies the pressure we *feel* to repair existing injuries' (Scarry, p. 57 – my emphasis). In developing her position, Scarry relies, on the one hand, on the Kantian analysis of the way in which beauty, unlike what is merely preferred, makes an immediate claim upon our regard that we expect others to recognize as well (Scarry, p. 67). Hence, it is something universal. On the other, she cites the 'distributional' character of beauty, thus relying on Plato's analysis of the capacity of a beautiful particular to lead us by analogy to the contemplation of beautiful ideas and, ultimately, the moral good. Citing John Rawls' definition of fairness as 'a symmetry of everyone's relation to one another', Scarry defines beauty as a 'contract' between the viewer and the beautiful object in which the 'symmetry' of the beautiful object 'leads us to' the symmetry that defines justice or 'fraternity' (Scarry, pp. 95, 90, 114). Thus, Scarry's analysis of beauty leaves intact traditional philosophical conceptions of justice as the mutual recognition of equals, and it treats art and literature as heuristics which provide analogies or images for justice and the moral good.

In an equally elegant analysis Martha Nussbaum repeats this evaluation of literature as a 'good guide' in matters of justice (Nussbaum, p. 74). Nussbaum argues that literary understanding 'promotes habits of mind that lead toward social equality' (Nussbaum, p. 92). 'Sympathetic emotion' is essential to public judgment, and in teaching us compassion literature acts as an 'equalizer'. The good reader is akin to Adam Smith's 'judicious spectator' and exhibits a proper 'neutrality' and 'detachment' in reading critically and without prejudice. Thus, the reader's literary neutrality promotes the proper 'judicial neutrality'. Nussbaum insists that 'not all emotions are good guides' (Nussbaum, pp. 74, 92). The literary imagination must be properly 'tethered', and the feelings it invokes are instructive only if informed by rational belief and a 'true view of what is going on'. Thus, the literary imagination can aid rational analysis, and encourages the development of justice understood as reciprocity among equals.

In these contemporary cases, the traditional philosophical idea of justice as fraternity, symmetry, or the mutual recognition of equals, as well as the traditional philosophical evaluation of art as providing a 'symbol of morality' or an educative analogy of justice persist. The experience of art and literature may disturb prejudice, enlarge and inform the understanding, and inculcate habits of mind that contribute to moral reasoning, but it does not in any way disturb the idea of justice as fraternity or the concept of the agent as a rational deliberator among better and worse choices. Both Scarry and Nussbaum maintain the tradition's confidence in fraternity as a regulative ideal, and its belief that with the proper detachment judgment is always possible.

My chapter develops the idea that literature, rather than merely supplementing the concepts and project of moral philosophy, actually calls it into question. Rather than merely inducing feelings that are effective in turning the mind toward philosophy's ideas of the moral good and justice, literature produces significant conceptual effects that challenge those very ideas. If, as Nussbaum enjoined, we pay attention to the truth of what is really going on, we discover ourselves educated by literature about agency in ways that demand a critique of fraternity as a regulative ideal and rational deliberation as a description of moral experience. In particular, mystery and detective fiction display concepts of agency, judgment, and sociality that more adequately address our genuine experiences of ethical urgency than do those of moral philosophy.

First, moral philosophy is regulated by the false ideal of an unambiguous moral agency. Literature, conversely, demonstrates the ineluctable intertwining of good and evil in the same action or agency. Thus, it offers a critique of the purity of the good and justice as conceived by moral philosophy. Mystery and detective fiction demonstrates the *liminality* of the moral agent: the way in which transgression and violence are essential to moral action in a corrupt and absurd world.

Second, this literature demonstrates that moral agency is not only poorly represented by the concept of fraternity, but that it is often impossible within the institution of fraternity. Moral urgencies are, in fact, rarely conflicts of rights between equals. Almost any morally charged relation – parent/child, teacher/student, doctor/patient – is a relation among *unequal* subjects, and the concept of fraternity cannot capture its asymmetry. Moreover, power is exercised within the institutions of fraternity, not only to control or repress, but also to exclude. Power produces not only subjection or inequality, but the *impossibility* of agency.

Finally, this literature offers a critique of the moral agent as occupying the detached position of a generalized reasoner. Beyond the alternatives of universalism and relativism, it demonstrates the *specificity* of agency and suggests the idea of singular universals, multiple figurations of the universal. These images or figures delimit and supplement one another, and, while not detachable from their contexts, nevertheless circulate among a community of readers as regulative ideals. Thus, my chapter ends by returning to the very danger of literature that Plato cited – that its presentation of the differences of style or perspective as something real and morally valuable would undermine the idea of the universality or univocity of truth.

I. Ambiguous agencies

> Life and above all politics, are surely a struggle, and since the wicked carry every weapon, it is the duty of the righteous to carry the same weapons, if only in order to rescue justice. We could almost say . . . that justice perishes because it is inadequately armed.
>
> – Marcel Proust, *Jean Santeuil*

In his *Groundwork of the Metaphysic of Morals*, Kant argues that our moral agency derives from our free rationality. Only because we are both free and rational can we elect among alternatives and be held responsible for our choices. This dependence of moral agency on the freedom of reason requires that we recognize the moral worth of all other rational beings, who have the same capacity of agency as ourselves: hence the requirement that our judgments must be universalizable, recognized as valid by any moral agent. Moreover, it establishes the need for a *'pure* ethics'. If the moral law is to be universal, as Kant insists it must be, then 'the ground of obligation must be looked for, not in the nature of man nor in the circumstances of the world in which he is placed, but solely *a priori* in the concepts of pure reason'. Moral agency must be pure both in the sense that it has purged itself of all inclination and interest and in the sense that it is absolutely self-consistent. In properly realized moral agency, the good is willed unambiguously, without any contamination of moral harm. The moral law 'in its *purity* and genuineness' produces the *'pure* will' of *'pure* ethics'.[4]

Detective fiction, on the contrary, pays attention to 'the circumstances of the world in which [the agent] is placed'. In 'The Simple Art of Murder', his famous essay in praise of American crime fiction, Raymond Chandler argues that the genius of this genre is to recast the problem of morality within the reality of a world that is essentially violent and malordered, a world of 'mean streets'. The moral problem for the detective is to discover how to be effective in a world of violence and injustice without being made mean by it. 'The realist in murder', Chandler remarks,

> writes of a world in which gangsters can rule nations and almost rule cities, in which hotels and apartment houses and celebrated restaurants are owned by men who made their money out of brothels, in which a screen star can be the finger man for a mob, and the nice man down the hall is a boss of the numbers racket; a world where a judge with a cellar full of bootleg liquor can send a man to jail for having a pint in his pocket, where the mayor of your town may have condoned murder as an instrument of money-making . . . It is not a very fragrant world, but it is the world you live in. (Chandler, p. 17)

In this inherently unjust world, key institutions such as the courts or the police regularly serve as corrupt tools of power. Violence, far from being an aberrant disruption of an otherwise well-ordered world, is, along with its ally money, the means by which power sustains and amplifies itself. Either defenceless citizens are manipulated and abused by the very institutions that are supposed to protect and assist them, or they are forced to live in circumstances that make avoiding violence and crime almost impossible. 'American violence is public life, it's a public way of life . . . ' (Williams, p. 35). This is 'the truth of what is really going on'.

Against this horizon, the 'purity' of the moral agent required by philosophy is an unaffordable self-indulgence, even an immoral concern with the beauty of one's own soul over the moral claims of others. These 'mean streets' test the character of those who walk them, and reveal a few uncommon 'common men' who are neither shark nor prey. 'Down these mean streets a man must go who is not himself mean . . . ' (Chandler, p. 18). Or, his meanness, his violence, is not itself mean, but the very weapon a righteous man must carry in order to rescue justice on behalf of the 'common man'. In this genre the detective's body and analytical powers seem to provide the only resistance to those social and institutional powers that continually feed themselves by subverting the law and subjecting the individual. The detective belongs to the class of those who are subject: he is, as Chandler remarks, a 'common man', else he 'would not be a detective' (Chandler, p. 18). Yet, because he is an effective moral agent in the world of violence and injustice, he is not himself subjected. In his liminality the detective is the violent agent of peace, the unlawful agent of justice, the undomesticated agent of domestic privacy.

Through their physical courage, their willingness to risk their own bodies, these liminal figures of counterviolence are often effective in protecting the bodies and domestic privacies of 'common men' from the violent and abusive incursions of the powerful. These heroic actions, however, do not imply any transformation of this ineluctably corrupt world. The genre is decidedly anti-utopian, presenting a world that cannot be purged of violence and corruption, where all redemptions are local and temporary. The detective practices his virtues of loyalty, honesty, and courage without believing in the reward of a happy ending.

Rarely, if ever, does the genre suggest political action or revolution as an appropriate response to the corruption of justice and the violence of subjection. In these novels and stories there is almost always a bad smell around anything political. The idea of delivering the world from its corruption and violence through political action is a utopian fancy that the hard-bitten social and moral realist cannot afford. In the Harlem novels of the African American expatriate Chester Himes, any movement promising liberation turns out to be a low and destructive con that his hero-detectives viciously attack.[5] Taking seriously the idea of a genuinely just society as an empirical aim would undermine the realism that is necessary to the detective's success as the violent counteragent of violence. His moral credibility depends upon his willingness to assert himself in the face of perpetual corruption.

Himes' detectives, Coffin Ed Johnson and Gravedigger Jones, are men of violence. They are also the most effective moral agents of their world. In a scene in which their superiors are reprimanding Coffin Ed and Gravedigger for their use of violence on the streets, Himes decries the life of crime and violence to which the African American man confined within the precincts of postwar Harlem seems condemned.

> The arteries stood out in Gravedigger's swollen neck and his voice came out cotton dry. 'We got the highest crime rate on earth among the colored people of Harlem. And there ain't but three things to do about it: Make the criminals pay for it – you don't want to do that; pay the people enough to live decently – you ain't going to do that; so all that's left is let 'em eat one another up.' (Himes, 1988, pp. 15–16)

The corruption of their world requires that the detectives take upon themselves actions that might seem inconsistent with moral agency: violent beatings, subterfuge, intimidation. Gravedigger's social commentary, however, suggests a more subtle dimension of the detectives' liminal moral agency. They are concerned to preserve and promote the agency of others.

The contradictory figure of the perpetrator who is also a victim appears repeatedly throughout Himes' work, but, perhaps, most poignantly and with the greatest complexity in the figure of Johnny Perry from *The Crazy Kill*. Perry is a perpetrator, a gambler, but also the kind of man who demands that the white police lieutenant call him 'Johnny', rather than 'boy', even though this puts him at risk of further violence and incarceration. He does so because he is an agent of his people, and his demand for respect is also a demand on their behalf. His agency restores theirs.

Solving the absurd 'crazy kill' of Johnny's brother-in-law recedes in importance next to the question of whether or not Johnny will be able to survive the investigation without being destroyed. The agents of justice, the detectives Gravedigger and Coffin Ed, as well as the local matriarch Mamie, anxiously focus on Johnny with affection and respect out of the fear that 'he's hotheaded enough to kill anybody in a rage' (Himes, 1989, p. 108). They treat him as a good man tested under dangerously stressful circumstances, and the detectives' drive to solve the crime derives largely from a desire to protect Johnny and to preserve his agency.

Johnny's moral liminality reflects the injustice of the absurd world in which he lives. A black man in postwar Harlem has two choices: he can take up the subjugated life of the porter or the waiter, remaining helplessly subject to the contingent and irrational violence of the white man, or he can attempt, not without danger, to achieve the moral dignity and efficacy exhibited in the liminal figures of perpetrators like Johnny or the detectives Gravedigger and Coffin Ed. Johnny and the detectives share as their first interest restoring the agency of their community. The task often requires them to undertake actions that compromise their own moral agency. At the end of the first book of his autobiography, Himes writes,

> Obviously, and unavoidably, the American black man is the most neurotic, complicated, schizophrenic, unanalyzed, anthropologically advanced specimen of mankind in the history of the world. The American black is a new race of man; the only new race of man to come into being in modern time. (Himes, 1972, p. 285)

The black man's exclusion from the conditions of agency in the fraternity of whiteness produces a new subjectivity beyond the purity of moral philosophy. Johnny's pride and self-control reflect the injuries and injustices that he has mastered, as he mastered the insulting white lieutenant. His moral dignity, his concern to preserve not only his own agency but the agency of his people, reflects the depth of his sufferings and subjections, and the violent strategies it has required.

Gravedigger and Coffin Ed believe that it is worth risking themselves, compromising their moral purity, engaging in violence, and thwarting authority in order to preserve the agency of such a man whose dignity restores the dignity of his people. In a world of racism and sexism, where money and violence are the determining forces, the ambiguous agency of Johnny or the 'hard-boiled' detectives serves as a point of resistance around which the subjected coalesce not only for protection, but for moral inspiration.

II. Impossible agencies

While Chester Himes' texts search for strategies of moral agency within the confines of racism, Thomas Harris' three volumes – *Red Dragon* (1980), *The*

Silence of the Lambs (1988), and *Hannibal* (1999) – explore the impossibility of female agency within the context of fraternity. Throughout these novels, virtue is associated with a womanhood that is neither the other to masculinity, nor defined by the economics of masculine desire: a womanhood, in short, beyond the figure of the sister.

Too often, feminism has focused its critique of the subjection of women on the family. When the domestic space of the family is considered in isolation as the unit of social analysis, the hegemony of man appears to take the form of patriarchy, as if the subjection of women is primarily a subjection to the father, whether as his daughter or his wife. The family itself, however, is situated in the public, political space of fraternity. As Hegel argued, it is not the relation of man and wife, but of brother and sister, that founds civil society, for it is the brother's exchange of his sister for the sister of another that establishes his fraternal bonds (Hegel, 1977, VI.A.a, pp. 267–78). Legally defined as property in the West well into the nineteenth century and still so defined in many parts of the world, woman is the first possession, the figure of property. Through this exchange of women, each man recognizes the right of the other to his own property, and in this exchange the mutual recognition of the brothers is made actual. Thus, the taboo against incest, as Levi-Strauss argues, is not so much a prohibition, as a positive prescription to exchange women in order to build the bonds of brotherhood in which society is realized. The other becomes my brother when I take/receive his sister, and thus, the links of community are elaborated (see Levi-Strauss, pp. 483–9).

Moreover, man's freedom to participate in the public domains of law, science, and philosophy is contingent on the containment of the sister in the domestic space of the family. If she shirks this duty and attempts to enter the discursive domains, Hegel argues, she puts those domains themselves 'in danger'. As Irigaray argues, woman provides the flesh and blood out of which the institutions and practices of fraternity are made; thus, she is its eternal irony, at once totally excluded and absolutely necessary (see Irigaray, pp. 214–26). The origin of fraternity excludes in principle her participation in it as an agent, rather than an object of exchange.

Freud's analysis of the origins of the family and civil society confirms those of Hegel and Levi-Strauss. The community of mutual recognition is established by the band of brothers who rebel against the father in order to take possession of the paradigm of property, the sister. In Freud's account, as in that of Levi-Strauss, the taboo against incest is joined to the taboo against cannibalism. Together they comprise the mutual pact of the fraternal order. In *Three Essays on Sexuality*, Freud identifies cannibalism with the most primitive intertwining of the sexual and aggressive instincts (Freud, p. 199). Its purpose is not the ingestion of the other's power, but the complete annihilation of the other. The alterity of the other is canceled, as he is ingested and no corpse remains to exert an ethical claim. The other's elimination opens up a new social space. Thus, fraternity arises in the intertwining of the two taboos: the father is eaten to end his exclusive possession of the women of the horde. Eating the father initiates the exchange of women and, thereby, the society of mutual recognition.

While the mythical father is eliminated in being eaten, woman's life is represented as food. Aristotle defines woman as the 'nutritive medium' of human life, while all form and identity are contributed by man. Hegel similarly identifies woman with 'a passive principle of nourishment', and explicitly invokes the necessity of woman's sacrifice of herself to the destiny of man (Aristotle, p. 98; Hegel, 1970, p. 175).

Hannibal analyzes the impossible attempt of a woman to become an agent within the structure of fraternity, and locates her agency on the other side of the founding taboos of this brotherhood. Harris gives a painful account of the injustices to which Clarice is subjected, by which she is nearly destroyed, and an even more painful and disturbing account of the role of Hannibal the Cannibal in securing for her a domain of agency.

Lecter's killings always depend upon the collusion of the victim's own vices. Thinking to dupe the psychiatrist into supplying him with recreational drugs, Mason Verger, a child molester, visits Lecter, only to find himself unwittingly drugged and convinced to slice off his own face, an act that leaves him an invalid on a respirator. A consummate player in the 'old-boy network' even in his debilitated state, Verger manages his fortune, owns large portions of Congress, and manipulates the FBI at will. While he continues to take pleasure in tormenting young children, Mason's overriding obsession in *Hannibal* is to take revenge upon Lecter. Against this figure of evil, and his ally Paul Krendler, Lecter emerges as a figure of justice.

Krendler, like Mason, shrinks at no evil in pursuing revenge. Krendler hates Clarice for overshadowing him professionally by catching Buffalo Bill, but her dismissal of his sexual demands enrages him. For Krendler the truth of Clarice's body is *his* desire, and when he cannot possess her body, he undertakes a campaign of annihilation, 'sticking a knife into her', and destroying her career.

As an agent of justice, Lecter exposes not only the corruption and subversion of the law, but the way in which violence against women is intrinsic to fraternity. *Hannibal* depicts the 'old-boy network' 'wolfing down' Clarice, who can be saved only through an apocalyptic transgression. In a cataclysmic metamorphosis, Clarice Starling, the pride of the FBI, the extraordinary heroine of the Buffalo Bill case, becomes the intimate, even sexually intimate, and more importantly, dietarily intimate, protégé of the cannibal Hannibal Lecter.

From the beginning Lecter approaches Clarice with respect and informed admiration. He admires what she admires about herself, when others fail to see these qualities or, as in the case of Krendler, despise her for these very virtues. Even when he uses his considerable psychological powers to manipulate her into revealing her most intimate history, Lecter gives her something in return: he helps her catch Buffalo Bill. Lecter never *preys* on Clarice.

While Lecter has been likened mistakenly to the vampire, who preys on his victims in order to subjugate them to his will, Lecter, in fact, preys on his victims only in order to eliminate them. He identifies his victims only by the necessity of self-preservation or by their own cruelty. Both in his relation to Clarice and in his choice of victims, Lecter is represented as applying the discernment of good and evil.

Yet Lecter's agency violates the founding taboos of civil society. In an apocalyptic transgression, Hannibal comes unexpectedly across the Alps of these taboos to challenge the law and rescue Clarice from its attempt to feed on her.

Krendler, whose desire for revenge trumps even his greed and ambition, engineers Clarice's suspension from the FBI. Relieved of her credentials and her official weapon, she loses any ability to act within the law. Within the fraternal order, she is no longer an agent. Discovering that Mason Verger, assisted by the law, has captured Lecter, and foreseeing the torture he will inflict on Hannibal, she crosses the threshold of the order established on the double taboo against cannibalism and the failure to exchange women.

Clarice's decision to rescue Lecter is based, first, on the realization that it is Lecter, even more than her allies in the FBI, who has known and appreciated her, and, second, on her revulsion at the connivance of the law in Verger's lurid desires. Dismissing this corrupt justice as 'the way of the world', Clarice 'made a simple decision: *The world will not be this way within the reach of my arm*' (Harris, p. 397). Undertaking Lecter's rescue, she finds herself 'a thirty-three-year-old woman, alone, with a ruined civil service career and no shotgun, standing in a forest at night' (Harris, p. 417).

In rescuing Lecter she is herself tranquilized to the point of death and, in turn, rescued by Lecter. He nurses her back to health, at the same time that he manipulates her psychological reawakening. Harris emphasizes Lecter's desire to nourish all Clarice's talents and discernment. Finally, Lecter restores her autonomy along with her gun. 'It occurred to Dr. Lecter in the moment that with all his knowledge and intrusion, he could never entirely predict her, or own her at all' (Harris, pp. 465–6).

Beyond fraternity's origin in the exchange of women, their mutual recognition does not depend on the law of property. It arises, rather, in their mutual transcendence of the objectification of the sister as property in the fraternal order, and in their genuine appreciation of the other, not as an object of desire, but as a bearer of virtues. In the moment he returns her gun, she joins him in a realm not prefigured by the law of the brothers. Having captured Krendler, Lecter presents him to Clarice at dinner one night. There Lecter slices up Krendler's prefontal lobe and serves it to Clarice in a black truffle sauce. This American girl from the hills of West Virginia, who became an FBI hero only to be betrayed by the fraternity, pronounces it 'really excellent' and, like Oliver Twist, asks for more (Harris, pp. 473–4). Lecter feeds

Clarice's needs and tastes, restoring her, body and mind, beyond the limes of the brothers' twin taboos.

A metamorphosis occurs in Lecter as well. Harris reminds the reader how shocking it is to see him uncaged and unrestrained, as he can chew off a man's face or disembowel him in a matter of moments. And, it is shocking when, one night after dinner, as Lecter considers that one day it might be necessary to eat her, Clarice responds by reaching into her gown with a cupped hand to free her breast. With her trigger finger she takes warm wine from her mouth to daub the breast. 'He came swiftly from his chair to her, went on a knee before her chair, and bent to her coral and cream in the firelight his dark sleek head' (Harris, p. 477). Clarice allies herself with Lecter's transgressions against the fraternal economy, at the same time that her companionship relieves him of his cannibalism.

As Chester Himes' novels demonstrate the impossibility of the black man's agency in the white world of racism, Harris' analysis of Clarice Starling shifts the question of ethics from a focus on conflicting rights and duties within the fraternal economy to a critique of the moral corruption of the economy itself and the impossibility of female agency within it. His apocalyptic argument repositions the moral agent at the edge of an unjust social order, delimiting a moral agency that exceeds the analysis of intentions and the calculus of rights and duties. Clarice's transgressive action is required by nothing other than her virtue, and her virtue puts at stake nothing less than the founding tropes of the social order itself. In the bureaucracies and institutions of the fraternal economy, her moral agency finds expression only in a liminal ethics.

III. Singular universals

Literary characters are both specific and general. True and false statements can be made about them: it would be false to say that Clarice Starling was from California or that Gravedigger Jones was a white man. Their specificity constrains us to attend to them as determinate, differentiated beings, rather than abstract, generalized subjects, such as the 'any possible rational being' of moral philosophy. On the other hand, they are disseminated across an open-ended community of readers. These characters figure moral agencies that are neither particular nor universal. They arise out of specific worlds and are solutions to specific problems. Yet, in their specificity, they are accessible indefinitely to the other moral agents, the readers, who revive them. Moreover, these forms are not given abstractly, but through the engagement of all the faculties, from sensation and feeling to the cognitive imagination. They are given not as propositions to be argued, but as immediacies that have been lived. Having realized them imaginatively, we find ourselves already engaged in their conviction. It may not be a world that I would like or that I would choose, but it *is*.

If we are to pay attention to 'the truth of what is really going on', we cannot escape engagement with these figures of liminal agency. Unlike rules and principles, these figures operate less by prescribing action and more by disturbing intention. They make us hesitant in our moral confidence, ambivalent in moral judgment, and skeptical of programs of redemption and salvation. Yet, they insist on the necessity of action in spite of this moral uncertainty. They require us to take on the obligations of moral agents with none of the reassurances that moral philosophy gives. Far from inscribing an horizon of moral purity, they remind us constantly of the necessity to make choices that inevitably involve moral harm. They refocus our attention away from the purity of our moral intentions or the regulative ideal of a fraternal justice, toward the specificity of the other's agency and the task of restoring and promoting it. They enjoin me as a moral agent to become a force that promotes agency against the subjections and exclusions of the corrupt justice of the fraternal order.

In the absence of rules or universals, we can see, nonetheless, that Clarice is morally better than Paul Krendler or that Johnny is morally admirable, despite his violent acts. We can make judgments. Against the meanness of racism and sexism, against the individual meanness of Mason Verger or the white police lieutenant, we can pose an agency that serves the agency of others without subscribing to the dangerous fiction of fraternal justice. Singular, yet universal as accessible to all, the figures of literature offer a moral challenge to philosophy's notion of the univocity of truth. Perhaps, neither the unity of a system of rules, nor the discourse of the fraternity of mutual recognition adequately captures moral experience. No doubt the rules and the discourse are necessary, but, perhaps, they are the heuristics to 'what is really going on' in the irreducibly specific solutions hazarded by moral agents amid the ambiguities and impossibilities of moral urgency.

Notes

1. Plato specifically refers here to painting, but he frequently draws an analogy between painting and writing as forms of illusion (see, e.g., *Phaedrus*, line 275d). He makes reference later in this passage to the illusionism of the 'maker of tragedies'.
2. Plato identifies only two licit purposes for writing: to serve old age as a mnemonic aid and to provide a record of itself for a community of discussion. We may assume that the dialogues were meant to serve the latter function. What were meant to be reminders of a living dialogue have become canonized and reproduced as the originary treatises of Western philosophy. Still, it is, perhaps, a mistake to identify Plato too closely with his representation of Socrates, even if this view of the waywardness of writing and its philosophical subordination to speech became fixed in Western philosophy. Perhaps, the argument I have outlined here belongs not to Plato, but to Platonism, to the dissemination of Plato throughout the Western tradition. In this regard, see 'Plato's Pharmacy' in Derrida (1981).

3. See the *Poetics*. It is through the production of compassion that tragedy educates the soul, for the viewer feels the suffering of the characters and undergoes with them their moral crises.
4. See the discussion of purity in the Preface to Kant's *Groundwork of the Metaphysic of Morals*, and the discussion of self-contradiction in the Formula of the Law of Nature in Chapter II.
5. Toward the end of his life, Himes did attempt to write a novel depicting an '*organized* black rebellion', but the effort, by his own account, proved impossible and resulted only in scenes of violent conflagration. The work was published unfinished. Himes remarked, 'I lost myself in trying to write a successful story about black people' (Williams, p. 42).

Works cited

Aristotle, *Generation of Animals*, trans. A.I. Peck (Cambridge, MA: Harvard University Press, 1963).

Chandler, Raymond, 'The Simple Art of Murder: An Essay', *The Simple Art of Murder* (New York: Vintage Crime, 1988).

Derrida, Jacques, *Dissemination*, trans. Barbara Johnson (Chicago: University of Chicago Press, 1981).

Freud, Sigmund, *Three Essays on Sexuality*, trans. J. Strachey (New York: Basic Books, 1975).

Harris, Thomas, *Hannibal* (New York: Delacorte Press, 1999).

Hegel, Georg Wilhelm Friedrich, *Philosophy of Nature*, ed. and trans. M.J. Petry (London: Allen & Unwin, 1970).

—— *Aesthetics: Lectures on Fine Art*, trans. T.M. Knox (Oxford: Oxford University Press, 1975).

—— *Phenomenology of Spirit*, trans. A.V. Miller (Oxford: Oxford University Press, 1977).

Himes, Chester, *The Quality of Hurt* (New York: Thunder's Mouth Press, 1972).

—— *Cotton Comes to Harlem* (New York: Vintage Crime, 1988).

—— *The Crazy Kill* (New York: Vintage Crime, 1989).

Irigaray, Luce, 'The Eternal Irony of the Community', in *Speculum of the Other Woman*, trans. Gillian C. Gill (Ithaca: Cornell University Press, 1985).

Kant, Immanuel, *Groundwork of the Metaphysic of Morals*, trans. H.J. Paton (New York: Harper & Row, 1964).

—— *Critique of Judgment*, trans. Werner S. Pluhar (Indianapolis: Hackett Publishing Company, 1987).

Levi-Strauss, Claude, *The Elementary Structures of Kinship* (Boston: Beacon Press, 1969).

Nussbaum, Martha, *Poetic Justice: The Literary Imagination and Public Life* (Boston: Beacon Press, 1995).

Plato, *Phaedrus*, Loeb Classical Edition (Cambridge, MA: Harvard University Press, 1914).

—— *Republic*, Loeb Classical Edition (Cambridge, MA: Harvard University Press, 1930).

Scarry, Elaine, *On Beauty and Being Just* (Princeton: Princeton University Press, 1999).

Williams, John A., 'My Man Himes: An Interview with Chester Himes', *Amistad I* (New York: Random House, 1970).

10
Is Forgiveness Ever Possible At All?
Rupert Read

In order to get a grip on this extreme question, it will be handy to have a good example or two to hand of situations where forgiveness clearly seems called for.

[A] You are reading this paper along with somebody else. As you go to turn the page, they rather clumsily knock their coffee over, spilling it all over you and your book. Imagine something like the following dialogue then ensuing.

They: 'Oh I'm terribly sorry; that was clumsy and stupid of me. Here, let me help clean you up; sorry!'

You: 'Don't worry, it's not important; I know you didn't "mean it".'

They: 'No no, really, it was very stupid; oh dear . . . do please forgive me.' Now, if they, in their agitation and regret really did say this, what would be your response to this request for absolution? In the case of such a trivial event, it's likely that you would soon enough say something like the following:

You: 'Don't worry, don't be silly, there's nothing to forgive, really; it's nothing.'

Let's ponder that phrase a moment – 'There's nothing to forgive'. Let's assume that you actually meant what you said (and were not, for example, merely being polite, while deep down you seethed and said to yourself, 'That was simply *unforgivably* clumsy!'). If so, it will be important and unavoidable to pay attention to the way that this piece of language actually works. If we can, we should try to take seriously the use of locutions such as 'There's nothing to forgive' (*Perhaps* we can't). It's only the exception, not the rule, I would suggest, that we – and our words – don't mean what we (they) say.

So, if we take the string 'There's nothing to forgive' seriously, then there is really nothing to forgive in the example we have sketched; so then quite clearly we haven't as yet got before us an example where forgiveness is relevant.

Let's try another example:

[B] Imagine that the person sitting beside you, while the two of you were silently reading, simply picked up the cup of coffee and quite deliberately *threw* it all over you.

Or:

[C] Think – actually think, right now – of an example – a real instance – where you have been deliberately or at least knowingly treated badly/maliciously in the past, e.g. a betrayal or a serious deception practised upon you by someone you trusted.

If we're thinking of an action like B or C, then the question I think is not, is forgiveness necessary at all here, but rather, *how can forgiveness happen at all here?*

Some wrong actions can in a way be undone. For instance, if I accidentally spill coffee over your beloved book, maybe I can buy you another one, just the same as the first. But actions that stand in need of forgiveness are often not like this. Something is broken, that cannot be *simply* replaced/repaired. If there is to be repair in the relationship, something more is required. Say, repentance and forgiveness?

But again, how to forgive, even the repentant, in a case like B or C, above? How to forgive, when forgiveness is required? When a breach has been effected, when something unundoable has been done?

Now, it would seem reasonable to suppose that it would be *straightforward* to answer that question if forgiveness were of the following nature: *If the past actually changed, when forgiveness was sought and granted.* If by being asked for forgiveness, and then granting that forgiveness, the past could be altered, the deed undone. Then, I take it, it would be clear why in many cases forgiveness was desirable, why it was engaged in – and why it was/is wonderful. But this scenario is of course utter fantasy.[1]

What actually happens is:

A harm or wrong is done, it remains a wrong, but yet it gets... forgiven. This is the extraordinary thing, the thing that somehow we have to hang on to: that a wrong that remains a wrong, that is not undone, somehow gets transformed in its felt meaning. It is no longer felt bitterly, and/or acted upon accordingly.

When we think of an action such as B or C, and we think of its being forgiven, the whole thing can come to seem more and more bizarre or remarkable. What is this thing called... forgiveness? What can it mean, for something like – something called – 'forgiving' to happen?

Now typically, when philosophers start asking themselves a question like that, they start to try to think of some set of concepts or categories which they might effectively use to explicate, analyze, or at least analogize the troublesome concept in question. So, I'm starting to have some real trouble getting a grip on what forgiveness is, on what 'forgiveness' could possibly be said to intelligibly mean – on how forgiveness is possible.[2] What forgiveness is, how forgiveness is possible at all...I'm starting to have trouble with that, so I'll try looking to other concepts which I have less trouble with.

I. Ceasing to punish X/ceasing to demand that X repay a debt

Etymology-fans tend to like this rendition of forgiveness. And more importantly, we know what it means to do one of these things. So these formulations *could* help us.

But a moment's reflection makes it evident that these concepts are not going to give us nearly enough resources with which to understand forgiveness. One can decide to forgive a debt, for example, because, hey, it's only money; or just because it will be really difficult in practical terms to get the money back. But in the latter case, for instance, one may well nevertheless feel considerable bitterness against the debtor.

There are all sorts of practical reasons why one might cease to demand the repayment of a debt, or cease to punish – but what forgiveness is, for us, is clearly more than (I). The harm was done, it – in itself – can't be undone; forgiveness is more than (I).

Unless we are to understand the sense of 'punish' or 'debt' here in a 'full' or 'deep' sense. Unless, for example, we mean by ceasing to punish, something like 'ceasing to harbour resentment'. But in that case, we have merely redescribed the problem. For this is what we want to understand: how can it be possible to cease to harbour resentment for a wrong that can't be undone?

II. Understanding

A second candidate: Is *understanding* sufficient for forgiveness? Is it the case that when one comes to *understand* why x did y, then that can be tantamount to or at least directly and immediately conducive to forgiveness? If so, then might we be in good shape, because surely we understand what 'understanding' is?

I shall come back to that latter question later. But first, to tackle the question of whether really understanding why x did y can directly yield forgiving. Because I'm not at all sure that it can.

A slogan perhaps comes to mind: 'To understand all is to forgive all.' But is that claim actually true? For sure, sometimes one finds that upon closer investigation, having made an effort to understand the 'forgivee', one changes one's view of the incident in question substantively – one comes to identify with the 'wrongdoer', to such an extent that one no longer thinks that any wrong was done, but thinks that, on the contrary, they acted rightly. And for sure, sometimes one finds that, in the case of an apparent betrayal or deception, the whole thing rested on . . . a misunderstanding. There was an equivocation on a word, or a word was misheard or misattributed, for example. The 'betrayal' was *merely* accidental; in other words, non-existent. So, for sure, sometimes – in both the above kinds of cases – understanding why someone did something results in its turning out that there's nothing to forgive. But then we are back to case A. And so we do not have here any cases where forgiveness is in question. 'To understand all', in these cases,[3] is actually to see that no forgiveness is required.

If we turn to cases which *are* within our purview, where forgiveness *is* 'required', then it is much less obvious that 'understanding all' will solve the problem. Sometimes one hopes, perhaps desperately, that talking with the person who wronged one will enable one to see their action in quite a new light, but (sometimes) what actually emerges is that they were doing the whole thing *more* maliciously than one had at first thought; for example, 'What, you mean actually that this . . . this *affair* has been going on for *years*, and you've systematically deceived and betrayed me over this person, even knowing that I was practically bound to find out in the end?!!' (At the close of this chapter, I consider in a little more detail a set of literary examples of just this form.)

It seems to me quite evident that there are at least some cases – important cases – where understanding is not equal to forgiving, but where in fact *the contrary* is most likely to be true. (And it seems evident also that, as we saw above, where understanding does apparently lead to forgiveness, what actually happens is that the action is removed from the set of actions that produce a need for forgiveness.)

And after all, none of this should much surprise us, because the idea that to understand all is to forgive all is not an idea that suggests a laudable tolerance and empathy, but rather a dubious relativism. There are at least some cases where, even if understanding can be achieved, it is not evident that forgiveness should or could be granted.[4] (And, concomitantly, if there is real forgiveness, it cannot be that the wrong done is in any way changed or lessened – indeed that would often be a failure, a moral failure, a suspect weakening of moral judgement. Whereas my sense is that a remarkable feature of true forgiveness is that it involves a kind of moral *strengthening*.)

So it seems to me that, for the reasons just given, the concept of understanding offers us very little help in the project of understanding *forgiveness*. For where it most powerfully can appear to offer such help, it only does so by removing actions from the category of 'wrong'.

Let us then try another candidate.

III. Forgetting

Is 'forgetting' the key to forgiving? Another popular slogan comes to mind, 'Forgive and forget'. Right away we notice that the slogan says 'Forgive *and* forget', suggesting a differentiation. And while I think that there is an important connection between forgiving and forgetting – indeed, that forgetting is in some cases[5] *criterial* for forgiving – it is relatively easy to show that understanding 'forgetting' will not enable us to understand forgiving, that there remains a gulf between them. A cute philosopher's counter-example should be enough to make clear that not just any mode of forgetting will amount to forgiveness.

Imagine case C again. Soon after the betrayal or whatever, imagine that you suffer an accident – a serious head injury. You wake up in hospital. Your friend/lover/whoever comes to visit. You act very nicely towards them. They may well think that you have forgiven them, and are quite ready to be reconciled with them, to accept them back into your life and so forth – but actually, unfortunately, it's just that you've suffered a head injury. You've forgotten all about their heinous act . . .

Forgetting is obviously not sufficient for forgiveness; but it does offer a clue: There is a serious question about whether forgiveness can survive continual reminiscence. If one continually, or obsessively, remembers, then one surely hasn't forgiven.

What we want out of 'forgiveness' is for something not to be continually present to one, but for one to be able to look at the person who has done the wrongful act, recognize that it was them who carried it out, and yet somehow overcome resentment. 'Forgetting' offers a clue – but no more than that.

One more try, a concept which has already crept into the margins of this chapter and may appear to offer our best last hope.

IV. Acceptance

Straightways, we must sub-divide 'acceptance' into at least two different kinds, and consider these more or less separately.

Accepting *that* something has happened

Is forgiveness that? Again, this concept seems to me to offer a clue – but to remain less than forgiveness. One can come to accept that a wrong act took place, and not feel that it is literally unbelievable that this horrible thing should have happened – one can, as it were, reconcile *with oneself* that one was betrayed – and yet resentment against the other may not be overcome.

Accepting an apology

A second variety of acceptance, and the one which will most intensively require our attention: Is forgiveness relevantly analogous to accepting an apology? It would be great if it were, for accepting an apology is, roughly,[6] a speech act, and, after J.L. Austin, many will agree that we – typically – understand speech acts. And starting with 'accepting an apology' seems particularly promising – because it suggests the element of 'contrition' and dialogic reciprocity which seems crucial to any wise forgiving.

But, regrettably . . . no. Forgiveness cannot be well understood as a speech act. Accepting an apology, sure, that can be pretty much understood in classical Austinian fashion, just like promising can be. When I accept an apology, I understand that you are regretful, and sincere in that regret, and I show this. But I may yet regret having to accept the apology, or find it hard to do so. I may, literally or metaphorically, accept an apology through gritted teeth.

But there cannot, I submit, be any such thing as forgiving through gritted teeth. Uttering the words 'I forgive you' with an ugly scowl around one's face – or simply in one's mind – is *not* forgiving someone. Roughly, if one says 'I forgive you' through gritted teeth, one is lying or, at best, deceiving oneself. So, forgiveness is clearly more than acceptance of an apology.

But what if someone were to respond, 'Maybe; but nevertheless "I forgive you" is itself a form of words, and its utterance must have some felicity conditions; why should we not understand forgiveness adequately just through understanding the speech act of saying "I forgive you"?'

But a direct speech-act-analysis of 'I forgive you' is not – for reasons already indicated – going to work, either. We *can*, for sure, have a fairly effective speech-act analysis/understanding of 'accepting an apology' or, to return to the *locus classicus*, of 'promising'. If I say to you, 'I promise you that I'll go to the cinema with you next weekend', and then I don't go . . . well, in that case I have broken my promise. There are only some very specific circumstances, delineated by Austin, in which a promise can be shown to be null and void, to have been infelicitously made or otherwise rendered invalid. But in the case of forgiveness, things are very different. You may have said to your betrayer, 'I forgive you for *y*', and a week passes, or a year passes . . . and it can *turn out* that you haven't in fact forgiven them. It can turn out, when one, as it were, looks within oneself, later, or if one *or if others* look at one's actual actions towards the wrongdoer since the declaration of forgiveness . . . it can turn out that one hasn't in fact forgiven them.

Circumstances, cases in which it can turn out that re-occurrences of resentment – in mind or action[7] – show this, perhaps much to one's – sometimes to everyone's – regret. Such re-occurrences can at virtually any time defeat the *attempt* one has made to forgive. This is how forgivers – all of us, potentially, not just an unsuccessful or 'hysterical' minority – suffer from reminiscences.

It seems then that, regrettably, the speech-act analysis of forgiveness is by no means sufficient,[8] and that the additional component needed to yield a potentially adequate account of forgiveness is perhaps twofold. On the one hand, we might want to talk about ACCEPTING SOMEONE BACK INTO ONE'S LIFE, about certain kinds of behavioural changes. But it is dangerous to say that this is *in general* necessary for forgiveness. There may be circumstances in which we might wish to allow for the possibility of forgiveness – for example, a physically or psychologically abused child might forgive – but not want to insist that the forgiver literally accept the forgivee back into his/her life, on pain of the forgiveness being otherwise described as fake. It is a common circumstance that one severely wronged will not forgive and so will not accept the wrongdoer back into their life; but I believe that there are cases where forgiveness too can accompany non-acceptance, in the sense currently under discussion.[9]

Now, can one accept someone back into one's life *without* having forgiven them? Surely yes, for various imaginable practical purposes. Perhaps not, if the acceptance is deep and full and true... in which case we are just, familiarly now, repeating the mystery, and the explanandum.

Rather than focusing upon changes in action, we might want to talk about a DEEP 'INNER' ACCEPTANCE, to talk about certain crucial kinds of emotional and mental changes, about a *change of heart* that takes place over time.[10] Maybe such talk is after all the best we can do.

Is that the best we can do? We might talk about how such a 'change of heart' is very often tied to a changed attitude on the part of the wrongdoer. Is this as good as it gets? Is it good enough? Are we really any closer to understanding forgiveness – what it is, how it is possible – than we were at the start? Have all the 'clues' which I have assembled added up to a full and coherent story, an outline of *the* explanation or correct philosophical account of forgiveness? Have I told you anything you didn't already know? Well, perhaps not – but then perhaps you only need to be reminded of what you already knew, anyway. Perhaps the best we can do, in philosophy, *vis-a-vis* forgiveness, is to point up how we play this game, how we – sometimes, apparently – do this amazing, ordinary thing. I have tried to emphasize the '*extraordinariness*' of this 'ordinary' thing.

But in case anyone thinks that any more than that has been achieved, in case one is tempted to think that a distinctive and powerful philosophical understanding of or account of forgiveness has been – could be? – achieved, it is worth remarking bluntly that the kinds of things that I have been led to speak of – a change of heart, an elusive change in one's way of being-in-the-world – are so vague, so untheorizable, that I don't think what I'm saying amounts to anything more than what religious folks have spoken of for centuries, when they've said things like, 'Forgiveness is only possible through the grace of God', or 'She must truly be a saint, to have forgiven them for that.' Now, maybe that kind of thing is exactly what we should say; or even, 'Only God can truly forgive.' Just two points:

(1) It is not at all obvious that such sentiments as these are *explanations/analyses*, at all, as opposed to cover stories (cover-ups) for a lack of explanation/analysis. (Likewise, it is all the same to me whether one says, 'There isn't any such thing as counting to infinity' or 'There's nothing

that would count as counting to infinity', or 'Only God can count to infinity'; only provided that whichever of these one chooses to say, it is said (and heard) in the right spirit . . .)

(2) Again, I want to understand forgiveness as a human phenomenon, as something that happens between people, which it seems to me is how the term is overwhelmingly used, nowadays (e.g. in quite secular contexts), and it's just not going to be good enough to *rely upon* concepts of God/divinity.

But it seems to me that the religious version of forgiveness offers, too, a clue. The clue is this: Perhaps we need to *accept* that there is something truly worth calling mysterious about forgiveness. Not 'supernatural', but surprising, *perplexing*, not open to explication in terms other than its own, certainly not in the terms of any academic discipline. Perhaps we need to accept that there are strict limitations on the extent of any would-be social scientific or linguistic or philosophical account of certain things that go on between human beings. And if all we can end up saying is, for example, 'Well, it requires a special kind of change of heart . . . and I can't really tell you in which circumstances that change of heart will or will not take place', then we might as well say, 'It's a mystery, there isn't going to be any successful account of forgiveness of the kind which one naturally wishes to imagine.' This is in fact the kind of stance that I am inclined to take up (and talk up).

The considerations I have so far adduced might lead someone to conclude that forgiveness is impossible (but just *what* is it that would then be being said to be impossible?), or that it is through and through paradoxical. They might lead someone to conclude that 'forgiveness' is a dead letter in a post-Christian world, as dead as 'tabu' or 'virtue' have elsewhere been argued to be.

I myself am strongly inclined rather to look for – to see – the order in this human practice, even if its order is far less evident – and far less 'account-able'[11] – than is the order of many other practices. I think that we don't know what we're saying if we assert that forgiveness is impossible, or literally supernatural. We have incoherent desires with regard to our words; we want those words to function in ways in which they do not function, while continuing to want them to function in enough of the same old way as to make the label ('forgiveness') fit at all. We incoherently want to say that there is something-which-we-can-make-no-sense-of which is impossible, or possible through supernatural intervention. But if we can really make no sense of it, then even to say that it is impossible is to say too much. (I will return and explain this thought more fully at the conclusion of this chapter.)

I think we ought to be humble in face of some things that people apparently do, things which we cannot get our heads around. I see forgiveness as a human phenomenon. This language-game is played, and without the dubious theoretical assumptions of certain other would-be language-games (e.g. water-divining, metaphysical philosophy). But some language-games don't take to *any* kind of theorization or analysis of themselves. I don't say that there is no forgiving or that the very concept of forgiving is confused; I say that forgiveness is remarkable, and rather mysterious, that it happens if at all in ways which fit quite poorly its 'surface grammar' – and that it is rare.

Let me turn to a couple of major objections to my line of thought, to my provisional conclusion here, two objections at least which must be responded to:

> 'A problem with your account – or non-account – is that you focus too much on the act of forgiveness – and on *the act to be forgiven,* on the betrayal, or whatever. You ought instead to focus on the person doing the forgiving, and on *the person to be forgiven.* You ought to separate out the act from the person, and understand that forgiveness is indeed something that happens between *persons – not* "between actions"!'

I will not deny that this objection too contains a clue – the last half of its last sentence is surely right, and important. But I'm unhappy with the first half of that sentence. It seems to me very problematic to rigorously separate act from actor, 'sin' from 'sinner'. If we take this objection seriously, then we must think of the kind of effect it has radically to split act from actor, as for example in cases of diminished responsibility in the courts, or in cases of Dissociative Identity Disorder/Multiple Personality Disorder: 'It wasn't really *you*, it was your 'alter' personality.' There may be contexts – in particular, specific legal and medical contexts – in which these are the right things to say. But I think that it would be extremely unsatisfactory if our general understanding of forgiveness had to rely upon such notions. I think that what we need always to keep in mind – and here I follow R.G. Collingwood[12] – is that forgiveness is supposed to be about a-person-who-*did*-something-*wrong*. You've got to keep the act and the actor in the frame together. Unless these two are kept as it were *internally related*, unless you keep a notion of the integrity of the person, unless you can take *that* seriously, then you're not going to be talking about forgiveness *at all*.

The second objection turns the focus from the 'sinner' more explicitly to the 'sinned against':

> 'Maybe you're concentrating too much on the act/person to be forgiven. Maybe you need to focus on *you*, the person betrayed, the would-be-forgiver. Maybe you yourself, the wounded party, is the key here – for isn't the ultimate reason to forgive because it will yield private spiritual and personal gain, and healing? The resentment, after all, is almost certainly hurting you more than it hurts the wrongdoer.'

This kind of view – that forgiveness is essentially something that you do for yourself – underlies most of the burgeoning forgiveness-as-self-help literature of the present time. Again, though, this line of objection, while popular – and perhaps potentially healthy in asking and saying what forgiveness can do for you, rather than endlessly only asking what you can do for forgiveness (for God) – is highly problematic. To say why, let me turn to Jacques Derrida. Derrida has not said a great deal in print about forgiveness, but I want to invoke his powerful deconstruction of the concept of 'the gift' here (and see what its morals are for the concept of the 'forgift'). What Derrida says, in essence, is roughly this:

> 'If you really look at examples of so-called gift-giving, what you find is that they amount to exchanges, to gifts being "given" simultaneously or interleaved in time. So, for example, if you are giving x a present, but expecting a "gift" in return, at least a gift of gratitude or a sense of ongoing indebtedness, then in what sense is it really a *gift* that you have given them? Our ethically-imbued perception of what a gift is or should be seems to call out for something beyond that.'[13]

A full discussion of these matters would take us too far beyond the present context, into (fascinating) questions of the possibility of altruism, the absurdities and vacuities of psychological hedonism and psychological egoism, the difficult issue of how and when human behaviour can be 'authentic', 'spontaneous', and/or 'natural'. But I think that – without begging too many questions on these weighty matters – we can say at least this: that what Derrida contends of giving can at least plainly be said, with some real and immediate plausibility, of forgiving. In specific relation to the objection we are considering, how should Derrida's thought be applied? Well, if forgiveness is a gift that one gives essentially to oneself, this seems to short-circuit the presence of the other person altogether. Derrida would surely say that if you are 'giving' the benediction of forgiveness only so as to use the other person to gain something for yourself – for example a new set of feelings of ease and tranquillity – then you're not really giving a gift at all.[14] If you're forgiving for your own benefit, is that really *forgiveness* at *all*?

This is important enough for it to be worth circling the same terrain with a couple of re-statements: Doesn't forgiveness have to be, as it were, essentially other-directed? Doesn't it have to be... truly a gift, freely *given*? If Derrida is right, then surely the objection to my argument which we have been considering *fails*; and, more generally, support is given to my 'positive' characterization of forgiveness as elusive, mysterious, and rare.

The objector might yet try again, though, roughly thus:

> 'Your Derridean argument is all very well; but there remains an ordinary sense in which there is an ordinary practice/language-game of gift-giving.

Surely you cannot square this Derridean move with your general Wittgensteinian orientation. Surely we can and do still talk, quite intelligibly,
about giving each other presents at Christmas, for example. That's how
our language-game is.'

And this last point is true. But there remains a response that can be given
to the objection, a response which will take us back to the structure of my
response to the would-be speech-act-analysis of forgiveness:

Imagine that you've been given a Christmas present. The following
summer, you somehow find yourself asking the giver, 'But have you really
given me this present?' What a very bizarre question. Under almost any
imaginable circumstances, the answer would probably be something like,
'Well *of course* – and anyway, what are you talking about, why are you asking
me this, what are you trying to say?'

So, Derrida notwithstanding, there *does* remain a straightforward, ordinary
sense in which, once a gift is given, then there you have it. But I want to say,
once again, that *forgiveness isn't like that*. This time, imagine that *you* were the
perpetrator. It *can* be to the point, if someone made a declaration of forgiveness to you at Christmas-time, say, to ask them, the following summer,
perhaps after overhearing an off-colour remark, or observing an ongoing
pattern of behaviour:[15] 'But have you really forgiven me for doing *y*?'

So, even if Derrida stretches things *vis-a-vis* 'the gift', I think that the
morals of his account carry over *clearly and plausibly* to the 'forgift'.[16]

What, in sum, do I want say about forgiveness? Let me return you to the
first things I did in this chapter. I asked you to imagine a wrong done to
you – a deception or betrayal, or even 'just' a deliberate spillage of coffee
over you. I didn't ask you to imagine a rape or murder, or a brutalizing
deep-set institutionalized racism, still less an extermination. But even in the
case only of a coffee being spilt over you, or of a deception by a friend, we
have found it near-impossible to understand intellectually/philosophically
how one could forgive, and what it could mean to do so. I think that most
wrongs done to people, not just the most extreme wrongs, *are not forgiven*.
They are unforgiven, or they are simply forgotten. Years pass, and one forgets
the innumerable petty wrongs that remain wrongs that were done to one
(and that one did) – usually. And in some *rare* cases, a wrong is remembered,
and yet forgiven. How does forgiveness happen? My suggestion is that, in
all but a tiny minority of cases, it does not. Either because it is not required,
or because it is sidelined by something else happening (e.g. a forgetting, or
a practical decision) – or because it just does not. And often, in a relatively
short amount of time there is no one left who could do the forgiving.
(Who, now, is well-placed to forgive perpetrators of the major genocides of
the first half of the twentieth century? It takes enough temerity to fancy
oneself well-placed even to forgive those who have harmed just one of those
nearest and dearest to one.) We are left, perhaps, just wishing desperately
that things had been different. But they weren't; they aren't.

And with that thought, we need to return to another moment early in this chapter. I wrote earlier that it would seemingly be straightforward to understand how forgiveness can happen at all, if forgiveness were of the following nature: If the past actually changed, if the deed were literally undone, when forgiveness was sought and granted. Then, I took it, it would be clear why forgiveness was desirable, why it was engaged in – and why it was wonderful. But the scenario I have just sketched is *utter* fantasy. By which I mean, I don't think we have any clear idea of what it would be even to understand such a 'scenario'. What sense can we make, for example, of sentences which speak of the past as subject to change? If the past could be changed, would it any longer be anything we would properly wish to call 'the past'? We have all seen sci-fi films involving 'time travel' 'back' 'into the past'; how many of us, seriously, think we are doing anything other than engaging with a charming illusion of sense – imagining that we imagine something, 'picturing' what is through and through an illusion – when we entertain ourselves by means of such mind-boggling 'scenarios' (e.g. the utterly absurd scenario of the powerful and highly entertaining *Terminator 2*)? Indeed, isn't much of the entertainment derived precisely *from* the utter boggle we experience in watching such films?

We very easily find ourselves with incoherent desires with regard to our words, when we speak of forgiveness, as when we speak of time. These incoherent desires lead us to say (incoherent) things like 'Forgiveness is impossible', or 'Forgiveness is incoherent', or 'Forgiveness would be possible if only time travel were possible.'

What we ought to say, I think, is that there is *no* way that we can think ourselves into a 'superior' position for comprehending what forgiveness is and how it is possible. And again, let the language here not mislead us – this is not because of an incapacity on our parts. To say 'God alone understands forgiveness; and we forgive through God alone' is, outside perhaps of some very specific religious context(s) where it may have its sense, to say as much and as little as saying 'Forgiveness is simply incomprehensible.' But what we must also say, if we are to say anything, it seems, is 'Forgiveness (sometimes) occurs.' This language-game – this interweaving of actions and words – is 'simply', sometimes, played. And perhaps most of those times will not end up being times in which, without taking up a controversial political or ethical stance, we can say that the game transparently should not be played, and/or is obfuscatory or *dangerous*.

But if words such as these don't satisfy you, then all the philosophizing in the world will add nothing further. And nor even, I suspect, may examples of the unforgivable more literary than those I have woven through this essay, not even great works such as Sylvia Plath's *Ariel*, Salman Rushdie's *The Satanic Verses* or the very first classic of stubborn unforgiving, Homer's *The Iliad*.[17]

Yet let me close by briefly trying. The *oeuvre* of Salman Rushdie can be compellingly read as an extended literary (and indeed quasi-philosophical) meditation on the great and sometimes insuperable (and sometimes *rightly so*) difficulty in forgiving – and on the wonder and beauty of some actual acts of forgiveness. If there is any living writer of fiction who has dwelt on the unforgivable to good effect virtually throughout his corpus, it is Rushdie. His two magnificent works on the birth and (simultaneous?) corruption and living death of India and Pakistan, *Midnight's Children* and *Shame* respectively, both end with a savage sense – and scene – of unforgiving, and indeed of unforgivability. *Midnight's Children* ends with a brilliant evocation and summation of the protagonist's sense of the terrible, crushing legacy left to the children of India's birth by its creators and betrayers. And for 'terrible', one might substitute 'unforgivable'. *Shame* ends with the leading protagonist suffering a terrifying death, revenge at the hands of the fury whom he can be read as having wronged horribly, earlier in the novel. Both endings are entirely bleak.

These two novels, then, can be read as anticipating *The Satanic Verses*. They take the same kind of risks that it does, only less dramatically, less single-mindedly. When one reads *The Satanic Verses* with those previous books as a backdrop, one sees the huge scale of the calculated risk that Rushdie took with the later book. I would be inclined to put the point as strongly as this: *The Satanic Verses* is a long and *self-reflexive* meditation on the committing of unforgivable acts. The central characters in the book are two men, Chamcha and Gibreel. Gibreel is a Bollywood film-star who becomes transposed through typical Rushdie 'magic realism' into the angel Gabriel. He speaks the Koran to Mohammed, but some of what he speaks Mohammed later denounces as having been satanic. Yet Gibreel insists that it was not Satan who spoke; it was he, Gibreel/Gabriel, throughout.

The central unforgivable acts in question in Rushdie's novel are all writings of literature. They are (1) Saladin Chamcha's tormenting revelation to Gibreel (via a series of odes he writes him) of an affair he is allegedly having with Gibreel's woman; (2) the extreme satirical mocking that Rushdie has the poet Baal undertake of the prophet Mohammed, based in part upon his cuckolding of the prophet; . . . and (3) . . . the writing of *The Satanic Verses*. This great prose-poem is an utterly calculated extended insult to fundamentalist/literalist Islam. Its characterization of the angel Gabriel who spoke the Koran to Mohammed as 'really' Gibreel, a Bollywood actor, and of the allegedly 'Satanic Verses' as actually just as valid (or not) – just as Revealed (or not) – as the rest of the Koran; combined with its depiction of the prophet's wives as whores and of the prophet as a humourless tyrant . . . what did Rushdie expect? Did he really think it conceivable that religious fanatics would ever be able to forgive what he had now done, and let life go on? Once it was so obvious that he (like the equally devilish, equally anti-theocratic and anti-Revelation, equally literarily talented Phillip Pullman, whose *His Dark Materials* trilogy makes quite plain how he, too, is very much 'of the devil's party') was writing a novel that, unlike its predecessors, put *centre-stage* its hatred for all they hold sacred (while simultaneously – and this is part of what makes the novel an astonishing achievement – capturing the supernaturalistic religious world-view very powerfully and very *sympathetically*, through the devices of magic realism, exploited fully in a way such as to make miracles manifest on the page)?

It is these three sets of 'verses', as much as the Satanic Verses expunged from the Koran, which give Rushdie's marvellous book – a book truly to die for – its title.

But one great irony, from our point of view in the present chapter, is that *The Satanic Verses*, unlike its two predecessors, ends upon a note of profound hope. It ends up with a reconciliation, a seemingly unlikely act of forgiveness between Chamcha (who has written the most calculatingly cruel verses of the whole novel) and his father. Saladin Chamcha is said in fact to 'fall in love' with the father whom he previously hated and blamed for many things (Rushdie, 1989, p. 523). Thus in the last full paragraph of the book, with a mood unutterably distant from those in which his two previous novels end, the narrator speaks of Saladin for the last time, and says of him, 'It seemed that in spite of all his wrong-doing, weakness, guilt – in spite of his humanity – he was getting another chance' (Rushdie, 1989, p. 547).

On the one hand, then, Rushdie portrays in this novel (and commits himself) heinous, deliberately unforgivable crimes (and here we see more fully the point of my discussion of (II) 'Understanding', earlier in this chapter). On the other, he manages this time to find a way to suggest that forgiveness is possible – even in very extreme cases. He pushes the limits, in terms of depicting and doing the extreme; and, as it were, asks His Father or his earthly representatives to give him a chance, all the same. Forgiveness is possible, he urges, paradoxically, in almost the same breath of showing just why it isn't . . .

Finally, it is worth adding that the three novels of Rushdie that we have briefly discussed above are in an important sense interchangeable, or (perhaps better) part of one, sprawling, tremendous trilogy. As Milan Kundera has helpfully written, every major novelist really writes only one novel: theme, and its variations; and so it is with Rushdie. His (mostly lower quality) production since the *fatwa* he suffered can quite easily be read as a set of further variations on the theme. Now, he writes for instance (in his *Haroun and the Sea of Stories*) so as to fight back at the unforgivable attack that fundamentalist Islam has wreaked upon his life. *Haroun* is a hymn to the literary, and a satire on the anti-writing fanaticism of the Shah of Blah (who is, I would suggest, transparently a transposed Khomeini – (then) the new Iranian dictator). It is a charming demonstration of what Rushdie *holds sacred*: the writerly (more than the ostensibly religious) sphere.

The greatest example I know of the *literature* of *forgiveness*, Antje Krog's *The Country of my Skull*, might take us further still than these great works of unforgivability that I have just been discussing. But where it takes us, I think, is more directly to ethics and politics (Krog's is a fictionalized account of her observation of South Africa's Truth and Reconciliation Commission) – as something that must be lived, and will never be 'fully understood' . . . and will never be philosophized into submission. And that area is certainly a topic for another occasion.[18]

Notes

1. I will explore the import and 'sense' of this fantasy towards the close of this chapter, where it will become important that it is *utter* fantasy.
2. I deliberately refuse to separate these questions out. A question of 'essence', a Kantianish question, a post-linguistic-turn question – they are all the same. It doesn't really matter what terms we use in order to frame our philosophical questions, the same difficulties and confusions can arise any which way. There is no privileged mode of philosophizing which is invulnerable to philosophic illusion – this, and not a formulaic emphasis upon, for example, what 'language-game' we are playing, is I think the true lesson of Wittgenstein's philosophy.
3. A rather fuller account of some such cases can be extracted from pp. 124–125 of J.L. Austin's 'A Plea for Excuses'. (I hope in this chapter also to be influenced by Stanley Cavell, especially by some of his work on 'the ordinary'.)
4. I have in mind, for example, the position of some of those in Ron Rosenbaum's intriguing book, *Explaining Hitler*, who argue that we must not allow our greater understanding of Hitler to lessen our condemnation of him, or to facilitate the perhaps-obscene act of 'forgiving' him. A minority position (held, for example, by Claude Lanzman), even more interesting for our present purposes, is that the very attempt to understand or explain Hitler is *itself* obscene. Advocates of this latter view – which I, for one, find a not entirely unpersuasive one – possibly fear that to understand all *is* inexorably to forgive all.
    In my 'Is forgiveness possible? The cases of Thoreau and Rushdie (on) (writing) the unforgivable', I present some further (real and fictional/literary) cases of malice and (consequent) lack of forgiveness, despite understanding. I urge in that paper that the power – and, in many cases, propriety – of *un*forgiving should not be underestimated. Central to that paper is the question of the unforgivability of the actions of the protagonists in Rushdie's *The Satanic Verses*, especially Saladin Chamcha – and the unforgivability of the writing of the novel. See the conclusion of this chapter for more on this theme.
5. See below. We should take care hereabouts; for it is sometimes suggested nowadays that 'Forgive and forget' is only sometimes an appropriate attitude; 'Forgive and remember' is quite reasonably said to be a desirable alternative in cases where there remains a risk of the perpetrator or his ilk striking again.
6. 'Roughly', because accepting an apology need not necessarily require any speech (sometimes the right kind of silence is enough to connote acceptance of an apology), nor even any particular non-verbal action. It would perhaps be more accurate – less misleading – to place all this within a Wittgensteinian context of 'language-games', where practices and words are thoroughly intermeshed in 'the stream of life' from the outset; but I think that using Austin's terms, as 'the literature' on forgiveness has tended to do, will be sufficient for our present purposes.

7. See below for detail. We need to take care when dealing with 'purely mental' resentment – because this notion can too easily encourage one of the more philosophically suspicious aspects of the recent 'self-help' vogue for forgiveness: the belief that 'forgiveness' is itself something fundamentally 'internal', and fundamentally undertaken for one's own good. I am endeavouring to keep in view forgiveness as something that happens paradigmatically *between persons*.

8. For this reason, I reject the conclusions of Joram Graf Haber. Haber claims, hopelessly over-optimistically, that trying to forgive is normally a sufficient condition for forgiving; so for him, sincerely saying 'I forgive you' *is* tantamount to forgiveness having been *achieved*. The only germ of truth in Haber's approach is this: that, often, the enunciating of 'I forgive you' could or even should be heard as amounting to 'I will try, over time, to forgive you.'

9. See for instance the first-person story told in Mariah Burton Nelson's *The Unburdened Heart*.

10. The process of forgiveness takes a long time. That, it has been suggested to me by Margaret Walker, could perhaps be correctly regarded as a grammatical remark. If so (see note 8, above), there are perhaps difficulties with the view that 'I forgive you' can ever be spoken unmisleadingly.

11. For full explication of this term, which means roughly 'able to have an account produced of it by its practitioners or those interested in understanding them', see Garfinkel, passim.

12. See his 'Punishment and Forgiveness', especially p. 128.

13. These are my words, my paraphrase; for Derrida's words and for details, see his 'The Time of the King', and also p. 40–41 of his *The Gift of Death*.

14. Of course, the very idea of a gift which you give to yourself is pretty peculiar. (As Wittgenstein asks, can my right hand give my left hand money?) This suggests that there must be real gift-giving to others.

15. If we changed the example slightly, and it was an off-colour remark or pattern of behaviour from *you* – the forgivee – which prompted some re-assessment, then that might be felt by the forgiver as an unexpected renewal of betrayal. They *might* then say, 'I forgave you last Christmas – but I guess that was a mistake, forgiving you.' However, I am stressing that, if the remark touched off/echoed any pre-existent feeling inside them or tendency in their behaviour, if they already still had any resentment, then they would most appropriately say something like, 'I guess I haven't really ever forgiven you at all – and what has just happened has merely reminded me – made me fully aware – of that.'

16. I leave aside here Derrida's eccentric explicit treatment of forgiveness in *On Cosmopolitanism and Forgiveness* which, in taking forgiveness *only* to be possible of things that are unforgivable, goes further than even I would want to into the realms of paradox. My suggestion is that the extension of the logic of Derrida's account of the gift into the realm of forgiveness works pretty well; I cannot say the same of Derrida's own, explicit, account of forgiveness. (Although it would be interesting to compare Derrida's discussion with Rushdie's, as discussed in my conclusion, below. The ultimate paradoxicality of the two is very similar.)

17. See Peter Winch's very fine discussion of Simone Weil's very fine discussion thereof, in the chapter on 'Incommensurability', in his *Simone Weil: The Just Balance*.

18. Thanks to David Rudrum, Andrew McGhee, Peter Kirkup, Dave Francis, Adrian Haddock, Emma Willmer, Francis Dunlop and Jeremy D.B. Keymer; to audiences at Manchester Metropolitan and Liverpool Universities; and to all at the

'Forgiveness: Traditions and Implications' Conference, April 12–15, 2000, Tanner Humanities Center, University of Utah, Salt Lake City USA, where this paper in very roughly its present form was first presented. Thanks to the late Jacques Derrida for oral comments which have helped me; this chapter is, I hope, a fond as well as justly combative 'memento'. Thanks also to the UK Arts and Humanities Research Board and to the British Academy for funding without which my attendance at that Conference would not have been possible. My final debt is to the writings of Aurel Kolnai, which I came across only recently, but which, from a very different starting point than my own, are the only works of philosophy that I have come across, which in their spirit and intent remotely approximate my own views concerning forgiveness.

Works cited

Austin, J.L., 'A Plea for Excuses', pp. 123–52 in *Philosophical Papers*, ed. J.O. Urmson and G.J. Warnock (Oxford: Clarendon, 1961).

Collingwood, R.G., 'Punishment and Forgiveness', pp. 124–32 in his *Essays in Political Philosophy*, ed. David Boucher (Oxford: Clarendon, 1989).

Derrida, Jacques, 'The Time of the King', pp. 1–33 in *Given Time: I: Counterfeit Money*, trans. Peggy Kamuf (Chicago: University of Chicago Press, 1992).

——*The Gift of Death*, trans. David Wills (Chicago: University of Chicago Press, 1995).

——*On Cosmopolitanism and Forgiveness*, trans. Mark Dooley and Michael Hughes (London: Routledge, 2001).

Garfinkel, Harold, *Studies In Ethnomethodology* (Cambridge: Polity, 1967).

Haber, Joram Graf, *Forgiveness* (Savage, Maryland: Rowman and Littlefield, 1991).

Nelson, Mariah Burton, *The Unburdened Heart: 5 Keys to Forgiveness and Freedom* (San Francisco: Harper, 1999).

Plath, Sylvia, *Ariel* (New York: Harper Collins, 1965).

Read, Rupert, 'Is Forgiveness Possible? The Cases of Thoreau and Rushdie (on) (writing) the Unforgivable', *Reason Papers*, 21 (Fall 1996), 15–35.

Rosenbaum, Ron, *Explaining Hitler: The Search for Origins of his Evil* (London: MacMillan, 1998).

Rushdie, Salman, *Midnight's Children* (London: Jonathan Cape, 1981).

——*Shame* (London: Jonathan Cape, 1983).

——*The Satanic Verses* (New York: Viking, 1989).

——*Haroun and the Sea of Stories* (London: Penguin, 1990).

——*Imaginary Homelands* (London: Granta, 1991).

Winch, Peter, *Simone Weil: The Just Balance* (Cambridge: Cambridge University Press, 1989).

Part V
Reading Philosophy as Literature

Introduction

Nowhere is the dynamic relationship between literature and philosophy more intricate than in the deceptively simple practice of reading. Ploughing through a text, whether a literary or a philosophical work, inevitably involves an amount of interpretation – at least some degree of inferring the 'meaning' of the work – yet within this activity there is rarely a readily apparent separation between the pursuit of the 'literary' aspects of the text (wondering what a certain metaphor suggests, or contemplating the implications of a troubling turn of phrase) and the more abstract activity that is commonly labelled 'doing philosophy'. For many thinkers – both philosophers and literary critics – this is a symptom of a deep-seated overlap between the genres of literature and philosophy.

There is, after all, no shortage of literary texts that debate or explore philosophical problems and issues. Indeed, many contemporary philosophers, spanning the broadest spectrum of thought (from Martha Nussbaum to Gilles Deleuze), have held that literature can, and indeed does, carry out work of the kind we would normally call 'philosophy'. Furthermore, many classic works of philosophy are shot through with stylistic or generic features that can only be described as 'literary': Rousseau's autobiographical confessions, Nietzsche's use of narrative, Heidegger's poetic style, or Wittgenstein's use of dialogue. Accordingly, some of the most distinguished of literary critics (ranging from Paul de Man to George Steiner) have turned their powers of critical observation upon the literary aspects of philosophical texts. But what does it mean to read literature 'as' philosophy, or to read philosophy 'as' literature? It is the second of these questions that will be tackled in this section. (The first has been broached by several of the preceding essays, which offer philosophical readings of various literary texts).

Consider, as an example, the prose of Wittgenstein. Wittgenstein writes in a *melange* of styles, ranging from aphorism to dialogue, and this array has drawn a tremendous amount of commentary. The philosopher Stanley

Cavell has claimed that Wittgenstein's style is intended to shape the experience we have when reading it, which in turn inevitably shapes our understanding of it: Wittgenstein's way of writing is parametrically linked to the kind of investigation of language he wants us to take part in (see 'The Availability of Wittgenstein's Later Philosophy' in his *Must We Mean What We Say? A Book of Essays* [Updated ed., Cambridge: Cambridge University Press, 2002]). The eminent literary critic Marjorie Perloff has also commented on Wittgenstein's style, locating him in the forefront of experimental, avant-garde modernist writers (see her *Wittgenstein's Ladder: Poetic Language and the Strangeness of the Ordinary* [Chicago: University of Chicago Press, 1996]). There need be no contradiction between these two approaches: indeed, philosophical and literary studies can effectively come together over this question to examine how it is that Wittgenstein's works can produce such startling effects.

A rather more radical approach to the question, however, has frequently been adopted by deconstructive critics, some of whom have sought to undermine the basis of any possible distinction between literature and philosophy. Indeed, one of the most astute 'literary' readers of 'philosophical' texts would be Derrida himself. According to his antifoundational viewpoint, philosophical texts are just that: texts. They inevitably produce rhetorical flourishes and figurative expressions, most of which lead to ambiguity, indeterminacy, and undecidability rather than to philosophical 'truth'. Furthermore, the concepts and theories that philosophy expounds cannot be thought independently of their embodiment in language – they are made up of the words that formulate them. So on this view, an emphasis on textuality transforms language from a vehicle for communicating philosophical ideas into the very crucible in which philosophy itself is formed. And philosophy shares this crucible with literature: like so many areas of human activity, both are endlessly, boundlessly textual. For a deconstructionist, this fact precedes and inevitably undermines any attempt to distinguish definitively between the two.

In Anglo-American circles, Richard Rorty has 'translated' this deconstructive argument into the more pragmatist claim that philosophy is just another kind of writing. Generations of philosophers have resisted this claim, and continue to resist it, because the value of philosophy as they see it lies in something that is extralinguistic – 'knowledge' or 'truth' – rather than in a mere trick of language. More precisely, then, philosophy is a kind of writing which would prefer to be something rather more than just another kind of writing. In Rorty's pragmatist version of Derrida's position, this remains wishful thinking because philosophy has no definitive truths to articulate. In the absence of such a content, philosophy becomes a genre of intertextual writing about other philosophical texts, and is best thought of as such. For more details, see 'Philosophy as a Kind of Writing' in Rorty's *Consequences of Pragmatism* (Brighton: Harvester, 1982).

A similar set of insights is explored by Arthur C. Danto, though to different conclusions. Danto is arguably more representative than Rorty of the mainstream of Anglo-American analytic philosophy, which has typically lacked patience with philosophy's literary or aesthetic pretensions, seeing them as distractions from philosophy itself. However, Danto does not share this traditional view, and voices scepticism towards it: like Rorty, he sees philosophy as a mode of discourse, and emphasizes its intertextual nature. He also investigates parallels between philosophical discourse and fictional or metaphorical discourse: both involve references or comparisons to things that are not, in any obvious sense, 'real'. Ultimately, however, Danto goes beyond Rorty in locating the difference between literature and philosophy in the figure of the reader of the text in question. Whether this position will dissolve or exacerbate the tensions between critics and philosophers, however, is doubtless a subject for further debate (see A.C. Danto, 'Philosophy as/and/of Literature' in *Literature and the Question of Philosophy*, ed. Anthony J. Cascardi [Baltimore: Johns Hopkins University Press, 1987]).

That literature and philosophy share certain linguistic, textual, and even conceptual properties is a point that goes all the way back to the first encounter between the two in Plato's *Republic* – as does the sense of competition or rivalry between them. Probably the most lucid, sophisticated, and entertaining commentator on the general question of 'reading philosophy as literature' is Berel Lang. (See his *Philosophy and the Art of Writing: Studies in Philosophical and Literary Style* [Lewisburg: Bucknell University Press, 1983], *Philosophical Style: An Anthology about the Writing and Reading of Philosophy* [Chicago: Nelson Hall, 1980], and *The Anatomy of Philosophical Style: Literary Philosophy and the Philosophy of Literature* [Oxford: Blackwell, 1990]). Lang's work remains an invaluable resource for anyone interested in the issues raised here. Another good survey of 'the aesthetics of argument' is Martin Warner's *Philosophical Finesse: Studies in the Art of Rational Persuasion* (Oxford: Clarendon Press, 1989).

Michael Eskin's essay begins this section by asking how we, as readers, differentiate between texts that participate in philosophical discourse and texts that participate in literary discourse, given that there are often no clear generic demarcations between the two. His answer is essentially a pragmatist one – that the figure of the author marks a given text as 'literature' or as 'philosophy'. Andrew Benjamin's discussion offers a philosophical analogy between the activity of literary criticism and the activity of translation, exploring both issues in terms of the philosophy of language set out by Walter Benjamin and others.

Jonathan Rée's essay adopts a more historical approach, charting the rise (and fall) of various styles of philosophical expression. He documents the origins of the modern fetish for clarity – and its accompanying phobia of 'gibberish' – by returning to the reformation and to early modern thought. His essay demonstrates how styles of writing and styles of thought are interrelated. This insight also underwrites Robert Eaglestone's essay, which examines the use of metaphor in the writing of philosophers from a broad variety of traditions. Eaglestone demonstrates how metaphoricity – or, to use a deconstructive term, 'metaferocity' – can influence and shape philosophical thought. Metaphors can help us to 'do' philosophy, to understand or to express complex ideas clearly, yet they can also manipulate or distort both the form and the content of philosophical discourse.

Finally, my own essay is a literary reading of a philosophical classic: Ludwig Wittgenstein's *Philosophical Investigations*. Drawing on Bakhtinian literary criticism, it describes the importance of dialogue to Wittgenstein's text, showing how the interaction between the multiple voices and sources of *Philosophical Investigations* forms the driving force behind it. These voices engage in a variety of literary strategies – polemical, parodic, interrogative – that make the experience of reading Wittgenstein's work a richly stimulating dialogical encounter.

David Rudrum

11
Who is Speaking? Brodsky, Heidegger, Wittgenstein, and the Question of Genre

Michael Eskin

What are the parameters according to which we determine and decide on a text's genre? How does a text establish, enact, and safeguard its generic status? Do we map our generic expectations onto the text in interpreting it within a certain framework, or is it, rather, the text itself that enjoins us to read it as a certain kind of text? With these concerns in mind, I want to look at a particular instance of generic differentiation in this essay: the distinction we make between philosophy and literature. My guiding questions are as follows: How do we know that we are reading a philosophical and not a literary text? What is involved in our apprehension of a text as philosophical or as literary?

I should stress that I am concerned neither with defining 'literature' or 'philosophy', nor with defying the fact that we do indeed distinguish between the two in our quotidian pursuits as professional or lay readers. Beginning, rather, from the recognition that such a distinction is commonly made, I am interested in tracing and reflecting on some of the issues involved in its emergence and hold. I want to anchor my thoughts and ruminations in a number of passages from the essays of Joseph Brodsky, whose writings, as I will show, throw into relief the question of generic differentiation with particular acuity.

Let me commence with several quotations from Brodsky's essays, collected in *Less Than One* and *On Grief and Reason*, which shall be the points of reference for my subsequent observations.

'Writing [poetry]', Brodsky notes, 'is literally an existential process; it uses thinking for its own ends' (Brodsky, 1986, p. 124). 'In an anthropological respect', he observes,

> a human being is an aesthetic creature before he is an ethical one. There-fore, it is not that art, particularly literature, is a by-product of our species'

development, but just the reverse. If what distinguishes us from other members of the animal kingdom is speech, then literature – and poetry in particular, being the highest form of locution – is, to put it bluntly, the goal of our species. (Brodsky, 1995, p. 50)

Consequently, poetry can be said to 'bea[r] witness' to the 'vocal and ethical possibilities of man as a species' (Brodsky, 1986, p. 267). Waxing more 'philosophical', Brodsky proclaims,

> The philosophy of the state, its ethics – not to mention its aesthetics – are always 'yesterday'. Language and literature are always 'today', and often – particularly in the case where a political system is orthodox – they may even constitute 'tomorrow'. One of literature's merits is precisely that it helps a person to make the time of his existence more specific... On the whole, every new aesthetic reality makes man's ethical reality more precise. For aesthetics is the mother of ethics... As a form of moral insurance... literature is much more dependable than a system of beliefs or a philosophical doctrine... Beauty and its attendant truth are not to be subordinated to any philosophical, political, or even ethical doctrine, since aesthetics is the mother of ethics and not the other way around. Should you think otherwise, try to recall the circumstances in which you fall in love. (Brodsky, 1995, pp. 48–49, 52, 208)

Having established the anthropological significance of poetry, as well as the relationship between aesthetics and ethics, Brodsky turns to the question of the poet and his (or her) relationship to language:

> a poet always knows that what in the vernacular is called the voice of the Muse is, in reality, the dictate of language; that it's not the language that happens to be his instrument, but that he is language's means toward the continuation of its existence. Language, however, even if one imagines it as a certain animate creature (which would only be just), is not capable of ethical choice.... The poet, I wish to repeat, is language's means for existence... he is the one by whom it lives... The one who writes a poem writes it above all because verse writing is an extraordinary accelerator of consciousness, of thinking, of comprehending the universe. Having experienced this acceleration once... one falls into dependency on this process... One who finds himself in this sort of dependency on language is... what they call a poet... The only evidence of human manufacture is that [the poem] is indeed being 'written'; and it gives you a sense that language is capable of arrangements that reduce a human being to, at best, the function of a scribe. That it is language that utilizes a human being, not the other way around. That language flows into the human domain from the realm of nonhuman truths and dependencies,

that it is ultimately the voice of inanimate matter, and that poetry just registers now and then its ripple effect . . . language is the inanimate's first line of information about itself, released to the animate. Or, to put it more accurately, language is a diluted aspect of matter. (Brodksy, 1995, pp. 56–58, 333, 374)

How do we read these passages, in which Brodsky addresses such philosophical issues as the existential role of poetry, its ethical and aesthetic significance, its ontological import, and its relation to other modes of discourse – philosophy, politics, and morals in particular? Do we read these passages as literature or as philosophy?

Given their explicit thematic concern with such deeply philosophical topics as ontology, aesthetics, and ethics, these passages are particularly conducive to bringing into focus any attempt to distinguish between philosophy and literature. For, irrespective of their philosophical gist, we do read Brodsky's essays, I venture to say, as poetological, rather than philosophical interventions and, hence, as literature. Why?

Rather than immediately responding to this question, let me further complicate the issue by juxtaposing Brodsky's text with a couple of other texts addressing similar issues and commonly categorized as philosophy: Martin Heidegger's *Unterwegs zur Sprache* and Ludwig Wittgenstein's *Tractatus* and 'A Lecture on Ethics'.

Such pronouncements by Brodsky as 'poetry, being the highest form of locution'; 'it is language that utilizes the human being, not the other way around'; '[language] is . . . the voice of inanimate matter, and . . . poetry registers . . . its ripple effect' echo in impetus and content Heidegger's reflections on language and poetry:

> Language speaks . . . Insofar as we have to look for the speaking of language in the spoken . . . we ought to find something purely spoken. The purely spoken is that in which the perfection of [language's] speaking . . . is a beginning one. The purely spoken is the poem. (Heidegger, p. 16) . . . Language speaks . . . in gestating . . . things . . . Language . . . *needs* the speaking of mortals [i.e. humans] in order to be heard . . . Humans speak insofar as they correspond to language . . . Its speaking speaks to us in and through the [purely] spoken. (Heidegger, p. 30 – my translation)

Thematically, the following links can be established between Brodsky's and Heidegger's texts: the voice of inanimate matter registered by poetry in terms of a ripple effect (Brodsky) is analogous to the speaking of language qua gestation of things and its concomitant resounding in poetry (Heidegger); poetry as the highest form of locution (Brodsky) parallels poetry as the purely spoken (Heidegger); language's utilization of the poet (Brodsky) echoes language's need for humans (Heidegger). In view of these thematic parallels between the poet and the philosopher it would seem impossible to stipulate a discursive distinction between the two based on content or theme. It is equally impossible, I should stress, to posit a generic distinction between the two authors' respective texts based on 'style' (in a broad sense): the prose of both is 'philosophical', apophantic, *and* what one may call 'intuitive' and 'divinatory'.

Yet, a generic distinction is made. It comes to the fore saliently in the fact that we typically refer to Brodsky's (and other poets') philosophical pronouncements as 'poetics' while calling Heidegger's (and other philosophers') pronouncements on language and poetry 'philosophy of language (or poetry)'.

Since a comparison of Brodsky's with Heidegger's text in particular may be considered tendentious and thus heuristically tainted – given that Heidegger's style has been depicted as 'pseudopoetic', as 'anal poetry [Afterpoesie]' (Adorno, p. 453) – let me juxtapose Brodsky's text with several passages from Wittgenstein, whom no one has, to my knowledge, seriously 'accused' of writing '(pseudo)poetry'. (David Rozema's attempt to read the *Tractatus* as a poem, although suggestive, does not change our view of Wittgenstein's texts as 'philosophy'.) Here are some quotes from the *Tractatus* and the 'Lecture on Ethics':

> 6.42 So too it is impossible for there to be propositions of ethics . . .
> 6.421 It is clear that ethics cannot be put into words.
> Ethics is transcendental.
> (Ethics and aesthetics are one and the same.) (Wittgenstein, 2001)

> Now I am going to use the term Ethics . . . in a sense . . . which includes what I believe to be the most essential part of what is generally called Aesthetics. (Wittgenstein, 1965, p. 4) My whole tendency and I believe the tendency of all men who ever tried to write or talk Ethics or Religion was to run against the boundaries of language. (Wittgenstein, 1965, pp. 11–12)

It is clear that Brodsky's ruminations on ethics, aesthetics, and their relationship fall, thematically, into the same domain of ethical-aesthetic inquiry as Wittgenstein's. Moreover, although in obvious thematic disagreement with Wittgenstein's views, Brodsky's text does not seem in any way to differ, from a purely rhetorical-discursive, that is, stylistic viewpoint, from Wittgenstein's (and Heidegger's, for that matter). Such apophantic statements as 'every new aesthetic reality makes man's ethical reality more precise. For aesthetics is the mother of ethics . . . ', or –

> Beauty and its attendant truth are not to be subordinated to any philosophical, political, or even ethical doctrine, since aesthetics is the mother of ethics and not the other way around. Should you think otherwise, try to recall the circumstances in which you fall in love. (Brodsky, 1995)

– could equally be found in a strictly philosophical work, such as Wittgenstein's. And even Brodsky's recourse to the example of falling in love, which adds a presumably 'unscientific', personal note to the text, finds its direct complement in Wittgenstein's recourse to personal experience in his attempt to understand ethics:

> Then what have all of us who, like myself, are still tempted to use such expressions as 'absolute good', 'absolute value', etc., what have we in mind and what do we try to express? Now whenever I try to make this clear to myself it is natural that I should recall cases in which I would certainly use these expressions and I am then in the situation in which you would be if, for instance, I were to give you a lecture on the psychology of pleasure. What you would do then would be to try and recall some typical situation in which you always felt pleasure. (Wittgenstein, 1965, pp. 7–8)

Thus, even at its presumably most 'unphilosophical' and 'unrigorous' – 'Should you think otherwise, try to recall the circumstances in which you fall in love' – Brodsky's text cannot be said to be any less 'philosophical' or 'rigorous' than Wittgenstein's 'try and recall some typical situation in which you always felt pleasure'.

These few instances of comparison between literature and philosophy make it sufficiently clear that a distinction between the two genres cannot be based on essential differences in style, content, or propositional impetus, that is, their respective truth claims. Both use figures of speech – for example, the metaphoric employment of gestation in reference to language in Heidegger, the similaic recourse to experience in Wittgenstein ('in ethical . . . language we seem constantly to be using similes' [Wittgenstein, 1965, p. 19]); both share thematic interests; both are directly oriented – albeit not universally in the case of literature – toward propositional truth.

Even the most literary of the literary – the overtly poetic or the fictional text – is, essentially, indistinguishable from the philosophical:

> One must be passive to conceive the truth . . .
> One notices, if one will trust one's eyes,
> The shadow cast by language upon truth . . .
>
> Man today can do *more* than the culture heroes and half-gods . . .
>
> We must not . . . perform an act because abstractly it seems to be a good act if in fact it is so contrary to our instinctive apprehensions of spiritual reality that we cannot carry it through, that is, cannot . . . perform it. Each one of us apprehends a certain kind and degree of reality and from this springs our power to live as spiritual beings . . .

If we didn't know and hadn't initially seen these snippets of text in their print versions with all of their paratextual and formal paraphernalia, and the information provided thereby, would we be able to guess with certainty that the only quote taken from a philosophical work – Herbert Marcuse's *One-Dimensional Man* (p. 56) – is 'Man today...', while the first three lines are from W.H. Auden's poem 'Kairos and Logos' (Auden, p. 14) and the final passage from Iris Murdoch's novel *The Bell* (p. 189).

What I am suggesting then is simply this: all of the distinctions that we tend to bring to bear on literature and philosophy – such as fiction versus non-fiction, propositional versus non-propositional, and so on – are predicated on the fundamental lack of any essential difference between the two genres and are only possible due to pragmatic pointers provided by the entire set-up of publishing and performance. In other words, we simply have to be told whether to read a text as literature or as philosophy. This is the simple answer to my earlier question as to why we read Brodsky's essays as literature and not as philosophy although they may 'sound' like philosophy and deal with philosophical issues.

But, what does it mean 'to be told' how to read a text? Does it mean that every time we open a book we have to have the cover page with the generic designator? And what if the covers are missing? What needs to be clarified is the common denominator which would allow for an explanation of the commonly made distinction under discussion. I suggest that the common denominator is the very instance of the author, and not any intrinsic quality of the text itself. We know how to read a text because we are told who wrote it – a poet or a philosopher. Thus, in the end it is the instance or function of the author which determines the light in which we peruse a particular text. Because we know that Brodsky is a poet, because we know that Heidegger and Wittgenstein are philosophers, we read their texts as literature and philosophy, respectively.

I can imagine that this sounds too simplistic. So, let's take a brief look at two more instances of authorship. Two cases come to mind immediately: Nabokov and Celan, both of whom have put out an extensive amount of literary translation virtually equaling their 'original' output. Yet neither is commonly treated as a translator, but as writer and poet, respectively – so much so, in fact, that Celan's translations for instance tend to be subsumed within his original œuvre. In other words, we do not think of Nabokov or Celan as translators who also wrote fiction and poetry. Similarly, we would not speak of Heidegger as a poet even though he did write poetry. And, I venture to suggest, we don't even read his poetry *as* poetry but, probably, as a kind of poetic articulation of his philosophy. The question of generic status and its perception hinges, more often than not, on the question of authorial constitution and the concomitant production of interpretive frameworks. I should stress that this is not an essential but an empirical observation.

If the author has functioned and continues to function – irrespective of Foucault's vision of a 'culture where discourse would circulate without any need for an author' (Foucault, p. 138) – as a 'standard level of quality... of stylistic uniformity [and as] a . . . historical figure in which a series of events converge' (Foucault, p. 128), it is because we need the author as a sounding board for our own hermeneutic expectations. In this sense it matters a great deal 'who's speaking' (Foucault, p. 138) – at least when it comes to concretely authored texts, that is, to texts that are not simply part of our respective troves of folklore.

At this point – but this ought to be the subject of another essay – we would have to inquire into the various modes in which authors acquire certain kinds of reputation in terms of their generic citizenship. In other words, we have to pose the chicken–egg question: Does the text constitute its author or is it the other way round? How do we know that a newly published text is literature or philosophy in the case of a previously unpublished author? I am not sure that this question can ever be satisfactorily answered. What is certain, though, is the fact that even in the case of a first text, the author typically establishes himself as a writer of, for example, verse, fiction, or philosophy. What is equally certain – to this author at least – is that the all too tempting recourse to intrinsic (linguistic, pragmatic, semantic, prosodic, narratological), or essentializing textual criteria would lead us right back into the impasse of the generic indistinguishability between philosophy and literature.

Works cited

Adorno, Theodor W., *Noten zur Literatur* (Frankfurt: Suhrkamp, 1981).
Auden, W.H., *The Collected Poetry of W.H. Auden* (New York: Random House, 1945).
Brodsky, Joseph, *Less Than One: Selected Essays* (New York: Farrar, Straus, and Giroux, 1986).
——*On Grief and Reason: Essays* (New York: Farrar, Straus, and Giroux, 1995).
Foucault, Michel, *Language, Counter-Memory, Practice*, ed. Donald F. Bouchard (Ithaca: Cornell University Press, 1977).
Heidegger, Martin, *Unterwegs zur Sprache* (Pfullingen: Verlag Günter Neske, 1959).
Marcuse, Herbert, *One-Dimensional Man* (Boston: Beacon, 1991).
Murdoch, Iris, *The Bell* (Harmondsworth: Penguin, 1999).
Rozema, David, '*Tractatus logico-philosophicus*: A "Poem" by Ludwig Wittgenstein', *Journal of the History of Ideas*, 63, 2 (April 2002), 345–63.
Wittgenstein, Ludwig. 'A Lecture on Ethics', *The Philosophical Review*, 74, 1 (1965), 3–12.
——*Tractatus Logico-Philosophicus*, trans. D.F. Pears and B.F. McGuiness, introd. Bertand Russell (London: Routledge, 2001).

12
Literary Potential: The Release of Criticism

Andrew Benjamin

Literature already involves a relation to language; one complicated immediately by literature already being a form of language. Literature is language at work. Once preliminary moves of this nature are conceded then the immediate questions that follow will almost inevitably concern the specific form of language that can be described as literary. Again, to the extent that it becomes possible to detect the consistent use of literary language, what this opens up is the possible identification of literary language with the essence of literature itself. From within this framework, answers to the question 'what is literature?' would involve attempts to define or at least locate literature's essential quality. The difficulty with such an argument is not that it resists addressing literature and thus would refuse the position that held to literature's own particularity – literature as opposed to science, for example – but that it does so in terms of essences. This commitment to the essential is more than the simple use of the language of essences. Rather, the commitment is to the very idealism that sustains such a language. And yet, what would literature be if literature were not to have an essential quality? Responding to this question will allow for the development of a materialist account of literature; an account positioned beyond, and positioning literature beyond, the hold of idealism.

The philosophical question of the essential is therefore at the heart of these concerns. The problem posed by such a question is that it delimits the nature of the task in advance. Allowing for an essence means that the philosophical project becomes the pursuit of the essential in its radical differentiation from particulars. What has to be stated is the essence. Whether it resides in a certain use of language, or simply defined by the continual reiteration of 'fiction' – understood as the production of the imagination as opposed to the results of scientific discovery (experimental method) – a commitment to the essential already determines in advance the answer to the question of literature. (There are of course other forms that a commitment to an essence of literature will take.) In general terms, what such a commitment entails is that this quality can be abstracted from a particular work. To the extent that abstraction is possible, literature's essential quality has an existence independently of specific instances of literature. The further consequence is that the essential is then given a relation to particulars that necessarily involves a form of transcendence. As such, the question of literature is not only settled in advance, the possibility of literature being a contested site is also precluded. Indeed, this preclusion is true by definition. Contestation, in sum the site and activity of argumentation concerning literature's presence, gives to literature a different conception of history than would be found in linking history to the chronological unfolding of the generic determinations that are taken to comprise literature. The presence of contestation, and it would need to be added its ineliminability, always occurs in the name of literature. Allowing for contestation however reopens the naming relation. In general the naming relation gives rise to questions of the following form: What occurs in the name of literature? Moreover, what does literature name?

Initially, these latter questions do no more than reiterate the problem of the essence. It might always be the case that what is named is the essence of literature. With contestation, however, a different question arises: namely, within contestation, what is named? In other words, within a contestation concerning either literature's presence or its quality, what is named? As a point of departure, the response to this question is that what is named is the site of contestation, thereby entailing that the identity in question – in this instance the name *literature* as the site of original conflict – becomes identified with conflict concerning its identity.

What follows from this position is that *literature* – understood now as a name – is that which is able to sustain conflict concerning its nature. While this will be true of universals in general, part of the attempt to engage with this as a problem means accepting that there is an already given series of determinations as to what counts as literature. While this may reflect the reading habits within a given historical period, there is far more involved since what conflict refers to is the possibility that what counts as literature – the existence of literature as such – can only be sustained by claims about literature. These claims are not descriptive sociological claims that identify literature with its named presence. On the contrary, they are the claims of criticism. In other words, it is not just that contestation is central, it is rather that literature comes into its own – comes to be as literature – through the activity of the critical. What this points to is a quality within works of literature. This quality is what allows for such works to be identified as literature. Moreover, this will be the case even if the claims are disputed or advanced for fundamentally different reasons. (A minimal act of reference will have been given in order to delimit the dispute as an actual dispute.) In addition to content – though equally as content – the given particulars allow themselves to be identified as literature. The act of identification once given within an account of the act becomes the work of criticism. What is identified can be reformulated, if only provisionally, as the literary. The literary refers to literariness. While 'literariness' will be the term used to name the operative quality within literature, a way into understanding the move from literature to the literary is by allowing for a productive analogy with translation. More specifically, the analogy is with translation's formal presence – that is acts of translation – and to its possibility (i.e. the ontology of the object in question).[1]

The translation of a sentence from one language to another occurs without either a predetermined result or control if these latter constraints necessitate that the outcome will have been predicted in advance. And yet, of equal significance is that this absence does not mean that any translation is possible or that all translations are of equal merit. (Relativism is not the consequence of the absence of predictive structures.) From within this set-up two elements that define translation need to be noted. The first is that translations refer. The second is that the process of translation is, on one level, potentially endless. This endlessness can be more adequately described as the infinite of potentiality and as such the specific translation – the translation of sentence X in one language into sentence Y within another – becomes the realization of potentiality as finitude. Both these points need to be developed.

What it means for translation to refer is not just the claim that the translation refers back to the source and implicitly to other possible translations. Rather, the reference in question is, on the one hand, to language and, on the other, to conditions of communicability. The translation is not a unique event without an inbuilt sense of relatedness. It is a unique, situated event that is always already related. That to which it is related does not determine what it is, rather it allows it to be what it is, that is, what it is – what a translation *is* – is the reiteration of language. Not language understood in terms of essences or even of its having an essential quality existing independently of activity but in terms of language's operative quality. What this means is that fundamental to a distancing of essentialism, equally inherent in resisting the reduction of language to simples whose relation to externality has to be thought in terms of reference, is the work of repetition.

Translation is therefore contextual and consequently can be discussed in terms of its particularity; that is, in terms of its being *this* language, its having *that* content, its incorporation of *that* given context and so on. Equally, however, its contextual presence (in sum its 'contextuality') is inter-articulated with its presence as a singular instance of the rearticulation of language (hence, the primordiality of repetition) – the result of which is that contextuality is bound up with this specific conception of repetition. In addition, this conception of repetition is delimited by its being inextricably connected to potentiality. This set of interdependent entities is, of course, a reformulation of the relationship between the infinite, understood as potentiality, and the particular, understood as finitude. What this establishes is the point of connection to the second element noted above.

The endlessness of translation exists as a potentiality. Precisely because there cannot be a one-to-one correspondence between the two components of translation (source and object language), any act of translation is already the interruption of potentiality, interruption as a form of realization. The particular however – understood as the finite moment and thus to be explicated in terms of a more generalized account of finitude – has neither a necessary nor an already determined form. Its conditions of possibility, moreover, are given within what has already been identified as a conception of potentiality defined in terms of the infinite. There is, as was alluded to above, an important connection between contextuality and potentiality. The impossibility of the reference to context having an absolutely determined nature is due to the separation between context and potential. A way that such a position can be understood is in terms of the ineliminable capacity for a further translation. Such a possibility can never be precluded even though – given a certain context – a specific translation will hold sway. What allows for future translations – perhaps even the translation of the translation – is potentiality understood as the ontological condition of language. Potentiality attests to language as a state of continual becoming (hence the use of the term 'infinite'). This way of construing the relationship between potentiality – thought in terms of an ontology of becoming – and context, as the locus of finitude, provides the setting in relation to which a return can be made to the literary. If translation involves an examination of translatability articulated with an ontology of becoming, then a similar state of affairs will pertain in regard to literature in which the literary (or literariness) is articulated within a similar ontological configuration.

Translation occurs both through an act and as an act. In addition, translation is possible because of the operative quality of language, in which the infinite potentiality of becoming allows for finitude. However, the relation between the ontological nature of language as translation's condition of possibility and the act of translation has to take not just the centrality of the act into consideration, what also has to be recognized is that finitude, the result of the specific act, brings both together as the actual translation. The direct consequence of this argument is that as actualization is finitude it need not be thought in terms of either loss or impossibility.[2] In sum, translation becomes the name given to an occurrence in which there is an act of constitution. Translation, in this sense, is the release of potential. The question to be addressed is the way this complex set-up is at work with literature. If there is a corollary with literature then it is the act of criticism. And yet, it is a complex and exacting corollary.

Translation shows. What is shown is in excess of the finite act. While Walter Benjamin is correct to argue that what is significant about translation is language's inherent translatability, what was absent from that treatment was in the first instance a sustained investigation into this quality. Translatability is not simply an optional predicate of language. It reveals that which is proper to language itself. Secondly, what does not figure within his writings on translation is the recognition that what occurs with any translation is repetition. (Moreover, what occurs *as* a translation is also a form of repetition.) Language allows for its translation. In the act what is given is language. The gift has the twofold quality of referring – both to the original and to language – hence it repeats. However, it repeats in a way that defines the occurrence of the new. At its most emphatic it can be argued that translation allows language to be what it is. Language while referring is always, and inevitably, in excess of that possibility. The two combine and work together to provide what could be described as language's inherent complexity. Evidence for this is found in the 'fact' that a complex utterance can be simplified, a move that both transgresses the original while still maintaining some of its initial quality. (In other words, this becomes another instance of the interplay of repetition and the originating, thus 'new', occurrence.) Further evidence, were it to be necessary, resides in the joke that resists simplicity as it insists on a complex range of meanings all of which are inherent in the 'same' word or the 'same' sound. It should not be thought that there are not pragmatic instances that resist complexity. What they cannot resist however is the complex range of possibilities that they may occasion. The red traffic light has a pragmatic determination that functions as a simple.[3] What it designates resists any equivocation. However, precisely because it is simple and necessitates an unequivocal response, it entails that the correct response is itself predicated upon the possibility of a range of other responses. Indeed, its simplicity is tied up with complexity and, it would have to be added, an inherent complexity of response, such that each response would function as a decision. The formal nature of a decision is that which interrupts a potential infinite. Each decision does, as a result, delimit the locus of responsibility. Complexity therefore will have always defined the operational quality of sites of meaning or signification. Finitude exists within a system that allows it to emerge.

What then of the relationship between literature and criticism? While literature may resist the reduction to a form of pragmatic determination – understood as a founding and thus original state of affairs – the important question concerns how that occurs. Precisely because there may be an attempt to secure the singularity of the literary text, the way of approaching this question is not to argue that literature is inherently overdetermined and thus literary language is not truth functional in the way that philosophical or scientific language is taken to be. (This is of course a supposition that demands detailed analysis in its own right.) Instead of working with assumptions about the truth or falsity of either literary or philosophical language it needs to be argued that the truth of literature emerges within the act of criticism. In the same way as a translation was occasioned by language, and in being occasioned revealed what was essential to language – essential without there having to be an essence in and of itself – the act of criticism has the same relation to literature. The most succinct formulation of this position is that it is criticism that serves to establish literature as literature. Criticism is not concerned with the identification of literature. Its object is the way a particular work presents that singularity.

The argument needs to be precise. Literature, both as a form of language in its own right and as a series of generic determinations – for example poetry, theatre, and the novel – will always have had a history. What the existent state of affairs refers to is twofold. In the first instance, reference is to the necessary presence of relationality. A given work at the point of its creation – either within the actual act of writing or in the event of its publication – is already part of its genre. The 'new' is therefore determined by relationality. Its creation – the advent of the new – has to be understood therefore as a coming-into-relation. The second element emerges because of the necessary insistence of relation. Once it can be assumed that the advent of the new work is already in relation then the new work takes on the quality of a repetition. It is another instance of the specific genre of which it forms a part. Attributing centrality to relationality and repetition redefines the nature of the generic determination. Essentialism has two forms, both of which are effectively distanced by the productive incorporation of relation and repetition. In the first case, what is precluded is the possibility that a particular generic has either an already given form or seeks to attain *forma finalis*. The second is a more demanding sense of the essence. Within it, while generic determinations are allowed, in the end they are effaced insofar as each genre refers in its own distinct way to something that is other than it but to which it gives privileged access. The first of these forms of the essence is of direct relevance within this argument. The latter, despite the demands it may make, can be immediately distanced insofar as it refuses the project of criticism by locating the 'truth' of literature in an external relation that only allows for the particular because the particular may function as an exemplary instance. In other words, it precludes the possibility of thinking particularity and thus of thinking the object with the practice of criticism.

What characterizes the first type of essentialism is the acceptance, on the one hand, of an already determined form and, on the other, the commitment – one thought within the inexorability of development conceived as teleology – of the eventual realization of final form. (Final form as an idealization of form returns, for example, as the positing of the 'ideal book'; cf., Mann, Mallarmé.) Finality, therefore, either as a given or as an end, establishes limits and closures. As opposed to a conception of the new understood as the continuity of a coming-into-relation there would be presence of the already determined. The question of literature would work, indeed would have to work, as an assumption. Given the determination in advance this would close down not just the question of literature but the need to uncover the nature of a given particular's relation to the genre of which it formed a part. Obviating the possibility of such a question would reduce criticism either to description or to the identification, within the content of a given literary work, of positions that could be generalized such that they were not reducible to mere literary creations (as would occur in reading literature as no more than a series of moral or ethical concerns; clearly this is only one example among a range of possible examples). The reason why either description, on the one hand, or generalization, on the other, is in the end the result of working with literature's assumed presence is straightforward. Once a work is assumed to be given and therefore is already present as literature then the question of the way in which it is present as literature is precluded. (In sum, within such a set-up interest would have moved from literature's having been constituted to the simple assumption of its presence.) Again, working with the *assumption* that the status of the literary text is given in advance, what becomes important is not the relationship between its formal presence as literature and content – this must be the case as the former element would have already been assumed – but either its content or its locations with the genre, where location and genre were thought in terms of perfectibility. In regard to content, the interesting consequence is that once the status of the work is assumed, then the content is already disconnected to its being as literature in any profound sense such that the lives of a work's characters can be taken as either cautionary or illuminating.

Once repetition and relation are reintroduced then there is a radical departure from the set-up sketched above. The status of the particular understood as a repetition means that the question does not concern the *that* of its presence but the *how*. In other words, that a given work is a work of literature is already established through relationality. The question of criticism becomes how it is what it is. From the philosophical standpoint, what is being investigated is the specific nature of a particular moment of finitude – the presence of a given work – within the infinite of potentiality. The latter is the continuity of the genre continuing to find form. The continuity of its finding form cannot be interrupted in an absolute sense by the presence of a given work – this is precluded for straightforwardly ontological reasons – nonetheless the locus of criticism is constituted by that specific form of interruption which in being held apart from finality emerges as finitude and thus as the particular work.

And yet, precisely because of the excision of structures of finality and determination, the interruption of criticism – an interruption that will always address the *how* of a work, and in so doing constitutes the work (and it will be important to return to this act of constitution) – must itself operate beyond the hold of completion. The specific literary text cannot be completed by the act of criticism. Again this is not relativism. Rather it is the inevitable position that stems from the demands of finitude. As such, what it enjoins in addition, and the addition brings with it an insistent necessity and thus demands its location within possibility and the affirmative, is the responsibility of criticism. Responsibility arises because the act of criticism – an act thought within finitude but which has its ground in the work's potential – has the structure of a decision.

Finally, therefore, criticism in addressing the *how* of a given work constitutes that work's particularity. The constitution in question establishes the work as literature. This end is achieved not by bestowing a quality of the work, nor by making claims about the operations of literature's essential quality within the work. Rather, constitution takes particularity as its point of departure. What is constituted therefore is the detail of the particular in question. The ground of that constitution is literariness understood as continuity of literature's finding form. Literariness refers to the ontological dimension that has already been identified as the infinite of potentiality. Criticism in addressing the individual work – working with it in order to establish the detail of a given instance – has to be understood as that which releases this potential, which releases works to establish the particularity of literature (and thus literary particularity).

Notes

1. I have addressed the question of the relationship between criticism and literature in a number of instances. See my 'Including transformation: notes on the art of the contemporary', and *Philosophy's Literature*. In addition, the argument presented in this chapter takes up and develops that engagement with Walter Benjamin on language and translation that appears in my *Translation and the Nature of Philosophy*, as well as in the texts cited above. The limits of Benjamin reside in the necessity for there to be an engagement with repetition and then the ensuing refusal to do so.
2. There is an important shift therefore from a conception of the incomplete constrained to be thought in terms of a structure of melancholia and one in which the complementarity between finitude and the incomplete overcomes the structure of melancholia due to the location of that relation – finitude and the incomplete – within an ontology of becoming. A mode of thinking which takes place *contra melancholia* affirms the centrality of finitude (and thus the incomplete) as an original condition. As such it is not the result of a loss of plenitude, and thus has to be thought within plentitude's eventual recovery. Finitude, as has been indicated, is positioned within a different ontological configuration.
3. The expression 'pragmatic determination' is used rather than the more standard term 'meaning' for the straightforward reason that meaning seems to suggest a structure of contestability. While the response to the traffic light may open a range of possible actions, it is unclear – as will be argued – that there is a meaning other than the one determined in advance by the light's color. The argument advanced through this chapter does not concern relativism as an epistemological state of affairs. The contrast to 'pragmatic determination' is not the relativity of meaning. On the contrary, the argument involves three elements. In the first instance,

finitude takes as its condition of possibility the ineliminable and productive presence of a potential infinite. Secondly, finite acts, which take the forms of translations or critical engagement, deal with what is fundamental to the object being considered. Thirdly, while finitude cannot be determined absolutely there has to be a relation to the ground of finitude. That relation establishes a site of regulation and engagement in advance.

Works cited

Benjamin, Andrew, *Translation and the Nature of Philosophy* (London: Routledge, 1988).
——*Philosophy's Literature* (Manchester: Clinamen Press, 2001).
——'Including transformation: notes on the art of the contemporary', pp. 208–18 in John J. Joughin and Simon Malpas, eds *The New Aestheticism* (Manchester: Manchester University Press, 2003).

13
Gibberophobia: Philosophy, Fear, and the Plain Style

Jonathan Rée

We philosophers are not, on the whole, particularly fussy when it comes to questions of style. We like to think that philosophy is about cutting through linguistic surfaces and getting straight to the point, so we do not want stylistic foibles to detain us. But that does not mean we do not care about style; quite the contrary, it implies that we have to be constantly vigilant, on our guard against stylistic excess, making endless war on the rampant flowers of rhetoric that threaten to invade the fields of truth and suffocate their mighty harvest.

This attitude involves an obvious paradox. Insouciance turns into obsession, as philosophy is sent off on a quest for a style without style – or any style at all, as long as it is plain. And this paradox is more than a theoretical curiosity: it is a looming practical presence as well. Modern philosophical authors may be uninterested in the positive principles that govern fine writing; but they are never indifferent to the stylistic demons they have learned to see lurking in every linguistic corner: the ever-present dangers of obscurity, self-indulgence, vagueness, ambiguity, pretentiousness, imprecision and muddle. No one will understand modern philosophical culture if they have not passed through dark nights of anxiety about the aseptic purity of their prose.

G.E. Moore's linguistic fastidiousness has been blamed for 'silencing a generation' in Cambridge, England, at the beginning of the twentieth century. ('I didn't want to be silent', he said, unanswerably: but 'I couldn't think of anything to say.' [Bell, p. 215]). J.L. Austin presided over a similar reign of terror in Oxford in the 1950s. Aspiring linguistic philosophers, according to one witness, used to 'wake up in the night with a vision of the stringy, wiry Austin standing over their pillow like a bird of prey'. By day they might settle down and 'write some philosophical sentences', and even take a momentary pleasure in them; but afterwards they would 'read them over as Austin might, in an expressionless, frigid voice.' Their nocturnal terrors would return; 'and their blood would run cold.' The 'mere fact of his

[Austin's] existence' was said to be enough to blight any dreams they might have of becoming philosophical authors.[1]

The same cold wind was felt in Cambridge, Massachusetts. No one would deny the greatness of the Harvard logician Henry Sheffer, originator of the 'Sheffer stroke'; but after publishing a celebrated seven-page article in 1913, he refused to release anything else of significance over a career that lasted another 40 years. He was known to have written extensively on 'Notational Relativity' and 'Analytic Knowledge', and it is possible that he spoke about his works-in-progress to admirers like A.N. Whitehead and Bertrand Russell; but he was so tormented by the fear that there might be something wrong with his formulations that he added arbitrary sheets of paper to his manuscripts and cut them into one-inch strips which he kept in little bundles held together by rubber bands, just to make sure they would never be exposed to public ridicule.[2]

Clearness

The American philosopher Brand Blanshard sought to articulate the paradoxical literary tastes of his colleagues in an essay called 'On Philosophical Style', which was published to an apathetic world in 1954. I came across my copy in the 1980s, at a time when Blanshard was already touchingly unfashionable on account of his idealistic pragmatism and his hostility to the high analytic tradition. And his remarks struck me at the time as not only interesting but useful, accurate and even wise.

Blanshard's starting-point was the fact that intelligent and well-disposed readers have often laboured over the works of great philosophers (Kant, Hegel and Dewey are his examples) only to end up suspecting that they were all 'talking gibberish' (Blanshard, p. 4). Of course any field of inquiry can be afflicted by gibberish, but philosophy is peculiarly vulnerable since it is also under constant suspicion of being its ultimate source. Gibberish, you might say, is philosophy's dark twin, or its besetting sin.

'In this matter of style philosophy is in a difficult position', Blanshard explained. On the one hand it 'belongs to the literature of knowledge', alongside the sciences; it is focused on sifting truth from error, and must therefore inhabit a 'drier climate' than most modern readers find comfortable. On the other hand, the truths that philosophy deals with are ones that engage our feelings, our moral convictions and our sense of self. There is more to them than abstracted cerebration, and philosophical authors who condemn themselves to 'roam a stylistic desert, and munch cactus as the sole article of their diet' are not only tormenting themselves unnecessarily, but betraying their intellectual vocation as well. They should not have allowed their commitment to exactitude to overwhelm their obligation to communicate with delicacy and 'clearness' (Blanshard, pp. 6, 15, 22, 15).

Blanshard admitted that it was hard 'to say what clearness means', but he thought he knew the best way to achieve it: keep in touch with the 'specific' or the 'concrete', and always illustrate your argument with examples drawn from 'experience' (Blanshard, p. 27). He then went on to explore the application of the principle at three different levels: words, then sentences and then discourses on a larger scale.

There were some philosophers – Burke, for example, or Brown, de Quincey, Ruskin or Santayana – who excelled in the use of gorgeously coloured words; but they were not good examples to follow. Their prose was 'like a window of stained glass which, because of its very richness, diverts attention to itself'. Serious practitioners of a 'literature of knowledge' would do better to confine themselves to words that create 'so transparent a medium that one looks straight through it at the object' (Blanshard, pp. 48–50).

But if colourful words were dangerous, grandiose ones were even worse. Philosophers should steer clear of 'Latinate' forms, and heed H.W. Fowler's lament over 'turgid flabby English ... full of abstract nouns' – especially verbs that had been uprooted from the soil of ordinary human activity by having an ending in '-*tion*' (or '-*ation*') tacked on to them.[3] All Latinate suffixes were suspect, but double ones were doubly so, and Blanshard shook his head over the gathering swarm of words where abstract nouns ending in '-*tion*' were turned into adjectives by the addition of a final '-*al*', as for example in neologisms like *exemplificational*, *observational*, *organizational* and *aspirational* (Blanshard, pp. 44–6).

When it came to sentences as opposed to words, Blanshard saw the main danger as issuing not from the Latin language but from German – or 'Teutonic' as he preferred to call it. Philosophical authors were like guides escorting us over tricky terrain, and it was 'a test of literary tact', as he put it, 'to know and take into account the length of the reader's stride'. They should not place their stepping stones too far apart, but nor should they adopt 'the method of the Teutonic sentence' which – by 'making each sentence into a miniature paragraph' – forces us to hobble ourselves with 'seven-league boots' and stumble, lunge, leap and lurch instead of marching purposefully onwards (Blanshard, pp. 51–4).

A good philosophical sentence called for the terse directness of plain conversation. 'Someone has said, "All peasants have style" ', Blanshard wrote, 'and philosophers cannot afford to get wholly out of touch with the fine economy of natural talk.' Berkeley was an ideal model: he had 'all the sharp-eyed wariness of the specialist', but even when his theories parted company with common sense, he carried on 'walking the road of ordinary speech'. According to Blanshard, 'Berkeley proved against all the Heideggers of the world that philosophy can be written clearly, against all the Hegels that it can be written simply, against all the Kants that it can be written with grace' (Blanshard, pp. 57, 62–3).

After his comments on words and sentences, Blanshard found little to say when he turned to 'units larger than the sentence'. He noted that essays and treatises were not the only possible forms of philosophical prose, and recommended dialogue as a refreshing alternative. Dialogue-writing was a difficult art, however, and most attempts ended in failure, either through making too much of 'the characters and their idiom' or through reducing them to 'mere philosophic abstractions'. Many philosophers had tried their hand at dialogues, but only a few (Plato, Berkeley and Lowes Dickinson, according to Blanshard) had made a success of it. The rest of us had better stick to plain expository prose, always taking care to keep it as transparent, concrete and clear as possible (Blanshard, p. 60–1).

I still share most of Blanshard's tastes in philosophical writing. But on re-reading him after twenty years, I am shocked by the habit, which he shared with many of his colleagues, of passing off doctrinal disagreements – about the value of the kinds of inquiry pursued by Kant, Hegel and Heidegger, for instance – as if they were self-evident judgements of taste rather than debatable theoretical contentions. Instead of offering reasoned objections to the authors he disliked, he was content to dismiss them for violating the supreme principle of philosophical style, the principle of absolute clarity.

There were some other gaps that struck me too. Why, for a start, did he assume that the range of large-scale literary forms available to philosophers was confined to dialogues on the one hand and treatises on the other? If only he had attended to a few serious works of philosophical fiction he would have noticed narrative forms far more interesting, those in which different 'characters' are called on to articulate various doctrinal positions. Kierkegaard's novelistic experiments in *Either/Or*, *Fear and Trembling* or *Repetition*, or Sartre's in *La Nausée*, for instance, show how an argumentative web can be woven out of implied narrative points of view, none of which need be stable, reliable or internally consistent. In Kierkegaard and Sartre, the philosophy resides not so much in explicit philosophical statements as in the unfolding of a story and the way it is told.

If he had been more sensitive to the philosophical uses of narrative, Blanshard might also have been less impatient with Hegel and Heidegger. Both of them had a talent for fine phrases ('the tremendous power of the negative' or the 'quiet force of the possible', for instance),[4] though they exercised it only intermittently; but they really made their mark as what might be called 'long-form' writers – authors who meant their sentences to function like the stones of a vault, each one held in place by all the others. The trick of Heidegger's *Being and Time* (or *Being and Time, Part One*, as it was originally called) was to promise an exposition of 'phenomenological ontology' but refuse to reveal what it might mean until a preliminary analysis has been completed, which of course it never is. The very form of the incomplete book is a celebration of the theme of incompletion. Hegel's *Phenomenology*, on the other hand, is an exercise in fully rounded story-telling. It is an epic narrative of the adventures and misadventures of 'spirit' in its search for the essential truth about the world, beginning when it sets out on its journey full of hope, continuing as it faces terrible ordeals on its way and finishing with its arrival, tired but happy, at its destination. Spirit starts by assuming that the truth it has set its heart on is something objective and separate from itself; but experience will eventually teach it that truth is really identical with self-knowledge, though it will have to pass through searing ordeals and humiliations before it reaches this conclusion. Hegel dramatizes the repeated postponement of enlightenment by constructing a counterpoint between things as spirit will know them once it has achieved perfect hindsight, and things as they seemed when it first encountered them. The *Phenomenology*, in other words, has the literary form of a classic autobiography: it is spirit's own memoir of its slow ascent to absolute knowledge.

Blanshard might possibly have argued that in relying on narrative techniques, Hegel and Heidegger were abandoning the 'literature of knowledge' in favour of something else – imagination, perhaps, or edification. But that would be a false dichotomy. The literary methods they adopted allowed them to explore various fragments of experience and let them jostle against each other to generate new kinds of knowledge – kinds of knowledge that promised to be less partial than their predecessors, and more flexible and robust. They created their account of philosophical knowledge by telling a more or less idealized story of the growth of a philosophical mind, rather than offering an all-out description of what you would know if you yourself were such a mind. The technique is fundamentally ironic. It is more like a Wordsworthian recollection than a set of statements saying 'this is how things are', and its object is to make us delay our interpretation of every statement we encounter, reserving judgement until we can appreciate its entire narrative context. It would not be unreasonable to regard it as, deep down, the literary technique most characteristic of modern philosophical writing as a whole, not just Hegel and Heidegger but Descartes, Spinoza and Kant as well, each of whom sought to guide their readers on an exemplary journey – a journey from lesser kinds of knowledge to better ones.

My re-reading of Blanshard revealed a similar gap at the second of his three stylistic levels, that of the sentence. His doctrine that 'each sentence should carry the thought one step forward' (Blanshard, p. 51) may seem unobjectionable, even platitudinous. In ordinary circumstances, we are entitled to expect the sentences we read to yield their meaning unreservedly to the kind of reader who is willing to pick up one foot after the other and trudge doggedly from foreword to postscript. But authors will sometimes find it necessary to create contexts that have rather less of the pedestrian one-way street about them – textual situations in which familiar terms are knocked off their customary perches in the hope that new semantic patterns will take shape; and philosophers are bound to be conspicuous amongst such authors. The sentence 'I am a thinking thing' is not so much a description of the person who utters it, as an attempt to precipitate a reconsideration of the meaning of 'I am'; and to say that '*esse* is *percipi*' is not to ascribe a specific quality to being, but to challenge certain assumptions about its relationship to experience. The same applies to all the other great philosophical sentences – Hume's 'reason is . . . the slave of the passions', Hegel's 'the real is the rational', Mill's 'actions are right in proportion as they tend to produce happiness', or Wittgenstein's 'the world is all that is the case'. They do not draw on pre-existing meanings in order to apply a self-contained predicate to a self-contained subject, like sticking a label on a jar. Their terms cannot be fully defined in advance, since the whole point of using them is to precipitate a questioning or even an alteration of their meanings. Hegel calls such sentences 'speculative propositions', suggesting that they create *specula* or mirrors in which their various terms can adjust themselves to each other.[5] We have to wait and see what meanings will accrue to the individual terms as they exercise their semantic charms on each other, and we are not supposed to exit from them with the same understanding we had when we came in. Blanshard's image of philosophical readers striding purposefully across the landscape, demanding that each sentence should take them 'one step forward', is flatly incompatible with the patient, delicate, attentive art of reading that speculative sentences call for.

I also find Blanshard's advice about words harder to accept than I used to, especially his prejudice against Latin-derived words. He cites the critic Walter Raleigh arguing that nonsense in Latinate English 'masquerades as profundity of abstract thought', whereas 'if you talk nonsense in Saxon you are found out at once; you have a competent judge in every hearer' (Blanshard, p. 48). No doubt he would also have applauded George Orwell's lament, in 'Politics and the English Language', about words ending in '-*ize*' and more generally about the 'Latin or Greek words' that 'constantly gain ground from their Anglo-Saxon opposite numbers': we are, according to Orwell, 'haunted by the notion that Latin or Greek words are grander than Saxon ones' (Orwell, p. 131). It is a very familiar story, and its air of truculent populism may have a certain appeal; but still it is not very likely to be true. Even if some English words of Latin origin sound 'grand', that does not mean that Latin-derived words are inherently snobbish or obfuscatory. Is a comedian really posher than a wit, or a pub than a club, a story than a tale? The idea of a rugged old 'Saxon' heart to the modern English language owes more to nationalist myth-making than linguistic analysis; and if Blanshard had seriously meant to purify his language of all Latinate words then the title of his essay 'On Philosophical Style' would have been reduced to its first word: a Beckettian or Ginsbergian 'On'.

The reformation and the plain style

When I first came across them, I assumed that Blanshard's views of philosophical style – his gibberophobia – belonged very specifically to the twentieth century, and principally also to the English-speaking world. They certainly have considerable affinities with the attitudes of Russell and Moore in their revolt against German idealism, as well as with the more recent habit of demonizing something called 'continental philosophy' on account of its supposed offences against the principles of a good, clear writing-style. They also find an echo in the attitudes to logic and the natural sciences that culminated in logical positivism. (Blanshard acknowledged the resonance when he suggested that the central positivist doctrine – that a statement 'means the experience that would serve to verify it' – was 'at once deplorable philosophy and admirable literary advice' [Blanshard, p. 35]).

But in fact the philosophical obsession with 'clarity', and specifically with the idea of philosophy as both the source of gibberish and the antidote to it, has a history that goes back all the way to the Reformation. One of the main objections the reformers made to the influence of Rome was specifically about philosophy: that the Church had for centuries been distorting simple gospel truths by forcibly reformulating them in terms of Pagan doctrine, especially the works of Aristotle. Another was the way it treated Latin as the canonical Christian language, almost as if it had been the mother tongue of the Old Testament prophets, or of Christ and his disciples, or as if the Latin translation of the Bible were itself an inspired book. Hence Protestantism was born with an innate hostility both to Latinity and to the old philosophy, or in a word to 'the schools', or what would later be called 'scholasticism'.

Take John Cotton for instance. He was a Puritan who studied at Cambridge at the beginning of the seventeenth century, and noted a bitter stand-off between two different styles of preaching and lecturing there: on the one hand the rhetorical extravagances of those who liked to 'stuffe and fill their Sermons with as much Quotation and citing of Authors [i.e. classical author-ities] as might possibly be', and on the other 'the plain & profitable way, by raysing of *Doctrines*, with propounding the *Reasons* and *Uses* of the same' (see Miller, p. 331). Plainness was all. Cotton wanted his Christianity clear and unstuffed, and he was one of the many Cambridge graduates who emigrated to New England in the hope of establishing a pristine Christian tradition there – a Church that would keep itself free of the 'Empty, Trifling, Alter-cative Notions' (Mather, p. 25) of the schools, either by banishing philosophy entirely, as an inherently Pagan discipline, or by confining it to a kind of practical logic that would assist in the systematic exposition of Bible truths.

Antony Tuckney, who had been an assistant to Cotton before sailing for the American colonies, became one of the fountains of Puritan vehemency in Cambridge during the Civil War complaining about preachers who were so scholastic 'both for wordes and notions' that their congregations could not understand them. He liked to quote Paul's Epistle to the Corinthians ('In the Church I had rather speak five words with my understanding, that by my voice I might teach others also, than ten thousand words in an unknown tongue' – 1 Corinthians XIV, 19), and called for a 'plaine powerful ministry' which would take care 'not to speake in schoole-language, nor to runne out in schoole-notions' (see Salter, pp. 37–8, 93).

But if the advocates of plain-style Puritan preaching were hostile both to Aristotelianism and to Latinism, that did not mean they were comprehensively anti-philosophical. Some were (Tuckney, for example, regarded philosophy as irredeemably unchristian), but most of them made a distinction between the bad old philosophy and something 'new', initially in the form proposed by Peter Ramus, the anti-Aristotelian logician and Protestant martyr (he died in the St Bartholemew's Day Massacre in Paris in 1572), who sought to replace the forms of classical rhetoric with something plain and simple that the Puritans called 'Logicall Analysis'.[6]

The young Henry More, who sought to uphold both Plato and Descartes in opposition to the Aristotelian tradition, was to insist that the 'lean style' associated with Puritan preachers was also 'fittest for philosophy' (More, 1647, p. 107). And Thomas Hobbes devoted many pages of *Leviathan* to ridiculing the 'metaphors, and senseless and ambiguous words' of the Aristotelians, holding that superstitious notions about immortality and incorporeality would be banished at once if we could always steer clear of figuration and stick to 'proper words' instead (Hobbes, V, 19–20, p. 21–2, XXXVIII, 11, p. 243).

Hobbes's dream of reforming university education after the English Civil War turned above all on a campaign against 'insignificant speech' (Hobbes, I, 5, p. 4). He observed with regret that linguistic inanities had not died out with the Aristotelian 'Schoole-men'; indeed the sharp decline in Latin fluency during his lifetime meant that the old habit of lacing vernacular discourse with Latin phrases was becoming absurd. He argued that good sense comes naturally to 'the common sort of men' provided they stick to their mother tongue and do not seek to spin it out with 'Latin or Greek names', or with mischievous suffixes like *-nesse*, *-tude*, or *-ity*, which turned honest perspicuous words like 'White', 'Magnus' or 'Corrupt' into dark abstractions like 'White*nesse*', 'Magni*tude*' and 'Corruptibil*ity*'. Anyone seeking a test of philosophical good sense, Hobbes suggested, need look no further than the vernacular:

> To be assured their words are without any thing correspondent to them in the mind . . . let him take a Schoole-man into his hands, and see if he can translate any one chapter . . . into any of the moderne tongues, so as to make the same intelligible.

Hobbes tried putting a passage from Francisco Suárez into ordinary English, with the following result:

> *The first cause does not necessarily inflow any thing into the second, by force of the Essential subordination of the second causes, by which it may help it to worke.*

'What is the meaning of these words?' Hobbes demanded with histrionic exasperation. Those honest enough to query them risked being dismissed as 'Idiots' by smug young muddleheads, but, Hobbes inquired, 'when men write whole volumes of such stuff, are they not mad, or intend to make others so?' (Hobbes, VIII, 27, p. 39; IV, 21, p. 17).

Hobbes's sense of the ridiculousness of Aristotelian Latinisms became full-fledged bluff buffoonery a few years later when Joseph Glanvill launched his attack on the 'verbosities' of Jesuits, Scholastics and Aristotelians in *The Vanity of Dogmatizing*.

> Though in *Greek* or *Latine* they amuse us, yet a *vernacular translation* unmasks them; and if we make them speak *English*, the cheat is transparent. Light is *energeia tou diaphanes* saith that *Philosophy*: in English, the *Act of a perspicuous body*. Sure . . . if this definition be clearer, and more known then the thing defin'd; *midnight* may vye for conspicuity with *noon*. . . . The Infant, that was last enlarged from its *maternal cels*, knows more what *light* is, then this *definition* teacheth. . . . Again, that motion is *entelecheia tou ontos en dynamei* &c is as insignificant as the former. By the most favourable interpretation of that unintelligible *Entelechy*; it is but an act of a being in *power*, as it is in *power*: The construing of which to any real meaning, is beyond the *criticisms* of a Mother *Tongue*; except it describes our modern Acts of *Parliaments*. (Glanvill, 1661, pp. 150, 156–7)

By the end of the seventeenth century, large tracts of philosophy were set aside for the cruel sport of gibberish-hunting, often conducted in a spirit of raucous hilarity.[7] After Ramus's logical analysis had gone out of fashion, it was replaced by the 'new philosophy' of Descartes and his followers, which was thought to have ousted Aristotelian natural science in the name of 'atomism' or 'corpuscularianism'. In 1694 an influential manual of Cartesianism argued that the 'Occult Qualities', 'Substantial Forms' and 'Hidden Powers' that cluttered up the old philosophy were mere figments of superstition and ignorance, so that 'our *Modern Philosophers* are at a loss about what the ARISTOTELEANS means by all this *Gibberish*'.[8] One philosophical satirist described the quiddities of Duns Scotus as 'insipid Trifles' and '*Irish Gibbrish*'.[9] And the Irish Cartesian William Molyneux suggested that the school philosophers had been infected with 'a Spice of Madness, whereby they *feign'd a Knowledge where they had none*', and that with all their 'Gibberish' they could have 'disputed to all Eternity' without ever discovering any plain and simple truth (Molyneux, 1692, sigs A2^v, B1^r). Those who wished to pursue the more spiritual side of the Cartesian philosophy, meanwhile, were obliged to explain that the new theory of ideas had nothing in common with the old '*Platonick Gibberish*' (Norris, 1690, p. ii). By the turn of the eighteenth century, it was taken as a matter of course that the old philosophy served 'to little better use, than so much *gibberish*' (F.B. [Francis Brokesby], 1701, p. 44). It should not be taken too far however, and the third Earl of Shaftesbury would caution against the ecstacies of being 'Emancipated from that egregious Form of Intellectual Bondage' which was the 'Gibberish of the Schools' (Shaftesbury, p. 41).

Universal translation

It might seem, then, that the attitudes to philosophical style that Blanshard was promoting half a century ago – a wariness of Latinisms, especially Latinate suffixes, an appeal to plain vernaculars as a touchstone of philosophical good sense, and a habit of harping on the word *gibberish* – were simply a continuation of the passionately sectarian anti-Aristotelianism of Protestants and new philosophers in seventeenth-century Britain and America. But they can also be seen as part of a larger transformation, affecting the whole of what might be called the linguistic situation of philosophy.

The first philosophers to try their hand at composing philosophy in modern languages – Montaigne, Charron, Bacon, Descartes and Gassendi, as well as Hobbes and Glanville – did so with considerable misgivings. They were at least as fluent in Latin as in their mother tongue, and as far as philosophy was concerned, one might say that Latin was really their first language: they would all have learned to think philosophically through Latin expositions of Latin texts (including Latin translations from the Greek of Aristotle and, increasingly, Plato). They were conscious that writing philosophy in a vernacular was a bold initiative, paralleled only by Cicero's achievement, one and a half millennia before, in 'teaching philosophy to speak Latin'[10]. The vocabulary of philosophical Latin had always been frankly modelled on Greek, either by way of simple transliterations which might or might not be subjected to Latin grammar (Greek-Latin words like *phenomenon* or *idea* or indeed *philosophia*), or by way of conventional equivalences, as when the Latin *natura* deputized for the Greek *physis*; and for those who were fluent in Greek it was still possible to hear the Greek behind philosophical Latin even after one and a half millennia.

That raised the question, for seventeenth-century philosophers experimenting with the vernacular, whether they wanted their Latin to show through their modern prose, and whether they minded if their works sounded more like translations than new-born originals. Descartes is famous for having launched himself on his literary career in French rather than Latin. But it was a very Latinate French, as his titles made clear: his *Discours de la Méthode pour bien conduire sa raison et chercher la vérité dans les sciences*, followed by *La Dioptrique*, *Les Météores* and *La Géométrie* all sound as though they had been conceived in Latin and then given a little nudge in a French direction. Descartes's French works lent themselves easily to the Latin translations in which they would become known throughout Europe – right down to the famous sentence (a translator's sentence from the Latin version of the *Discours*), *cogito ergo sum*. It is curious that when he changed his mind and reverted to Latin in his *Meditationes* a few years later, Descartes expressed the opposite worry – that his Latin was beginning to sound like a translation from French.[11]

In English, however, the tide was running in the other direction. Philosophers like Hobbes were anxious that their vernacular prose should not sound like Latin, and the path had been prepared for them by a handful of translators (then as now an unjustly neglected sector of the intellectual workforce) who had already started the assault on the idea of Latin as the natural medium for philosophy, and specifically for logic. In 1573 an English translator called Ralph Lever set out 'to prove that the arte of Reasoning may be taughte in Englishe', since 'we Englishmen have wits [and] . . . we have also framed our selves a language'. Instead of cluttering his translation with the 'inkhorne termes' of transliterated Latin, he undertook to 'devise understandable termes, compounded of true and ancient English words': for example *ifsaye* (for 'conditional proposition'), *backsette* (for 'predicate') or *bounder* (for 'terminus'). In the same way, for this early poet of English logic, a conclusion was an *endsay*, an opposite a *gaynset*, an accident an *inbeer* and a definition a *saywhat*. And the maxims of logic – or rather *Witcraft*, as Lever thought it should be called in English – could be expressed in robust vernacular statements such as 'every simple shewsay . . . is either a yeasay or a naysay'.[12] It was a heroic attempt, and it is interesting to daydream about how philosophy might have fared in the English language if Lever's initiative had caught on. Within a few years, however, it had been faced down by the work of a rival translator, who argued that

> it is no shame nor robberie to borrowe tearmes . . . from the Latines, as well as they did from the Greekes: and speciallie such tearmes as can not be aptlie expressed in our native speech . . . thinking it much better so to doe, then to fayne new words improper for the purpose, as some of late have done. (Blundevile, 1599, sig. A3ʳ)

The author of the first English translation of Plato's *Apology* and *Phaedo* (published in 1675) made a suggestive contrast between Socrates and Plato. Socrates was not a pusillanimous, parochial Master of Arts, but a man of action – a soldier who stood for '*Wisedom* reconciled to *Warre*', and hence for a rugged kind of virtue that could be recognized immediately, in all seasons and climes. Plato, on the other hand, with his 'Atticism and admirable Civility', was a local boy, and his spell would not work on those who did not know Greek. The new English version of Plato would be a genuine 'Translation' (as opposed to a 'Paraphrase'), aiming to 'trace out his [Plato's] very Expressions, and render them even word for word'. But it would not linger over the 'graceful *Phrases*' that were 'much more agreeably and pathetically expressed by one Tongue, than by another', and hence 'incapable of alienation or traduction'. By 'preferring plain *imitation* to more artificial ornament', the translation would provide a clearer portrait of Plato's philosophy than could ever be derived from his own beguiling Greek.[13]

The same issues confronted translators of contemporary works, as William Molyneux realized a few years later when he made the first English translation of Descartes's *Meditationes*, published in 1680. Like the anonymous translator of Plato, he was impressed by the fact that his hero had been a soldier. 'He had a Genius fitted . . . for the Pike as well as Pen,' as Molyneux put it, commending the military briskness with which Descartes expressed his 'dislike to the unsatisfactory Notions, and verbose emptiness of the Peripatetick Philosophy'. Although he prided himself on his accuracy as a translator, he was prepared to ignore 'smoothness of phrase or quaintness of expression' in Descartes's Latin in order to do better justice to his 'Physico-Mathematical Argumentation'. Hence, Molyneux said defiantly, 'the Philosophical plain stile and rough Language of the following Translation' (Molyneux, 1680, sigs A2^v–A5^r).

It seems that something was changing in the relationship between philosophy and language. Philosophers who experimented with vernaculars, and philosophical translators working in modern languages, were committed to Puritan principles of good prose: they were wary of waywardness and idiosyncrasy and stern in their advocacy of a clear, plain style, purged of all vestiges of Latin.[14] Together they were trying to topple Latin from its traditional supremacy as the language of western learning, and indeed of western Christianity; but they were not interested in promoting some other language – English or French or perhaps Dutch – as the new Latin. They were beginning to imagine knowledge as a commodity that belonged equally to all languages, or to none: a notion that the classical philosophers, wedded to the peculiar resonances of Latin or Greek, would have found ridiculous.[15] They were becoming suspicious of notions that seemed to adhere to particular languages or particular forms of words, and wished to deal only in meanings which, as they saw it, could be expressed in indefinitely many different ways without losing their identity. That is how modern philosophy contracted its chronic gibberophobia, and bound itself to something called 'clarity' as the alpha to omega of philosophical style.

The modernization of philosophy in the seventeenth century is usually thought of as a great leap forward – the European mind liberating itself from the dictatorship of Aristotelian Latin, extending the usable intellectual past to include thousands of philosophies in dozens of different languages and generally limbering up for the Enlightenment.

But if there were gains, there were surely losses as well. In a world that acknowledged no real philosopher apart from Aristotle, philosophical reading was as free as the wind: the arts of interpretation flourished as readers sought to explore the entire gamut of meanings that his texts could be made to express. And where Latin was the only language, philosophical writing was as free as poetry: thinkers could exploit the full range of its idioms, and where necessary expand them at will, without worrying about whether equivalents could be found in clear vernacular paraphrases. But when the repertory expanded, the horizons of philosophical reading narrowed: interpretation was reduced to finding a simple and unambiguous meaning for each of thousands of different texts, and dismissing anything left over as mere gibberish. Meanwhile philosophical writing declined into the menial role of expressing such universally available meanings in the plainest possible style.

Blanshard was not insensitive to these ambiguities, and he concluded his essay with a doubt. 'Should any of us wish', he asked, 'that Hobbes was less unmistakably Hobbes in his writing, or Bradley Bradley, or Moore his repetitious, lucid, vehement, painstakingly precise self?' The answer had to be no. 'The problem of style', Blanshard concluded, 'is not a problem of words and sentences merely, but of being the right kind of mind.' (Blanshard, pp. 64, 69). That is not the kind of thing that anyone would say today without embarrassment; nor does it fit in with the idea of 'clarity' as the supreme principle of philosophical conduct. But Blanshard had a point all the same. The greatest of the modern philosophers – from Descartes and Locke to Rousseau, Hume and Kant, from Hegel, Kierkegaard and Nietzsche, to Wittgenstein, Heidegger and Derrida – have all been through a similar experience. First they have internalized a passion for clarity, and then they have moved beyond it. They have done their time trying to give clear and definitive answers to simple and univocal questions before embarking on something rather more daring – before trying to foster, in themselves and in others, 'the right kind of mind'. They have thrown off the halter of the plain philosophical style and fought to regain some of the intellectual freedoms that philosophy lost when it graduated to modernity. In short, they have developed philosophical courage. They have overcome their fear of the fate that waits for us all: the inevitable lapse into stylistic imperfection, into ambiguity and idiom – in short, into gibberish.

Notes

1. Mehta, citing G.J. Warnock, pp. 53–4.
2. Henry Sheffer's 'A Set of Five Independent Postulates for Boolean Algebras with Application to Logical Constants' appeared in the *Transactions of the American Mathematical Society* in 1913. It was quickly recognized as a classic, but Sheffer's authorial anxieties were never appeased. Luckily, he found speech far easier than writing, and was able to communicate memorably in lectures and seminars. In the twenties he came close to losing his job, but was saved by a colleague who testified that 'He raises the standard and is a living example of mental integrity and high-mindedness whether he publishes a book or not.' In the end it came to be accepted that 'although he has published little, he has created greatly'. See Henle *et al.*, pp. x, v. It appears that Sheffer was also handicapped by his reputation as a 'sensitive' Jew; see Kuklick, pp. 457–8, 569–70.
3. Fowler continues his strictures on 'nouny abstract style' as follows: 'to count the *-tion* words in what one has written, or, better, to cultivate an ear that without special orders challenges them as they come, is one of the simplest & most effective means of making oneself less unreadable'. See H.W. Fowler, *A Dictionary of Modern English Usage, s.v.* -tion.

4. For 'die ungeheure Macht des Negativen' see Hegel, *The Phenomenology of Spirit*, Preface, p. 19, §32; for 'die stille Kraft des Möglichen' see Martin Heidegger, *Being and Time*, p. 446, §76.

5. See Hegel, p. 38, §61: 'The general nature of the judgement or proposition, which involves the distinction of Subject and Predicate, is destroyed by the speculative proposition [*durch den spekulativen Satz zerstört wird*].'

6. For the term 'Logicall Analysis' see Abraham Fraunce's work of 1588, *The Lawiers Logike*, pp. 120–39.

7. Rabelais played an important role in it too, especially the passage where the student from Limoges exasperates Pantagruel with his habit of Latinifying his French. The student explains himself: 'Signor Missayre, mon génie n'est poinct apte nate à ce que dict ce flagitiose nebulon pour escorier la cuticule de nostre vernacule Gallicque, mais viceversement je gnave opere, et par veles et rames je me enite de le locupleter de la redundance latinicome' (Rabelais, p. 246).

8. See Anthony Le Grand, *An Entire Body of Philosophy, According to the Principles of the Famous Renate Des Cartes*, Book II, p. 50; the comment is due to the translator and has no equivalent in the Latin original, *Historia naturae, variis experimentis et ratiociniis elucidata*, 2nd edition (London: J. Martin, 1680), p. 99.

9. Gabriel Daniel, *A Voyage to the World of Cartesius*, p. 125. The original French phrase is: 'de toutes ces fadaises . . . c'étoit là du gibier d'Hybernois'; see *Voiage du monde de Descartes* (Paris: Simon Benard, 1691), p. 130.

10. This much-quoted phrase began life in Cicero's *De Finibus* III, xii: 'Itaque mihi videris Latine docere philosophiam et ei quasi civitatem dare; quae quidem adhuc peregrinari Romae videbatur.' ('Indeed, Cato, I feel you are teaching philosophy to speak Latin, and naturalising her as a Roman citizen. Hitherto she has seemed as a foreigner at Rome . . . '; see Cicero, p. 259).

11. In his letter to Marin Mersenne of 24 December 1640, Descartes reproaches himself for 'ce qui peut sentir la phrase française' in his Latin; see Descartes, p. 267. Specifically, he was uneasy about having used *in dubium revocari* instead of *in dubium ponere* in the title of the First Meditation.

12. See Raphe Lever, *The Arte of Reason, Rightly Termed, Witcraft, Teaching a Perfect Way to Argue and Dispute* (London: 1573), sig. iiii^r, p. 84, pp.235–9.

13. Anon, translator, *Plato his* Apology of Socrates *and* Pheado (London: James Magnes and Richard Bentley, 1675), Epistle Dedicatory, n.p., sigs A1^r–A3^v.

14. Molyneux himself noted the connection, comparing his own vocation for 'Communicating the Methods of Truth to those that have only the English Tongue' to that of the New England preachers who were translating the Gospels into Algonquin. See Moylneux, 1680, sig. A7^r.

15. In the same passage where he wrote of 'teaching philosophy to speak Latin', Cicero mentioned certain disreputable 'philosophers . . . who could express their ideas in any language, for they ignore Division and Definition altogether'. ('Scio enim esse quosdam qui quavis lingua philosophari possint; nullis enim partitionibus, nullis definitionibus utuntur'; see Cicero, p. 259.

Works cited

Anon, (trans.) *Plato his* Apology of Socrates *and* Pheado (London: James Magnes and Richard Bentley, 1675).

Bell, Quentin, *Virginia Woolf*, vol. 2 (London: Hogarth, 1972).

Blanshard, Brand, *On Philosophical Style* (Manchester: Manchester University Press, 1954).

Blundevile, M., *The Art of Logike, Plainely Taught in the English Tongue* (London: John Windert, 1599).

F.B. (Brokesby, Francis), *Of Education, with Respect to Grammar Schools and the Universities* (London: John Hartley, 1701).

Cicero, *De Finibus bonorum et malorum*, trans. H. Rackham. Loeb Classical Library (1914). (London: Heinemann, 1961).

Daniel, Gabriel, *A Voyage to the World of Cartesius*, trans. T. Taylor (London: Thomas Bennet, 1692).

Descartes, René, *Oeuvres*, eds Charles Adam and Paul Tannéry (Paris: Cerf, 1897–1913).

Fowler, H.W., *A Dictionary of Modern English Usage* (Oxford: Oxford University Press, [1926], 1940).

Fraunce, Abraham, *The Lawiers Logike* (London: William How, 1588).

Glanvill, Joseph, *The Vanity of Dogmatizing* (London: Henry Eversden, 1661).

Hegel, G.W.F., *The Phenomenology of Spirit*, trans. A.V. Miller (Oxford: Oxford University Press, 1977).

Heidegger, Martin, *Being and Time*, trans. John Macquarrie and Edward Robinson (Oxford: Blackwell, 1962).

Henle, Paul, Horace M. Kallen, Susan K. Langer (eds), *Structure, Method and Meaning: Essays in Honor of Henry M. Sheffer* (New York: Liberal Arts Press, 1951).

Hobbes, Thomas, *Leviathan* (London: Andrew Crooke, 1651).

Kuklick, Bruce, *The Rise of American Philosophy* (New Haven and London: Yale University Press, 1977).

Le Grand, Anthony, *An Entire Body of Philosophy, According to the Principles of the Famous Renate Des Cartes*, trans. Richard Blome (London, Richard Blome, 1694).

Lever, Raphe, *The Arte of Reason, Rightly Termed, Witcraft, Teaching a Perfect Way to Argue and Dispute* (London: 1573).

Mather, Cotton, *Magnalia Christi Americana*, Book 3 (London: Thomas Parkhurst, 1702).

Mehta, Ved, *The Fly and the Fly-bottle: Encounters with British Intellectuals* (London: Weidenfeld and Nicolson, 1963).

Miller, Perry, *The New England Mind: The Seventeenth Century* (New York: Macmillan, 1939).

Molyneux, William, (trans.) *Six Metaphysical Meditations . . . written originally in Latin by Renatus Des-Cartes* (London: Benjamin Tooke, 1680).

——*Dioptrica Nova: A Treatise of Dioptricks* (London: Benjamin Tooke, 1692).

More, Henry, *Philosophicall Poems* (Cambridge: Roger Daniel, 1647).

Norris, John, *Reflections upon the Conduct of Human Life* (London: S. Manship, 1690).

Orwell, George, 'Politics and the English Language' (1946), in *The Collected Essays, Journalism and Letters of George Orwell*, vol. 4, eds Sonia Orwell and Ian Angus (London: Secker & Warburg, 1968).

Rabelais, François, *Pantagruel*, in *Oeuvres Complètes*, ed. Pierre Jourda (Paris: Garnier, 1962).

Salter, Samuel, (ed.), 'Eight Letters of Dr Antony Tuckney and Dr Benjamin Whichcote written in 1651,' appended to *Moral and Religious Aphorisms of . . . Doctor Whichcote* (London: J. Payne, 1753).

Shaftesbury, Lord Anthony Ashley Cooper, *Several Letters Written by a Noble Lord to a Young Man at the University* (London: J. Roberts, 1716).

14
Philosophy's Metaphors: Dennett, Midgley, and Derrida

Robert Eaglestone

Literature, for philosophy and for philosophers, is like the 'Irish Question' for nineteenth-century British politicians. Not only does 'the literary' resemble a colonized land which, at once both inside and outside the imperial power of 'philosophy', continuously disturbs the seemingly ordered doings of the colonizing centre, but also, as soon as a 'philosophical' answer to the problem is arrived at, the question – the subjects – change. Of course, this is in part what Jacques Derrida is hinting at when he discusses the 'strange institution' of literature. More prosaically, it reflects a common and important teaching experience: for every assertion about literature, a literary counter-example can be found; for nearly every interpretation another equally plausible interpretation can be discussed. These pedagogic experiences are not just accidents, but, I suspect, deeply ingrained in the very experience of the literary.

The aim of this chapter is to explore this relationship, too briefly, by looking at one area (among many) in which philosophy, quite broadly understood, has trouble with literature: the area of metaphor. However, rather than discussing what philosophers have thought of these two areas (either philosophers of science like Dan Sperber, or more mainstream thinkers like Donald Davison, for example), I want to explore how philosophers have consciously used metaphors themselves. The aim is not (only) to show that metaphor is unavoidable in writing (by now rather an old and respectable argument) but to hint at what this unavoidability might mean for a range of thinkers. How a thinker uses metaphors shapes and reflects both what they think metaphor is (in its use) and, in turn, what their own philosophy attempts to do.

Some thinkers, like Berel Lang, suggest that the analysis of philosophical style is not 'decisive for every or any particular instance of reading or interpretation' (though any reading will, 'unavoidably, take a position with respect to the literary or stylistic character of those works'), which suggests that it is not important for the meaning of a work (Lang, p. 23). In contrast, others, often followers of Derrida influenced by essays like 'White

194

Mythology', find in the style, the writing, a total shaping of meaning – 'metaferocity' (see Derrida, 1974). Some, like Stanley Cavell, argue that, for example, Wittgenstein's style is inextricable from what the *Investigations* means. Others argue that style is a guide to what is really going on or to make taxonomies of thinkers (Wheeler makes an off-hand – but very illuminating – remark: 'You are an analytic philosopher if you think Kripke writes clearly; you are a continental philosopher if you think Heidegger writes clearly') (Wheeler, p. 2).

The point of these differences is important. A tradition dating from Hume, at least, and one which includes Austin, differentiates between words about words and words about things. (One could refine this much further, of course: when a theoretical physicist discusses infinitesimal forces, and when an aeronautical engineer discusses parts of an aeroplane, how much is the former a thing compared to the latter?) Implicit in this is a complex and difficult claim about the nature of reference. Do words about words and words about things function in the same way? (That is, do the words relate or refer to the words in the same way as they do to the things? If so, then, in fact, words and things – the word 'justice' and a table – are not different. If they do not, then these are different things.) Donald Davidson writes that

> We don't need the concept of reference; neither do we need reference itself, whatever that may be. For if there is one way of assigning entities to expressions (a way of characterizing 'satisfaction') that yields acceptable results with respect to the truth conditions of sentences, there will be endless other ways that do as well. There is no reason, then, to call any of these semantic relations 'reference' or 'satisfaction'. (Davidson, p. 224)

I do not go so far as this: what I want to suggest is that there are different forms of reference, and that (to use this simplistic distinction as a guide) when we talk about words, or when we talk about things, we employ different forms of reference, and, indeed, then different forms of truth condition and ontological assumptions about what we are doing. The metaphors philosophers use to describe what they do illuminate these different forms of reference, and in turn offer a picture of what philosophy thinks it is about. I want, then, to contrast the use of metaphor in three thinkers roughly in three different traditions – Daniel Dennett, Mary Midgley and Jacques Derrida – and to show to what other ideas the use of metaphor leads.

Daniel Dennett might seem to be an odd figure with which to begin. As a leading analytic philosopher of science, he is often contemptuous of the 'linguistic turn' and of 'French colleagues' with their 'deliberate obscurantism and . . . striking of stylized poses', though he does share odd affinities with much work in this other strand of philosophy (Dennett, 1993, p. 203). However, he does write very well: his major works (after *Content and Consciousness*, his first book) are not only accessible to scholars and scientists in a number of disciplines but also to the informed general reader. (This is one part of the reason for his influence in a range of fields – consciousness studies, philosophy of science and so on.) Part of this is his ability to coin good metaphors – literary thought experiments? – and to 'tell a good story': indeed, Bo Dahlbom writes that when 'other philosophers use definitions and arguments, Daniel Dennett will make his point by telling a story . . . His philosophy is in his stories' (Dahlbom, p. 1). And he is self-conscious about this. He writes: 'I view philosophical writing in an engineering spirit: I design and build devices – arguments, intuition pumps, metaphor machines – that are supposed to achieve certain effects. When they work, I'm exultant and when they don't, I'm surprised and annoyed' (Dennett, 1993, p. 203).

Engineering is very close to Dennett's heart: while 'engineering has always had second-class status in the intellectual world . . . regarded with a certain measure of condescension by the mandarin elite of science and the arts' it 'harbors some of the deepest, most beautiful, most important thinking ever done' (Dennett, 1995, p. 188). Thus, it shouldn't surprise us that his explanation of consciousness and for the 'evolution and meaning of life' is, basically, that it's just good engineering. He uses the engineering metaphor in two closely interlinked ways. First, his work is full of engineering language and examples: pumps, cranes, hooks, design space, forced design moves and so on. His examples and argumentative steps are often taken from engineering, or from the resolution of engineering problems. For example: in *Consciousness Explained*, his discussion of mental images, itself a step in his development of a phenomenology, is taken from robotics – the development of the Shakey robot at the Stanford Research Institute in the 1960s: the problem Shakey solved was the recognition of blocks of different shapes (see Dennett, 1991, pp. 85–95). Second, his overall argument or construction is built like an engineering project, taking small, narrative, steps towards an overall conclusion. In a sense, to see his overall style of writing as 'engineering' is a defence from attacks like those of Searle in *The Mystery of Consciousness* where Searle accuses him of writing in bad faith with a dishonest style. One critic of Dennett describes his *Consciousness Explained* as a 'collage' and the style of taking 'small steps' as the rhetorical trick of the 'Slippery Slope' (Vorhees, pp. 54, 55). But this is to fail to see how his philosophy is not a collage, but a carefully constructed engineering project. Indeed, accounts of the mind like Dennett's have been described as 'reverse bio-engineering' (Harnad, p. 195).

But, of course, this engineering metaphor, this version of 'what philosophy is', is not a neutral one. Despite Dennett's claims that he is avoiding the 'rarefied atmosphere' of what Rorty describes as metaphilosophy, Dennett's work, in as much as it is metonymically described as 'engineering', brings in implicitly a range of undisclosed philosophical presuppositions (Dennett, 1993, p. 205).[1] First, to understand philosophy as engineering, as drawing in a range of materials to build, implies that it is systematic: that it is not simply a 'collage' but part of an overall scheme or overarching system. This 'engineering plan' understands the whole world, even the stones the builder rejects, as possible material for its system, and everything is seen in relation to that system: 'once you have explained everything that happens, you've explained everything'; to 'reduce', 'unite' and 'explain'; his slogan 'we want to know why' (Dennett, 1995, p. 22). This belief in systems is part of the analytic tradition. It reveals what I call a metaphysics of comprehension – comprehension both in the sense of understanding and in the sense of grabbing, taking power over – behind Dennett's work. That is, Dennett's metaphysics is thrown into relief by thinkers like Emmanuel Levinas: this sort of comprehension Levinas understands as a 'philosophy of injustice' which works by 'a reduction of the other to the same by interposition of a middle and neutral term' (Levinas, pp. 46, 43). These terms – which include 'Hegel's universal, Durkheim's social . . . Freud's unconscious', Heideggerian 'Being' and, we could add, Dennett's 'Universal Acid' of Darwinism – 'know only themselves', declare themselves self-sufficient and engage with 'nothing of the Other but what is in me' (Levinas, pp. 272, 43). The differences between Levinas's and Derrida's conception of ethics and Dennett's 'engineering' approach is demonstrated most clearly, perhaps, in the closing stages of *Darwin's Dangerous Idea*, where Dennett writes that 'no remotely compelling system of ethics has ever been made *computationally tractable*, even indirectly, for real-world moral problems' (Dennett, 1995, p. 500). Of course, for Levinas and Derrida, this is true, for how could a 'computationally tractable' system, stemming from the machine of Western metaphysics which puts truth first, not ethics, resolve a moral problem? It is precisely the idea of a 'computationally tractable' system that suppresses what Levinas, for example, understands as the ethical: from this point of view, is 'moral problem' – with its tang of a universalizing calculus – even an appropriate term?

Second, the engineering metaphor implies a world which the machine then matches, against which things can be verified. This seems to suggest that the claim that Dennett is a verificiationist has some accuracy. His work relies on metaphysical *a priori* truths about the world. For example, he writes that we 'would not be surprised to find that [aliens] . . . understood and used the same arithmetic that we do. Why not? Because arithmetic is *right*' (Dennett, 1995, p. 129). He goes on: the 'point is not restricted to arithmetic, but to all "necessary truths" – what philosophers since Plato have called *a priori* knowledge' (Dennett, 1995, p. 130).[2] Engineering implies a form of empiricism, itself a philosophical, metaphysical gesture, and his 'ground level engineering moves' rely on this assumption.

Third, as Dennett proclaims, this understanding of what philosophy is gives the impression that his work can avoid metaphysics and what he might see as the other trappings of philosophy: it is a sleight of hand and many critiques of this sort of argument have been made (most tellingly, perhaps, by Peter Winch's critique 'extra-scientific pretensions of science') (Winch, p. 2). One example is that, even though Dennett denies a teleology, his work is teleological: 'reverse bio-engineering' demands that we – the 'human' – are the telos that has arrived to be 'reverse engineered'.[3] All his attempts to show that humans and consciousness are not special, above being a fantastic piece of engineering, show precisely that we are special, as 'we' remain the horizon for his inquiry.[4]

Fourth, understanding philosophy as engineering makes the medium, language, invisible. This is not to say that Dennett is unaware of the difficulties of language. He spends much time, for example, clarifying 'metaphorical mistakes'. For example, he spends six pages clarifying the metaphor of the 'tree of life' to show that a living human is not 'higher on the evolutionary scale' than a living amoebae – more complex, perhaps, but, since each has been evolving for the same length of time, the height/depth metaphor is misleading (Dennett, 1995, pp. 85–91). However, in the very first chapter of his very first book, Dennett tries to bypass the problems of referentiality by suggesting what he calls 'tentative fusion'. There is not time to outline the argument here in detail, but, to summarize, Dennett divides language into two: those sentences that are referential and those that are non-referential. Those that are referential are then 'fused' – or correlated – to conditions in the world. Thus language – or at least language about the physical sciences – is reduced to algebra (see Dennett, 1986, pp. 3–18). And after this, Dennett never seems to worry about language again, except in two places. At the end of *Consciousness Explained* he writes:

> I haven't replaced a metaphorical theory... with a *non*-metaphorical ('literal, scientific') theory. All I have done, really, is to replace one family of metaphors and images with another... It's just a war of metaphors, you say – but metaphors are not 'just' metaphors; metaphors are the tools of thought. No one can think about consciousness without them, so it is important to equip yourself with the best set of tools available. (Dennett, 1991, p. 455)

Challenged by Richard Rorty and Bo Dahlbom over this, Dennett argued that

> I was not trying to say It's All Just Metaphor or anything remotely like that. I was just pointing out that however precise, literal, and non-metaphorical science may be in *some* of its accounts, it is never free of metaphors; some are good, some bad, and all are potent. I was proposing to replace some of the bad ones with some better ones. (Dennett, 1993, p. 204)

However, of course, the tools you use determine what you aim to do and what you are able to do. If you think you are doing engineering, engineering is probably what you will do: the metaphor and the method it inspires determines the output. In *Allegories of Reading*, Paul de Man writes of rhetoric which

> functions as a key to the discovery of the self, and it functions with such ease that one may well begin to wonder whether the lock indeed shapes

the key or whether it is not the other way around, that a lock (and a secret room or box behind it) had to be invented in order to give a function to the key. For what could be more distressing than a bunch of highly refined keys just lying around without any corresponding locks worthy of being opened? (de Man, p. 173)

Dennett has utilized a constructive and fertile way to do philosophy – as engineering – and is so carried away by its metaphorical strength – its *meta-ferocity* – that he forgets that it is only a metaphor.[5] 'Bending thought round to look critically at itself', as Mary Midgley writes with a very English litotes, 'is quite hard' (Midgley, 1996, p. 2). And it is to Midgley I now turn.

Mary Midgley asks: 'Is philosophy like plumbing?' (Midgley, 1996, p. 1). 'Both activities' she goes on 'arise because elaborate cultures like ours have, beneath their surface, a fairly complex system which is usually unnoticed, but which sometimes goes wrong' (Midgley, 1996, p. 1). Not only is this metaphor 'familiar and domestic' – which itself perhaps implies a critique of the more grandiose and gendered assumptions behind much philo-sophy – but also highlights, according to Midgley, our need for philosophy, because 'when the concepts we are living by work badly, they don't usually drip audibly through the ceiling or swamp the kitchen floor. They just quietly distort and obstruct our thinking' (Midgley, 1996, pp. 1–2). Much of Midgley's work is of this sort: patiently clarifying and 'explaining away' seeming problems and overstatements. For example, in *Evolution as a Religion: Strange Hopes and Stranger Fears* she discusses 'doctrines which are believed to be scientific, but are not actually so, and whose persuasiveness seems to be due to their serving some of the functions of a religion, even though they are seen by their promoters as being hostile to "religion" as such' (Midgley, 1985, p. 13).

Of course, this innovative metaphor and her work in general picks up on an analytic tradition that explains the aim of philosophy: 'to shew the fly the way out of the fly bottle' (Wittgenstein, §309). However, there is a key omission in Midgley's plumbing metaphor, which is very revealing. In his declarations of the point of philosophy, Wittgenstein makes clear the significance of language: 'Philosophy is a battle against the bewitchment of our intelligence by means of language' (Wittgenstein, §109).[6] Midgley's metaphor for what she does passes over this, or rather, does not suggest language is at the core: instead, she offers rather a more amorphous idea of 'concepts' but without the crucial rider, for analytic philosophy, that concepts are in language.[7] In turn, this suggestion reveals a much wider divergence between her work and analytic philosophy. Michael Dummett writes:

analytical philosophy is post-Fregean philosophy . . . Only with Frege was the proper object of philosophy finally established: namely, that the goal

of philosophy is the analysis of the structure of *thought*; secondly, that
the study of *thought* is to be sharply distinguished from the study of
the psychological process of *thinking*; and, finally, that the only proper
method for analysing thought consists in the analysis of *language*... the
acceptance of these three tenets is common to the entire analytical school.
(Dummett, pp. 441, 458)

Midgley decisively resists this for at least two reasons. First, she suspects
that the 'post-Fregean' debates have run aground, since the logic it demands
limits intellectual creativity and fails to clarify any specially important new
vision: 'Philosophy becomes scholastic, a specialized concern for skilled
plumbers doing fine plumbing, and sometimes doing it on their own in
laboratories... it has happened to Anglo-American philosophy during much
of this century' (Midgley, 1996, p. 3). Second, she is opposed to overarching
theories:

the strong unifying tendency that is natural to our thought keeps making
us hope that we have found a single pattern which is a Theory of
Everything – a key to all the mysteries, the secret of the universe... A
long series of failures has shown that this can't work. That realization
seems to be the sensible element at the core of the conceptual muddle
now known as Postmodernism. (Midgley, 1996, pp. 10–11)

Like Nietzsche, and unlike post-Fregean philosophy according, at least, to
Dummett, Midgley 'mistrusts all systematizers'.[8] More than her distaste for
contemporary scholasticism resulting from the decay of analytical philosophy, it is this system-mistrusting 'plumbing' – an English cousin to Continental *bricolage* – that means Midgley's work forms an interesting 'border
crossing' between the analytic and the European traditions.[9] Indeed, her
insistence on self-knowledge – or attempts at it and its difficulties – can be
read to sound like a 'common sense' version of one of Derrida's metaphors
for philosophy.[10]

The photographer Steve Pyke took portraits of a number of major philosophers and asked each one to define, in a hundred words, their understanding of what philosophy was. Derrida's response was aphoristic: 'The
philosopher should start by meditating on photography, that is to say the
writing of light before setting out towards a reflection on an impossible self-
portrait' (Pyke, no page). This metaphoric interweaving between philosophy
and photography gestures towards an array of implicit ideas, familiar from
Derrida's work.

The aphorism suggests that philosophy occurs only in a context (thus
the comparison with photography in a book of photographs): this puts
into question the idea of a universal explanatory system, as contexts are
limitless. Derrida's response is congruent with his well-known position that

deconstruction (Derrida's 'philosophy', at least, in the context of this book of photographs) is not a method, that it reads each text or situation as a singularity. The aphorism also shows that thinking is bound in with the metaphorical nature of language, that, as in much philosophy, it is involved with ideas about light ('photologocentrism'?).[11] It rejects systematic thought in its concern to be an 'impossible self portrait'. These reflections – combined with an explicit turn to ethics in the later work of Derrida and in continental philosophy as a whole – lead to a different approach to the metaphysics of comprehension. Where Dennett offers a grasping of everything with his machine of thought, Derrida, no less rigorous, and also using a technology metaphor, shows how philosophy can only fail to grasp, or can only grasp in a certain way.

Each of these three usages of metaphor, then, commits the thinker to an array of other beliefs and commitments, not least to ideas about how and why metaphors should function. Yet, this is not to say that these works of philosophy are 'only metaphorical', nor to say that by analysing the rhetoric the 'core' of each thinker is uncovered. It is to say that these different forms of metaphor work – 'metaphorize', perhaps? – in different ways. In his recent book, *The Singularity of Literature*, Derek Attridge argues that in literature, the 'words mean, and at the same time they show us what it is to mean': metaphor becomes literary when it 'involves the performance of metaphoricity' (Attridge, 109, p. 96). In these cases, the texts are not, or not only, using metaphors to mean and to resound in their metaphoricity, but are using, implicitly or explicitly, the metaphors to do philosophical work: that is, they have meaning and resound, but they also do something more. This is a philosophical use of metaphor, perhaps, and perhaps we might want to reconsider something that we may have taken for granted: that between 'passing through' language to meaning and reading the language of philosophy, there is, as it were – one step beyond simple meaning, one step to the side of the literary – a form of philosophical writing that is only barely beginning to be understood.

Notes

1. For Rorty's discussion, see his 'Holism, Intrinsicality, and the Ambition of Transcendence', in *Dennett and his Critics*, pp. 184–202.
2. Interestingly, this certitude, combined with his awe at the world, qualifies him for two of Midgley's three criteria of 'religious belief'. See Midgley (1985).
3. For another, more flagrant example of this 'backwards looking teleology', see Steven Mithen's *The Prehistory of the Mind: A Search for the Origins of Art, Religion and Science*.
4. Compare Nietzsche, 1986, pp. 12–13: 'All philosophers have the common failing of starting out from man as he is now and thinking they can reach their goal through an analysis of him. They involuntarily think of "man" as an *aeterna veritas*, as something that remains constant in the midst of all flux, as a

sure measure of things. Everything the philosopher has declared about man is, however, at bottom no more than a testimony as to the man of a limited period of time. Lack of historical sense is the family failing of all philosophers.' Compare also Harris (1997).

5. This also explains his attacks on French 'deliberate obscurantism' and on Wittgenstein: 'Wittgenstein famously stressed that in philosophy the process . . . is more important than the product . . . Though this is hotly (and correctly, in my opinion) disputed by many philosophers who aspire to solve real problems – and not just indulge in a sort of interminable logotherapy' (Dennett, 1995, p. 141).

6. See also, intra alia, '[T]he results of philosophy are the uncovering of one or another piece of plain nonsense and of bumps that the understanding has got by running its head up against the limits of language' (Wittgenstein, §119).

7. Dummett writes, summarizing Wittgenstein, 'to possess a concept is to be the master of a certain fragment of language' (Dummett, p. 438).

8. 'I mistrust all systematizers and avoid them. The will to a system is a lack of integrity' (Nietzsche, 1968, p. 25). In answer to his question, 'Can Analytical Philosophy be Systematic, and Ought it to be?', Dummett answers 'yes' and 'yes'. See Dummett, pp. 437–58.

9. Other interesting cases here might be the work of Alastair MacIntyre – a UK philosopher who is not 'post-Fregean' – and of Isaiah Berlin – who left 'philosophy' for 'the History of Ideas'.

10. See, for one example of this from many, Mary Midgley, 'Being Scientific about Our Selves', where she analyses the words 'scientific' and 'self knowledge'.

11. On this, see also Cathryn Vasseleu, *Textures of Light: Vision and Touch in Irigaray, Levinas and Merleau-Ponty* and Martin Jay, *Downcast Eyes: The Denigration of Vision in Twentieth Century French Thought.*

Works cited

Attridge, Derek, *The Singularity of Literature* (London: Routledge, 2004).
Dahlbom, Bo (ed.), *Dennett and His Critics: Demystifying Mind* (Oxford: Blackwell, 1993).
Davidson, Donald, 'Reality without Reference', in *Inquiries into Truth and Interpretation* (Oxford: Oxford University Press, 2001).
de Man, Paul, *Allegories of Reading: Figural Language in Rousseau, Nietzsche, Rilke, and Proust* (London: Yale University Press, 1979).
Dennett, Daniel, *Content and Consciousness* (2nd ed. London: Routledge, 1986).
——*Consciousness Explained* (London: Penguin, 1991).
—— 'Back from the Drawing Board', in *Dennett and His Critics: Demystifying Mind*, ed. Bo Dahlbom (Oxford: Blackwell, 1993).
——*Darwin's Dangerous Idea: Evolution and the Meanings of Life* (London: Penguin, 1995).
Derrida, Jacques, 'White Mythology: Metaphor in the text of Philosophy', *New Literary History*, 6 (1974), 8–74.
Dummett, Michael, *Truth and Other Enigmas* (London: Duckworth, 1978).
Harnad, Steven, 'Why and How We Are Not Zombies', *Journal of Consciousness Studies*, 1, 2 (1994), 195.
Harris, Roger, 'Social Darwinism for Postmodernists', review of Daniel Dennett's *Kinds of Minds*, in *Radical Philosophy*, 86 (1997), 42–6.
Jay, Martin, *Downcast Eyes: The Denigration of Vision in Twentieth Century French Thought* (Berkley: University of California Press, 1993).

Lang, Berel, *The Anatomy of Philosophical Style: Literary Philosophy and the Philosophy of Literature* (Oxford: Basil Blackwell, 1990).

Levinas, Emmanuel, *Totality and Infinity: An Essay on Exteriority*, trans. Alphonso Lingis (Pittsburgh: Duquesne University Press, 1969).

Midgley, Mary, *Evolution as a Religion: Strange Hopes and Stranger Fears* (London: Methuen, 1985).

——*Utopias, Dolphins and Computers: Problems of Philosophical Plumbing* (London: Routledge, 1996).

—— 'Being Scientific about Our Selves', *Journal of Consciousness Studies*, 6, 4 (1999), 85–98.

Mithen, Steven, *The Prehistory of the Mind: A Search for the Origins of Art, Religion and Science* (London: Phoenix, 1998).

Nietzsche, Friedrich, *Twilight of the Idols and The Anti Christ*, trans R.J. Hollingdale (London: Penguin, 1968).

——*Human, All too Human*, trans. R.J. Hollingdale (Cambridge: Cambridge University Press, 1986).

Pyke, Steve, *Philosophers* (Manchester: Cornerhouse Press, 1993).

Searle, John R., *The Mystery of Consciousness* (London: Granta, 1997).

Vasseleu, Cathryn, *Textures of Light: Vision and Touch in Irigaray, Levinas and Merleau-Ponty* (London: Routledge, 1998).

Voorhees, Burton, 'Dennett and the Deep Blue Sea', *Journal of Consciousness Studies*, Vol. 7, No. 3 (2000), 53–69.

Wheeler, Samuel C., *Deconstruction as Analytic Philosophy* (Stanford: Stanford University Press, 2000).

Winch, Peter, *The Idea of a Social Science, and Its Relation to Philosophy* (2nd ed., London: Routledge, 1991).

Wittgenstein, Ludwig, *Philosophical Investigations*, trans. G.E.M. Anscombe (2nd ed., Oxford: Blackwell, 1958).

15
Hearing Voices: A Dialogical Reading of Wittgenstein's *Philosophical Investigations*

David Rudrum

T.S. Eliot's early drafts of his poetic masterpiece *The Waste Land* famously used an offbeat line from Dickens as a rather cryptic working title: 'He Do the Police in Different Voices'. These words might serve equally well – perhaps, indeed, rather better – as a title to a philosophical masterpiece by one of Eliot's contemporaries: Ludwig Wittgenstein's *Philosophical Investigations*. At some points in *Philosophical Investigations*, Wittgenstein shamelessly violates the rules of ordinary language – only to be stopped and cautioned by another voice, which goes on to spell the rules out. At other times, he gets lost and asks for directions – whereupon a different voice emerges from the text to set him back on track. If the text is loitering, a voice will speak up to move it on; if the text is rushed, a voice will slow it down and pull it over for speeding. The word 'Investigations' in Wittgenstein's title suggests detective work,[1] but in actual fact his philosophical practice has as much in common with an old-fashioned bobby on the beat, walking down the mean streets of linguistic philosophy.[2]

This elaborate metaphor, however, is not the principal reason why I suggest that 'He Do the Police in Different Voices' would be a fitting title, or at any rate a good epigraph, for *Philosophical Investigations*. The main reason is exactly the same as that behind Eliot's original choice of the phrase: like *The Waste Land*, Wittgenstein's text is an intricate entanglement of many different voices, each of which speaks in an idiom replete with allusions, references, paraphrases, and quotations, all taken from the widest array of sources both ancient and modern, Christian and pagan, identifiable and obscure. The result, in both these works, is an intertextual morass that juxtaposes passages of aphoristic clarity with passages that are impenetrably baffling. Such texts inevitably invite endless exegesis, and it may seem natural for the baffled reader to resort to that perennial question of literary analysis, '*Qui parle?*' For example, in my experience of teaching *The Waste Land*, undergraduate students will typically assume that their essays will arrive at the bedrock of 'what Eliot meant' if only they could succeed in identifying who says what, where each of his indistinct voices begins and ends, and then in unpacking all of his manifold allusions. If this assumption seems naïve, it is perhaps no more so than the belief – still held by some of the most distinguished of analytic philosophers – that at the heart of Wittgenstein's text lies an inviolable kernel, a 'message' or 'doctrine' ('what Wittgenstein meant') that is independent of and separable from the different voices that make up his way of practising philosophy. In what follows, I want to argue that Wittgenstein takes his *Philosophical Investigations* far beyond the traditional genre of the philosophical dialogue, into a new form of philosophizing where the articulation of thought is a necessarily dialogical, interactive process.

That *Philosophical Investigations* bears more than a passing family resemblance to the ancient genre of philosophical dialogue is a point explored in some detail by Jane Heal:

> It is patent that Wittgenstein does not write dialogue in the sense in which we find it in Plato, Berkeley, Hume etc., i.e. with named characters to whom remarks are assigned, as in a play script. What, however, makes the term seem entirely apt is the strong impression that, from time to time, a voice other than Wittgenstein's speaks, i.e. that some thought other than one endorsed by Wittgenstein himself is being expressed. (Heal, p. 68)

Heal goes on to ground this impression in close reading of extracts from the *Investigations* that clearly involve exchanges of various kinds with some sort of interlocutor (e.g. §146–7, 208–11, 258).[3] Moreover, she demonstrates that 'in the course of the dialogue many different kinds of speech acts occur, among them assertions, objections, protests, questions, avowals etc.' (Heal, p. 73). It is clear from her analyses that a form of dialogue with an interlocutor takes place in *Philosophical Investigations*, that it is a richly complex interaction, and that Wittgenstein's interlocutor is not easily pinned down.

For many philosophers, this feature of Wittgenstein's prose has raised the obvious question: to whom is he talking? Who is this mysterious 'other' whom Wittgenstein addresses sometimes as 'you', sometimes as the other half of a 'we' or 'us', sometimes more vaguely as 'one', and sometimes more indirectly still? Since the *Investigations* often proceeds by interrogating this 'other', eliciting suggestions from it, and then criticizing these suggestions in order to formulate ways of moving on, one's reading of the text would presumably gain a great deal if one could identify the person with whom Wittgenstein is conversing, and, hence, the philosophical position he is addressing in his formulations. Those who investigate the *Investigations* in this way have rounded up several of the usual suspects, but two candidates in particular have attracted their scrutiny: the first is St Augustine (or, more precisely, the Augustine who gives us 'a particular picture of the essence of human language' [Wittgenstein, §1]); the second is Wittgenstein himself (or, more precisely, the Wittgenstein that wrote the *Tractatus Logico-Philosophicus*).

There is indeed much that recommends each of these candidates. In the first instance, it is Augustine's voice that we encounter at the very beginning of the *Investigations* – not Wittgenstein's. Augustine sets out a picture of language (and, by implication, of its relation to the world and the self) that Wittgenstein goes on to explore, to interrogate, and to criticize. Why, then, should we not read Wittgenstein as responding to Augustine? On the other hand, though, Wittgenstein frequently cites the *Tractatus* and engages with it – almost as often as Augustine's *Confessions* – and had originally planned to 'publish those old thoughts and the new ones together: . . . the latter could be seen in the right light only by contrast with and against the background of my old way of thinking' (Wittgenstein, p. viii). This points towards a reading of the interlocutor as Wittgenstein's alter ego, a younger version of himself, and towards a reading of his text as a dialogue between his early philosophy and his later philosophy.

Both these interpretations have plausible and attractive aspects. Whilst they may seem incompatible, assigning very different directions to *Philosophical Investigations*, they nevertheless share a common, basic point of agreement: that Wittgenstein is talking to one interlocutor; that this interlocutor holds one specific set of philosophical views and beliefs; and that both the interlocutor and his/her philosophical position can be clearly identified. This assumption that pinning down Wittgenstein's interlocutor, by assigning him/her an identity and a philosophical position, will in some way help explicate his text is an entirely reasonable one – much like wanting to know which author Eliot is referencing at a given line in *The Waste Land*. But it has its limits. For one thing, it assumes that the interlocutor's philosophical position is fixed, a given, or, as it were, a 'readymade'. If this were indeed the case, then why is there any need for dialogue here at all? Why create the voice of an 'other' and engage with it, instead of producing conventional philosophical forms like exposition, exegesis, and critique followed by alternative formulations? As Heal has it:

> Why did he not write such things as 'In my first chapter I shall set out what I call "the Augustinian view of language" – a view which we found powerfully attractive but which, I shall argue . . . The third chapter tackles what may be labelled "the private language argument" (hereafter PLA) and it applies the conclusions of the earlier chapters to the special case of . . . ' and so forth. What would have been distorted or gone missing if he had proceeded thus? (Heal, p. 73)

So, as in a text like *The Waste Land*, identifying the different voices merely raises questions of its own, and does nothing to address the burning question asked by so many philosophers, including Heal and Stanley Cavell: 'Why does he write that way?' (Cavell, p. 70).

To answer this question, I want to consider two further suggestions – by Cavell and Heal, respectively – as to the identity of the interlocutor. In 'The Availability of Wittgenstein's Later Philosophy', Cavell suggests that 'The voice of temptation and the voice of correctness are the antagonists in Wittgenstein's dialogues' (Cavell, p. 71), because, as in the genre of confession, the voices in dialogue express an impulse towards self-scrutiny, working through problems towards a therapeutic resolution. However, this description is resisted by Austin E. Quigley, because 'it would be more accurate to call the second voice the voice of correction' (Quigley, p. 6). That is, rather than a critique *of* a fixed philosophical position *from* a fixed philosophical position, the altercations in Wittgenstein's text are part and parcel of its philosophical labour, a style of thinking which emphasizes the *process* of philosophizing rather than the *product*, i.e., a fixed philosophical position. For Quigley (and presumably for Cavell), dialogue is essential to *Philosophical Investigations* because it involves 'less a philosophy, or a theory, or a position, than a technique of philosophizing, theorizing, positioning – a technique . . . that we are invited not just to learn, but to develop' (Quigley, p. 11). In a sense, dialogue is what enables *Philosophical Investigations* to 'do' what it is 'about'.

This sense of the importance of interactivity in Wittgenstein's dialogue is shared in Heal's suggestion of the interlocutor's identity, though it is a rather simpler and more direct suggestion:

> But who is Wittgenstein's interlocutor? Clearly it is whoever is addressed as 'you' and is the other part of the 'we'. And who is that? . . . [A]s suggested precisely by the use of the words 'you' and 'we' . . . the part of 'you' is played by whoever is reading the *Investigations*. Thus 'you' is me, *if* I find myself nodding when 'you' speaks and *if* I am willing to be counted a part of the 'we' invoked by Wittgenstein. And it is you, if you are similarly willing to join in. (Heal, pp. 72–3)

The simplicity of this suggestion is appealing. It chimes closely with Cavell's description of the self-scrutiny that Wittgenstein's dialogue entails. What both suggestions emphasize is the significance of the interactive dimension of Wittgenstein's text: it involves a form of negotiation, a productive, even creative engagement with another perspective rather than a simple confrontation between two opposed views, and it is this process, more than the content, that invites the reader to reflect on Wittgenstein's formulations as they are being formulated. This is why *Philosophical Investigations* is not reducible to the formulaic genre of philosophical dialogue practised by philosophers from Plato to Hume.

Yet Cavell's and Heal's readings share a weakness with all attempts to pin down Wittgenstein's interlocutor: plausible as these suggestions may seem, in Quigley's phrase, 'they by no means exhaust the voices of the text' (Quigley, p. 26). The assumption that *Philosophical Investigations* is a dialogue between two voices – and, with it, all the discussions about 'Wittgenstein's interlocutor' that are derived from this assumption – is based, I contend, on a simplified reading of the textual practice involved here. When we ask who Wittgenstein is talking to, we should not overlook the possibility that the dialogue practised in *Philosophical Investigations* involves more than just two voices, and that the voices involved in his philosophizing are plural, protean, and unfixed. He do linguistic philosophy in different voices.

As an example of this, consider this short excerpt from *Philosophical Investigations*:

> §253 'Another person can't have my pains.' – Which are *my* pains? What counts as a criterion of identity here? Consider what makes it possible in the case of physical objects to speak of 'two exactly the same', for example, to say 'This chair is not the one you saw here yesterday, but is exactly the same as it'.

How many voices are talking here? There is an assertion, then two questions, then a suggested analogy. Both the typography and the content seem to suggest that the assertion 'Another person can't have my pains' is made by a voice distinct from the rest of the passage, one that does not speak again in this excerpt. I take it, then, that the two questions are asked by a different voice from that which makes the assertion. But who suggests the analogy? Is this voice the same one that asks the questions? The tone is less radical, the style is less interrogative, and the content is less antifoundational and destabilizing. If the previous question – 'What counts as a criterion of identity here?' – is a genuine one (and it does indeed appear to be) then this suggestion answers it. It is possible, as Heal suggests, that Wittgenstein asks himself questions, and answers them (Heal, pp. 68–70). But it is also possible, and I maintain more likely, that a third voice is in play here. First we have the voice of someone trapped within a particular picture who articulates it; then we have a more radical, aporetic, proto-deconstructive voice interrogating the picture; then we have a voice seeking to point towards a way out of it. Such voices – and many others – resound throughout *Philosophical Investigations*. Is it possible to say for sure which of them is Wittgenstein's?

So, *qui parle*? It is all too easy to associate the third voice, the voice that seeks to dissolve constricting pictures and resolve troublesome questions, with Wittgenstein himself, in line with his approach to philosophy as a therapy that can 'shew the fly out of the fly-bottle' (Wittgenstein, §309). Note, though, that there are significant occasions when dialogue with the picture-enslaved voice leads the voice we have associated with 'Wittgenstein' not to clarity but to greater confusion:

§304 'But you will surely admit that there is a difference between pain-behaviour accompanied by pain and pain-behaviour without any pain?' – Admit it? What greater difference could there be? – 'And yet you again and again reach the conclusion that the sensation itself is a *nothing*.' – Not at all. It is not a *something*, but not a *nothing* either!

There are also times when this supposedly therapeutic voice opts to patronize and snub the picture-enslaved voice rather than help it:

Yes, but then how can these explanations satisfy us? – Well, your very questions were framed in this language, if there was anything to ask! And your scruples are misunderstandings. (Wittgenstein, §120)

Furthermore, it also responds to the aporetic voice with similar snubs and put-downs:

'But how does he know where and how he is to look up the word "red" and what he is to do with the word "five"?' – Well, I assume that he *acts* as I have described. Explanations come to an end somewhere. (Wittgenstein, §1)

What this suggests is that the voice traditionally associated with Wittgenstein does not always play the role of a patient explicator or therapist seeking to (re)solve his interlocutor's problems. This is not an all-knowing, all-powerful authorial voice. It has its limits, and like any other literary character – for that is what I maintain these voices amount to – it has flaws in its personality. (Much the same, of course, could be said of the impatient, hot-headed, impetuous, aporetic voice, and the slower, confused, exasperated and exasperating picture-enslaved voice.)

That is not to suggest that, instead of a dialogue, as has traditionally been assumed, *Philosophical Investigations* is a trialogue. Rather, there is a *multitude* of voices resounding through this text. Sometimes, we are being addressed by 'Wittgenstein's philosophical straight man' (Staten, p. 126). But sometimes Wittgenstein sets up a fall guy, a 'straw man': 'It is as if someone were to say: "A game consists in moving objects about on a surface according to certain rules . . ." – and we replied: You seem to be thinking of board games, but there are others' (Wittgenstein, §3). Sometimes he creates characters in fictional scenarios and endows them with their own voices and forms of discourse, such as the builders shouting 'block', 'pillar', 'slab', and 'beam' in *Philosophical Investigations* §2, or the shopkeeper and the customer in §1: how these scenarios and voices play out are of paramount importance in shaping his philosophizing. In addition to these characters, the voices of a number of philosophers have their say in the text (Socrates, Augustine, William James, Frank Ramsay, Bertrand Russell, and G.E. Moore). Sometimes they are directly cited ('Augustine says in the *Confessions* "quid est ergo tempus? si nemo ex me quaerat scio; si quaerenti explicare velim, nescio"' [§89]); sometimes loosely paraphrased ('James, in writing of this subject, is really trying to say: "What a remarkable experience! The word is not there yet, and yet in a certain sense is there…"' [Wittgenstein, p. 219]); and sometimes the subject of rather quirky personal anecdote ('F.P. Ramsay once emphasized in conversation with me that logic was a "normative science". I do not know exactly what he had in mind, but it was doubtless closely related to what only dawned on me later…' [§81]). In addition to the voices of these identifiable philosophers, *Philosophical Investigations* is also shot through with voices of other thinkers that are not referenced, directly cited, or even named, yet their influence can be heard in many of the views expressed by other voices in the text: Wittgenstein's personal friends like Piero Sraffa and Nikolai Bakhtin come in here,[4] as well as a number of more canonical figures like Schopenhauer, Nietzsche, or Spengler. On top of all this, there is the more self-referential citation of Wittgenstein himself, especially of his earlier work: 'It is interesting to compare … the multiplicity of kinds of word and sentence, with what logicians have said about the structure of language. (Including the author of the *Tractatus Logico-Philosophicus*)' (§23). Besides the philosophers, writers from Goethe to Lewis Carroll contribute to *Philosophical Investigations*, as do lines from an unidentified 'hard-boiled' novel ('He measured him with a hostile glance and said…' [§652]), snatches of the old song 'Lilliburlero' (§13), the musings of a deaf-mute called Mr Ballard (§342), and even an odd sound bite from a particularly obtuse French politician (§336).

Philosophical Investigations, then, is a tapestry woven together from all of these different strands and sources. We should not assume that they are simply 'thrown in' by Wittgenstein as mere citations or examples: rather, they take on active roles that play a crucial part in shaping his text. Each of them is, in some way, a 'contributor' to the book, a voice that speaks, a presence that makes itself felt. Viewed this way, we should describe *Philosophical Investigations* not as a dialogue, but as a thoroughly dialogical, polyphonic work.

To deploy these terms is to invoke the literary theory, philosophy, and criticism of Mikhail Bakhtin, whose thought has exerted a strong influence on literary studies from the 1980s onwards. Dialogism, according to Bakhtin, is one of the most basic conditions of language: the word spoken in dialogue is as it were turned inside out, orientated by a principle of addressivity towards an other (even if this other is the speaker's own self). On this view, language is necessarily interactive, in negotiation and in struggle with itself, as words run up against the competing forces of (for instance) the voices that speak them, the voices to whom they are spoken, the sources from which they are taken, the readers for whom they are intended, and so forth – each of which can and will exert a shaping force in the coming-into-being of any piece of discourse.[5] This process is fundamentally creative, as the various voices and discourses mutually enrich each other in 'critical interanimation' (Bakhtin, 1981, p. 296). As Bakhtin has it, 'Truth is not born nor is it to be found inside the head of an individual person, it is born *between people* . . . in the process of their dialogic interaction' (Bakhtin, 1984, p. 110). Dialogism, as a property and even a condition of discourse, is thus intimately bound up with what Bakhtin calls polyphony, or multivoicedness. In diagnosing polyphony at work in literature, Bakhtin describes it thus:

> *A plurality of independent and unmerged voices and consciousnesses, a genuine polyphony of fully valid voices* . . . What unfolds . . . is not a multitude of characters and fates in a single objective world, illuminated by a single authorial consciousness; rather a plurality of consciousnesses, with equal rights and each with its own world, combine but are not merged in the unity of the event. (Bakhtin, 1984, p. 6)

Polyphony and dialogism, often present in even the simplest of utterances, open up the text as a site of contestation over meaning, truth, authority, and anything else that might involve a 'last word' on the subject. They offer a way of hearing the plurality and the dynamism that are the life-blood of discourse (and I would suggest, as an aside, that Wittgenstein's philosophy offers another).

Bakhtinian analysis has, over the years, revealed the huge extent to which dialogism and polyphony subsist in both literary and everyday language. Indeed, the academic market was no doubt saturated with Bakhtinian readings of literary texts some time ago. So far as I am aware, however, there have been few attempts to apply it to philosophical discourse. In the case of Wittgenstein's *Philosophical Investigations*, there is good reason to do so. Like the polyphonic texts Bakhtin describes, this text is 'a whole formed by the interaction of several consciousnesses, none of which entirely becomes an object for the other; this interaction provides no support for the viewer who would objectify an entire event according to some ordinary mono-logic category . . . – and this consequently makes the viewer a participant' (Bakhtin, 1984, p. 18). Furthermore, the following characterization of the dialogical text also applies equally to Wittgenstein's philosophical dialogue: 'The entire work [is] constructed . . . as a great dialogue, but one where the author acts as organizer and participant in the dialogue without retaining for himself the final word; . . . reflected in his work [is] the dialogic nature of human life and human thought itself' (Bakhtin, 1984, pp. 72–3). Lastly, in *Philosophical Investigations*, as in the clearest articulations of dialogized, poly-phonic discourse, the interaction that generates the text is not something that is experienced as finalized and complete, but as an ongoing, unfolding event that we enter into:

> the 'great dialogue' . . . as a whole . . . takes place not in the past, but right now, that is, in the *real present* of the creative process. This is no stenographer's report of a *finished* dialogue, from which the author has already withdrawn and *over* which he is now located as if in some higher decision-making position: that would have turned an authentic and unfinished dialogue into an objectivized and finalized *image of a dialogue* . . . The great dialogue . . . is organized as an *unclosed whole* of life itself, life poised *on the threshold*. (Bakhtin, 1984, p. 63)

Viewed this way, the multitude of different voices and sources that make up *Philosophical Investigations* are not just a diverting feature of Wittgenstein's style – they are the driving force of his philosophy. The disputes, negotiations, and conflicts they enter into with one another are not ultimately subjected to any overarching unity, nor reduced to one final, 'correct' position. This is what makes *Philosophical Investigations* a veritably 'Bakhtopian' text.

Consider the following extract from Wittgenstein:

> §171 I might have used other words to hit off the experience I have when I read a word. Thus I might say that the written word intimates the sound to me. – Or again, that when one reads, letter and sound form a unity – as it were an alloy. . . . When I feel this unity, I might say, I see or hear the sound in the written word. –

> But now just read a few sentences in print as you usually do when you are not thinking about the concept of reading; and ask yourself whether you had such experiences of unity, of being influenced and the rest, as you read. – Don't say you had them unconsciously! Nor should we be misled by the picture which suggests that these phenomena came in sight 'on closer inspection'. If I am supposed to describe how an object looks from far off, I don't make the description more accurate by saying what can be noticed about the object on closer inspection.

At first blush, it appears that Wittgenstein is not actually arguing with *any* voices here: it seems, in line with Heal's reading, that the only person being directly addressed is the reader, who is asked to consider what reading is like as an activity. Perhaps there is an element of dialogism in the direct address of one's words to another, but, on a first reading, the altercations between voices that one finds throughout the *Investigations* do not appear to take place here.

A closer reading of the passage reveals this is a simplification. Wittgenstein begins by suggesting what we *might* say reading involves, and ends by telling us what we must *not* say reading involves. Why does he do this? If we look closer at what Wittgenstein tells us we might or must not do, an answer suggests itself: we *might* say that reading 'intimates' sound (that is, that it is a deeply personal, 'inner' experience); or we *might* say there is a 'unity' between sound and word (that is, that there is some sort of 'super-strong connexion' [Wittgenstein, §197] holding them together by philosophical necessity). We must *not* think of reading involving unconscious processes that are presumably hidden by some psychological phenomenon; nor are we allowed to think of it as something resolvable by looking at it more closely ('nothing is hidden'). It should be clear from this paraphrase that behind these suggestions and prohibitions lie the very views that Wittgenstein's interlocutors repeatedly advocate – the hidden, the inner, the unconscious, the psychological, the deeply metaphysical: all of these are repositories to which the voices of the antagonists in the *Investigations* regularly appeal. Rather than debating with them and inviting rejoinder, Wittgenstein here is launching pre-emptive strikes against his adversaries. As Bakhtin has it:

> The other's rejoinder wedges its way, as it were, into his speech, and although this rejoinder is in fact absent, its influence brings about a radical accentual and syntactic restructuring of that speech. The rejoinder is not actually present, but its shadow, its trace, falls on his speech, and that shadow, that trace is real. (Bakhtin, 1984, p. 208)

Wittgenstein's comments are gestures towards the other voices. The suggestions as to what we *might* say effectively set up his opponents' voices as straw targets which he will go on to demolish, while his prohibitions on what we must *not* say try to stave off potential objections from those same voices. True, there may be no rejoinders in the dialogue here, but the piece is nevertheless thoroughly addressed as much to his opponents as to us (the reader), and is dialogized by the fact of their (absent) presence. Just like the rejoinder itself, it is structured in anticipation of the other's answer, which it seeks to pre-empt. Bakhtin calls this kind of discourse 'hidden polemic':

> the other person's discourse remains outside the limits of the author's speech, but the author takes it into account and refers to it. Another's discourse in this case is not reproduced . . . but it acts upon, influences, and in one way or another determines the author's discourse, while remaining outside it. Such is the nature of discourse in the hidden polemic. . . . In a hidden polemic . . . every statement about the object is constructed in such a way that . . . a polemical blow is struck at the other's discourse on the same theme, at the other's statement about the same object. . . . The other's discourse is not itself reproduced, it is merely implied, but the entire structure of speech would be completely different if there were not this reaction to another person's implied words. . . . In a hidden polemic . . . the other's words are treated antagonistically, and this antagonism, no less than the very topic being discussed,

is what determines the author's discourse. This radically changes the semantics of the discourse involved: alongside its referential meaning there appears a second meaning – an intentional orientation toward someone else's words. (Bakhtin, 1984, pp. 195–6)

What may seem like an invitingly open, direct address to the reader turns out to be the pursuit of dialogue by other means. Similar devices abound throughout the *Investigations* – Wittgenstein frequently gives examples, draws analogies, or paraphrases ideas in terms that make a barbed dig at precisely the kind of thing the voices of his potential interlocutors might say.[6] Such comments are inevitably dialogized – they are addressed in at least two directions at once. To describe this phenomenon, Bakhtin coins the disarmingly apt neologism 'the word with a sideward glance at someone else's hostile word'[7] (Bakhtin, 1984, p. 196).

Another feature of words dialogized by this awareness of the presence of other voices is what Bakhtin calls the 'loophole'. An additional example of the 'word with a sideward glance', the loophole comes into being because one cannot help but try and steer one's words around an anticipated response, even though this response has not yet been (and may never be) spoken. In the case of the hidden polemic, the 'word with a sideward glance' takes on a combative approach towards the anticipated response, but the loophole is just the opposite: it acts as a get-out clause to enable the speaker to retract or modify his words in the event of a hostile reception. 'A loophole is the retention for oneself of the possibility for altering the ultimate, final meaning of one's words' (Bakhtin, 1984, p. 233). Any word spoken with a loophole is not finalized, it remains provisional, and this will 'inevitably be reflected in its structure. . . . Judged by its meaning alone, the word with a loophole should be an ultimate word and does present itself as such, but in fact it is only the penultimate word and places after itself only a conditional, not a final, period' (Bakhtin, 1984, p. 233).

The word with a loophole makes its presence felt throughout Wittgenstein's *Investigations*, owing to the highly dialogical nature of the text. For example, several of the voices, when pressed by others to describe or define some concept or phenomenon, begin with phrases like 'One would like to say . . .', 'I feel like saying . . .', 'We want to say . . .', or such like. After Stanley Cavell, Wittgensteinians have tended to assume that these phrases betoken the voice of temptation, confessing the desires that lure them into philosophical error. Yet on many occasions, these desires turn out to be legitimate, even correct, intuitions. So why the faltering provisionality? I contend that utterances like 'I want to say', 'One feels like saying' and so forth are first and foremost loopholes: they betoken the speaker's awareness that he/she is on unsafe philosophical ground, and that there are hostile voices out there just waiting to latch onto their words and expose them for the linguistic and grammatical illusions they are. Under such disputatious circumstances, one soon becomes hesitant to assert anything at all, let alone something one feels is unsound. So one asserts it provisionally, and uses words like 'We feel like saying...' to retain the possibility of retracting one's ideas if they meet with stiff resistance. Wittgenstein's internally dialogized voices, then, are closely accurate representations – literary representations, in a sense – of the kinds of expression his characters would use, as we all do, to negotiate their way through a prickly polyphonic speech environment.

In the case of the 'word with a sideward glance' – the hidden polemic and the loophole – the presence of another voice makes its dialogizing influence felt from within, rather than from without, as in a regular dialogue between separate voices. Words of this kind belong to a category Bakhtin calls 'double-voiced discourse', which, he says, 'is always internally dialogized' (Bakhtin, 1981, p. 324). Double-voiced discourse is a broad category, including literary techniques such as stylization and confession, as well as parody. According to Bakhtin, in parodic discourse the author 'speaks in someone else's discourse', however 'the voices are not only isolated from one another, separated by a distance, but are also hostilely opposed' (Bakhtin, 1984, p. 193).

Now parody is not, perhaps, a genre one might associate with philosophy, let alone with Wittgenstein. But it is a device by no means alien to the dialogical strategies of *Philosophical Investigations*. Consider this extract:

§297 Of course, if water boils in a pot, steam comes out of the pot, and also pictured steam comes out of the pictured pot. But what if one insisted on saying that there must also be something boiling in the picture of the pot?

On the face of it, it is hard to make out what Wittgenstein is saying here, if anything at all. It is not even clear whether he is asking a genuine or a rhetorical question. Why would he ask such a very strange thing?

Bearing in mind that throughout his *Vermischte Bemerkungen* (and occasionally in *Philosophical Investigations* too), Wittgenstein makes a series of comments exhorting us to pay attention to our nonsense, to enrich our philosophical diet with a sprinkling of silliness, and to see the value of games and jokes, we might do better *not* to take him seriously at moments like this. That is, there is something satirical, even parodic, about the nature of the above question. Who on earth would ever think that there must be something boiling in a picture of a boiling pot? Well, perhaps someone who believed that within a picture of the facts, there lies an internal structure that shares the same logical form as the facts themselves – that the picture and the facts must both correspond to the same underlying logical structure. In other words, someone who believed in the picture theory (*Abbildung*) that Wittgenstein advocated in his *Tractatus*. Read this way, the question becomes a *reductio ad absurdum* of Wittgenstein's earlier thought, a satirical exercise in philosophical parody that is all the more interesting for being a piece of self-parody. Of course, this reading depends on seeing the paragraph as a piece of double-voiced discourse: we have to be able to detect the trace of the voice being parodied (in this case, that of the *Tractatus*) as well as the fact that another voice – presumably endorsed by Wittgenstein – is parodying it, in order to read this as parody. And this is not easy, given that Wittgenstein last referenced the *Tractatus* 183 paragraphs earlier, in *Philosophical Investigations* §114, and does not explicitly do so again in the text. So the parody in this case also involves a 'word with a sideward glance' at another voice that might not be uppermost in the reader's mind. This gives some idea of the extent to which the voices in *Philosophical Investigations* are multilayered, overlapping, intersecting, and mutually critical – some idea, in short, of the extent of its polyphony.

This polyphony is made possible by one further aspect of *Philosophical Investigations* I would like to consider here. It has to do with the way Wittgenstein uses language in his own text, as for example in the following extract:

> §33 . . . But do you always do the *same* thing when you direct your attention to the colour? Imagine various different cases. To indicate a few:
>
> > 'Is this blue the same as the blue over there? Do you see any difference?' –
> > You are mixing paint and you say 'It's hard to get the blue of this sky.'
> > 'It's turning fine, you can already see blue sky again.'
> > 'Look what different effects these two blues have.'
> > 'Do you see that blue book over there? Bring it here.'
> > 'This blue signal-light means . . . .'
> > 'What's this blue called? Is it "indigo"?'

After further discussion of the use of the word 'blue', Wittgenstein asks 'Can I say "bububu" and mean "If it doesn't rain I shall go for a walk"?' (Wittgenstein, p. 18).

Wittgenstein's use of these lively, graphic examples imparts a highly interactive element to *Philosophical Investigations*. Why is it such an effective strategy? What Wittgenstein is doing involves *exhibiting* everyday language. His words therefore have a double aspect: they have their everyday uses, which are crucial, but no less important is their secondary status as philosophical *exempla*. They carry two different forces, yet the one cannot be disassociated from the other. In Bakhtinian terms, what Wittgenstein offers us is 'The image of another's language and outlook on the world, simultaneously represented *and* representing' (Bakhtin, 1981, p. 45). That is, as well as being a means of representation, the words themselves 'have here become the object of representation', so that '[t]hey both illuminate the world and are themselves illuminated' (Bakhtin, 1981, pp. 44–5). Such a strategy, in which language is simultaneously something that represents and something that is represented, involves what Bakhtin calls an 'image of a language'.

Wittgenstein is forever creating images of various languages – the *exempla* from everyday language blend with constructed images of philosophical discourse (and with nonsensical parodies of it), and also mix with examples derived from games, as well as fictitious images of languages based on the bizarre customs of imaginary tribes. At times, we are even asked to imagine what an image of a dog's language might be like. However, it is important to note that these representations of others' languages need not be (and often are not) 'faithful' or 'truthful' representations. Wittgenstein deploys a variety of techniques, ranging from parody and contrastive juxtapositioning to paraphrase or direct citation, when incorporating into *Philosophical Investigations* these images of various other languages (or, better, images of language games). Sometimes (as when setting up his 'fall guy') the technique with which he introduces these images of language games involves manipulating the form each image takes to suit his philosophical purposes:

> Therefore, the author is far from neutral in his relationship to this image: to a certain extent he even polemicizes with this language, argues with it, agrees with it (although with conditions), interrogates it, eavesdrops on it, but also ridicules it, parodically exaggerates it and so forth – in other words, the author is in a dialogical relationship with [this] language; the author is actually *conversing* with [it]. (Bakhtin, 1981, p. 46)

Language therefore works in a multitude of ways throughout *Philosophical Investigations*. How it works at any given point is, as much as anything else, a factor of how many voices are involved, either as interlocutors in a direct dialogue or as presences within an internal dialogue. The superb rigour of the analytic technique with which it formulates its propositions is bound up with the accountability of those propositions to a whole host of different voices within the text – including, of course, the reader's. This is what makes *Philosophical Investigations*, in Marjorie Perloff's apt phrase, 'so interactive a text' (Perloff, p. 66).

I began by highlighting *Philosophical Investigations'* dynamic relationship to a variety of intertexts – ranging from pulp fiction to the church fathers – and to the spectrum of viewpoints it displays, from impatient iconoclasm to stubbornly conservative enthrallment. If we learn to pay attention to these features, and to listen to the clash of voices in *Philosophical Investigations*, it will appear as a very different kind of work: an ever-unfolding, shifting, provisional set of formulations, a technique that involves not statement but negotiation (even confrontation), a dialogue that is unfinished and literally unfinishable. This, in turn, might help us understand the nature of Wittgenstein's fitting claim that 'In philosophy we do not draw conclusions' (Wittgenstein, §599).

Notes

1. For an unlikely comparison between Wittgenstein and Agatha Christie's *Miss Marple*, see Brill, pp. 42–4. For a work of detective fiction that claims a Wittgensteinian influence, see Philip Kerr, *A Philosophical Investigation.*
2. I would not suggest, though, that Wittgenstein's philosophical project can be reduced to this simple role. As Henry Staten observes, 'Wittgenstein is very badly served when he is understood as a policeman who enforces community standards in language use' (Staten, pp. 96–7). Perhaps this is a good example of the dangers of 'metaferocity' in philosophical discourse, as explored in Robert Eaglestone's preceding discussion.
3. Following standard practice, references to Wittgenstein's *Philosophical Investigations* are to the numbered paragraphs, unless otherwise indicated by a page number.
4. For a discussion of these influences, see Eagleton.
5. For the clearest summary of this aspect of Bakhtin's thought, see Bakhtin (1981, p. 276).
6. Wittgenstein even makes digs like these at his own work: 'It is interesting to compare . . . the multiplicity of kinds of word and sentence, with what logicians have said about the structure of language. (Including the author of the *Tractatus Logico-Philosophicus*)' (Wittgenstein, §23).
7. Wittgenstein is well aware of the phenomenon that Bakhtin identifies, and describes it in strikingly similar terms ('a furtive sidelong glance') in *Philosophical Investigations* §690.

Works cited

Bakhtin, Mikhail, *The Dialogic Imagination: Four Essays*, ed. Michael Holquist, trans. Caryl Emerson and Michael Holquist (Austin: University of Texas Press, 1981).

——*Problems of Dostoevsky's Poetics*, ed. & trans. Caryl Emerson, introduction by Wayne C. Booth (Minneapolis: University of Minnesota Press, 1984).

Brill, Susan B., *Wittgenstein and Critical Theory: Beyond Postmodernism and Toward Descriptive Investigations* (Athens: Ohio University Press, 1995).

Cavell, Stanley, 'The Availability of Wittgenstein's Later Philosophy', pp. 44–72 in *Must We Mean What We Say? A Book of Essays* (Updated ed., Cambridge: Cambridge University Press, 2002).

Eagleton, Terry, 'Wittgenstein's Friends', pp. 99–130 in *Against the Grain: Essays 1975–1985* (London: Verso, 1986).

Heal, Jane, 'Wittgenstein and Dialogue', pp. 63–83 in *Philosophical Dialogues: Plato, Hume, Wittgenstein*, ed. Timothy Smiley. *Dawes Hicks Lectures on Philosophy: Proceedings of the British Academy*, 85 (Oxford: Oxford University Press, 1995).

Kerr, Philip, *A Philosophical Investigation* (London: Vintage, 1996).

Perloff, Marjorie, *Wittgenstein's Ladder: Poetic Language and the Strangeness of the Ordinary* (Chicago: University of Chicago Press, 1996).

Quigley, Austin E., 'Wittgenstein's Philosophizing and Literary Theorizing', pp. 3–30 in *Ordinary Language Criticism: Literary Thinking After Cavell After Wittgenstein*, ed. Kenneth Dauber and Walter Jost (Evanston, IL: Northwestern University Press, 2003).

Staten, Henry, *Wittgenstein and Derrida* (Lincoln: University of Nebraska Press, 1984).

Wittgenstein, Ludwig, *Philosophical Investigations*, 2nd ed., trans. G.E.M. Anscombe (Oxford: Blackwell, 1958).

Part VI
Conclusion: Approaching the End

Introduction

By way of a conclusion, the essays in this section address one of the most burning issues confronting the literature–philosophy relationship today: namely, the thesis that art is coming (or has come) to an end. This idea, which has its origins in Hegel's aesthetics, has clear and dramatic consequences for the status of both literature and philosophy, and raises and begs many questions about the study of both. How do we approach the problem of the end of art itself?

It is indicative of the *rapprochement* between philosophy and literature in German thought and culture that many of the greatest philosophers in this tradition have broached this very question. Notoriously, in his *Aesthetics*, Georg Wilhelm Friedrich Hegel (1770–1831) viewed art as in a terminal decline, and foresaw an end to art altogether: the visual and plastic arts, he argued, were no longer adequate to embody the Idealistic nature of the truths they attempted to represent. Yet, crucially, Hegel's position negotiates a partial exemption clause for literature: unlike the fine arts, literature shares with philosophy the medium of language which, reasoned Hegel, was ultimately the only vehicle for expressing truth in the post-Classical world. Since Hegelian aesthetics has influenced the broadest possible spectrum of critical thought – from Marxism to deconstruction, from phenomenology to postmodernism – it has formed an important source of the growing rapport between literature and philosophy. Stephen Bungay's *Beauty and Truth: A Study of Hegel's Aesthetics* (Oxford: Oxford University Press, 1986) is an excellent reading of Hegel's position. Another discussion is Anne and Henry Paolucci's *Hegelian Literary Perspectives* (Smyrna: Griffon House, 2002), though its focus is confined mostly to dramatic literature.

Writing in the Marxist tradition, and with a strong Hegelian influence, Theodor Adorno (1903–69) is similarly pessimistic about the fate of art under the conditions of capitalism. Art, for Adorno, finds its autonomy under constant threat, and has become an alienating rather than an integrating experience. Modern art, in particular, with its rupture from tradition, its fragmentary forms, and its emptiness of content, reflects this situation. As regards literature, Adorno's oft-cited remark about the barbarity of writing poetry after Auschwitz summarizes his view that traditional aesthetic notions like beauty have reached their end in the contemporary world. Adorno's writings on literary themes, *Notes to Literature* (2 vols, ed. Rolf Tiedemann, trans. Shierry Weber Nicholsen. New York: Columbia University Press, 1991), are well worth reading, but are best understood in conjunction with his philosophical works. Useful discussions of the place of literature in Adorno's thought include Chapter Five of Simon Jarvis's *Adorno: A Critical Introduction* (Cambridge: Polity, 1998) and Chapter Two of Shierry Weber Nicholsen's *Exact Imagination, Late Work: On Adorno's Aesthetics* (Cambridge, MA: MIT Press, 1997).

The essays in this section grapple with the question of what happens after the end of art, and what the implications of this end might be for both philosophy and literature. Josh Cohen's essay draws on a variety of thinkers who follow Hegel in describing the contemporary artwork as a null, empty, self-negating entity. It explores the idea that art is fundamentally a vestige, an essentially negative gesture that lacks any substance or content. Simon Malpas's essay debates how both philosophical aesthetics and literary criticism might equip themselves to cope with the 'end of art', whether as a concept or as a phenomenon. Drawing more heavily on Adorno and the legacy of Romanticism, it seeks to re-evaluate and reappraise the status of the aesthetic for a climate that no longer recognizes the concepts on which our traditional ideas of aesthetics were founded.

A great deal of both philosophical and critical literature has been dedicated to the contemplation of this topic. Arthur C. Danto, one of the most influential voices in the philosophy/literature dialogue, has considered the theme in his *After the End of Art: Contemporary Art and the Pale of History* (Princeton, NJ: Princeton University Press, 1997). His position is discussed in *The End of Art and Beyond: Essays after Danto*, ed. Arto Haapala, Jerrold Levinson, and Veikko Rantala (Amherst, NY: Humanity Books, 1999).

David Rudrum

16
No Matter: Aesthetic Theory and the Self-annihilating Artwork

Josh Cohen

Introduction

To begin with, two artworks, one visual, one literary. (We may observe in passing the predicament of 'beginning with two' intimated by Jean-Luc Nancy: I am about to suggest that each text can be read as an attempt to present its own essence, that is art 'as such'; yet in the attempt to present itself 'as such', 'art' immediately finds itself consigned to its own ineluctable plurality [visual, literary, musical], that is to 'arts'.)[1]

The first is the winner of the 2001 Turner Prize, now difficult to dissociate from the ritual accompaniment of media-generated scandal and derision. The prize went to Martin Creed for a series of installations, the most notorious of which was 'Work 127: Lights Going On and Off'. As the title baldly indicates, the work consisted of a large and empty gallery in the Tate Modern building in which the lights were switched on and off at programmed intervals.

The second is in fact two stories from a collection by the American writer Lydia Davis, best known in literary and aesthetic theory circles as a translator of Blanchot (and others). In the first, she describes a 'thirteenth woman' who lived in 'a town of twelve women' (Davis, 2001a, p. 14). The woman, like the God of negative theology, is defined only via a series of negations:

> No one admitted she lived there, no mail came for her, no one spoke of her, no one asked after her, no one sold bread to her, no one bought anything from her, no one returned her glance, no one knocked on her door; (Davis, 2001a, p. 14)

And yet the woman continues living in the town in spite of the non-existence to which it consigns her, 'without resenting what it did to her'. In the second, the narrator describes (and therefore writes) a story which appears to be nothing more than the search for its own center. If we were to seek to distinguish this story from a large number of postmodernist counterparts, we might point to the unexpected if tentative 'success' of this search (as opposed to the 'failure' which would typically attend the postmodernist quest for the center). There may be no center, writes the anonymous narrator: 'Or – which is or is not the same thing – there is a center but the center is empty' (Davis, 2001b, p. 39).

These pieces by Creed and Davis, for all their differences of form and register, seem to beg the same question: what are they asking us to see? In the absence of a determinate object, does Work 127 ask us to see light itself, that is, art's very medium of transmission? Or a darkness anterior to light? Or, as the title suggests, the alternation of the two? What is signified by the titles of Davis's stories, given that in both cases they signal someone or something whose existence is voided by the stories themselves? In sum, the paradox is this: nothing is shown by these artworks, and yet they do not show us nothing.

The self-annihilating artwork

In beginning to come to grips with this paradox, we could do worse than remind ourselves once more that Davis is a translator of Blanchot. For Blanchot explicitly inaugurates a tendency in contemporary aesthetic theory which, reductively, is nothing more than the insistently repeated unfolding of this paradox. My intention here however is to approach Blanchot circuitously (is there another way to approach Blanchot?), via Giorgio Agamben's trenchant reading of modern aesthetics, *The Man Without Content* (Agamben, 1999). Agamben's book provides the most explicit genealogy for the self-annulling trajectory of art and aesthetic theory enacted by the artworks in question. Beginning from Kant's third *Critique*, Agamben's text shows how the negativity of Kant's criteria for the judgment of the beautiful – disinterestedness, representation outside of concepts, purposelessness and cognition outside of concepts – by depriving art of a positive content, consigns it to a state of nothingness or non-art: 'every time aesthetic judgment attempts to determine what the beautiful is, it holds in its hands not the beautiful but its shadow, as though its true object were not so much what art is but what it is not: not art but non-art' (Agamben, 1999, p. 42).

It is not, of course, that the Kantian aesthetic judgment does not determine particular objects as beautiful, but that in so doing it points to nothing that is *present* in the object or indeed its judge. An artwork earns the title of the beautiful when determined by no subjective interest, rule of representation, teleological purpose or cognitive concept. Under Kant's gaze, art's proper content – the beautiful – becomes a non-content:

> aesthetic judgment confronts us with the embarrassing paradox of an instrument that is indispensable to us in knowing the work of art, but

that not only does not allow us to penetrate its reality but also at the same time points us toward something other than art and represents art's reality to us as pure and simple nothingness. (Agamben, 1999, p. 43).

Hegel's proclamation of the 'end of art' ('art is a thing of the past') at the outset of the *Lectures on Aesthetics* can be understood as the attempt to diagnose and critique this voided content of art. Hegel attributes the nothingness of the Kantian aesthetic to the modern split between artistic subjectivity and the material it works upon: 'The works of the Muse', writes Hegel:

> now lack the power of the Spirit, for the Spirit has gained its certainty of itself from the crushing of gods and men... It cannot give us the actual life in which they existed, nor the tree that bore them, nor the earth and the elements which constituted their substance... (cited in Agamben, 1999, p. 123)

Art no longer constitutes the medium through which subjectivity unites with substance (as if ever it did!); indeed, the history of art is the history of the riven unity of artist and material, of form and content. No longer the medium through which a universal cosmos articulates itself, the artist becomes an 'absolute essence' which, Agamben writes, 'annihilates and dissolves every content in its continuous effort to transcend and actualize itself' (Agamben, 1999, p. 54).

This self-annihilating motion found its exemplary contemporary expression for Hegel in romantic irony. In the ironic, artistic consciousness is torn away from the external world, pulled toward its own self-transcending essence: '*Irony* meant that art had to become its own object, and, no longer finding real seriousness in any content, could from now on only represent the negative potentiality of the poetic I, which, denying, continues to elevate itself beyond itself in an infinite doubling' (Agamben, 1999, p. 55).

Hegel's diagnosis and ferocious critique of romantic irony, argues Agamben, acutely anticipated the condition of contemporary art. What is the meaning of the scandal, derision, perplexity, anger – of the cries of 'What does it mean?', 'But I could do that!' – that so insistently divides (and joins) art and its public, if not the disjunction of art from any content proper to itself?

Art 'ends' without disappearing, inasmuch as its perpetual dissolution of content cannot dissolve the motion of dissolution itself. Art itself has rather become this motion, Hegel's *ein Nichtiges, ein sich Vernichtendes*, which Agamben translates as 'a self-annihilating Nothing', eternally surviving itself (see Agamben, 1999, p. 56). From this perspective, Creed's installation and Davis's stories become both the logical culmination of the Kantian aesthetic and an ironic confirmation of Hegel's prognosis, actualizing themselves through the annihilation of their own content.

The empty center of the story

Davis's 'The Center of the Story' (Davis, 2001b), in fact, offers a compressed version of the Hegelian narrative of art's fate; its withdrawal first from the language of the gods, then from the active processes of history, and finally from content itself. Not that the story is – as if such a thing were possible – *without* content; on the contrary, its content, or at least that of the woman's story described in it, is announced at the very outset: 'A woman has written a story that has a hurricane in it, and a hurricane usually promises to be interesting' (Davis, 2001b, p. 35). But the promise of 'interest' – and it is hard here not to think of the paradoxically gratifying 'agitation' that Kant associates with contemplation of nature in its 'wildest and most ruleless disarray and devastation' (Kant, p. 100), not to mention the subjective 'interest' which invalidates an aesthetic judgment[2] – is quickly broken:

> But in this story the hurricane threatens the city without actually striking it. The story is flat and even, just as the earth seems flat and even when a hurricane is advancing over it, and if she were to show it to a friend, the friend would probably say that, unlike a hurricane, this story has no center. (Davis, 2001b, p. 35)

The story thus offers a kind of comic radicalization of Kant's insistence on distance (between subject and sublime object) as a condition for the experience of the sublime. The physical displacement (say the window of a secure house) required by Kant's beholder to appreciate the sublimity of nature's terrors becomes in Davis's story a kind of uncanny non-encounter.

The story repeats the doubled gesture of promise and betrayal, offering and withdrawal of center two further times: once in the story-within-the-story, in which a sick man fears he is being struck down for blaspheming; and once in the story 'itself', in which the writer, in the course of her researches into religion, finds 'an unusual, religious sort of peace' (Davis, 2001b, p. 39). Each of these non- or quasi-events – the hurricane that fails to strike, the sickness that fails to kill, the religious feeling that brings no faith – repeats the essential logic of the story:

> there is a center but the center is empty, either because she has not yet found what belongs there or because it is meant to be empty: there, but empty, in the same way that the man was sick but not dying, the hurricane approached but did not strike, and she had a religious calm but no faith. (Davis, 2001b, pp. 39–40).

It is hard to avoid noticing the very Blanchotian terms which fail to occupy the empty center: dying, faith, the 'disaster'. Each of these takes place only in its failure to take place, in its radical exteriority to experience: 'When the disaster comes upon us', writes Blanchot,

> it does not come. The disaster is its imminence but since the future, as we conceive of it in the order of lived time, belongs to the disaster, the disaster has always already withdrawn or dissuaded it; there is no future for the disaster, just as there is no time or space for its accomplishment. (Blanchot, 1995, pp. 1–2)

It is in this sense that 'the disaster ruins everything, all the while leaving everything intact' – that is, 'flat', 'even'.

The quasi-events related in Davis's story – the approaching hurricane, the man's sickness, the writer's religious feeling – all partake of this disastrous logic; none of them coincide with their own 'coming' or accomplishment. Indeed, for each of these events, 'the Bible' becomes the shared nexus of this non-coincidence, the already-betrayed promise of a transcendental meaning. The Bible is both cipher of the unity of form and content, center and story, and signifier of their ineluctable disjunction.

Translating

At the risk of yet another theoretical detour (one whose purpose should become clear), this invocation of the Bible as the end – in every sense – of language irresistibly evokes the conclusion of Walter Benjamin's famous essay on 'The Task of the Translator':

> meaning... is vouchsafed in Holy Writ alone, in which meaning has ceased to be the watershed for the flow of language and the flow of revelation. Where the literal quality of the text takes part directly, without any mediating sense, in true language, in the Truth, or in doctrine, this text is unconditionally translatable. (Benjamin, p. 262)

It is worth recalling the specific meaning Benjamin attaches to 'translatability'. A text is 'translatable' inasmuch as it intimates, beyond its communicable content, 'a language of truth, a tensionless and even silent depository of the ultimate secrets for which all thought strives...'(Benjamin, p. 259). The task of the translator is the 'divination and description' of this language of truth. Thus it is that 'the interlinear version of the Scriptures is the prototype or ideal of all translation' (Benjamin, p. 263); for if the original takes part in unmediated Truth, then it is 'unconditionally translatable' in the sense that it is *translatability itself*, language itself detached from this or that communicable content.

If the interlinear version of the Bible is for Benjamin the ideal of translation, however, the unsurpassed historical exemplar of translation is to be found in Hölderlin's translation of Sophocles's tragedies: 'In them the harmony of the languages is so profound that sense is touched by language only the way an aeolian harp is touched by the wind.' (Benjamin, p. 262). This near detachment of language from sense, in which the differences of the languages come close to dissolution, is glossed by Blanchot in 'Translating', a brief essay on – and in a sense a theoretical 'translation' of – Benjamin's essay. Hölderlin's translations of Sophocles, in forging a new and profound 'understanding' between Greek and German, gave rise to Goethe's icy laughter:

> At whom, indeed, was Goethe laughing? At a man who was no longer a poet, not a translator, but who was recklessly advancing toward the center in which he believed he would find collected the pure power of unifying, a center such that it would be able to give meaning, beyond all determined and limited meaning. (Blanchot, 1997, p. 61)

Is this not the very center to which, much more tentatively, the writer of 'The Center of the Story' (that 'of' in both senses) gestures? More tentatively because she knows, perhaps like Goethe, that her search for a meaning 'beyond all determined and limited meaning' – for meaning *itself*, a 'pure power of unifying' – can only void itself. For as Blanchot points out, translation lives in the shadow of its own predicament; it knows that the very possibility of its movement toward 'pure' language is conditioned by the *difference* of languages. Far from seeking to efface this difference, 'translation is the very life of this difference' (Blanchot, 1997, p. 59), its 'power of unification' issuing from the division which makes it possible.

The significance of Davis's role as translator of Blanchot should be coming into focus. For the paradox that recurs insistently throughout Blanchot's fiction and criticism alike is precisely this play of unity and difference, of an absolute that withdraws itself from presence, throwing the writer, the translator, the lover, the madman, back onto the finitude of existence. It is the paradox that is perpetually translated not only in Davis's renderings of Blanchot, but in the very different register – opaquely simple, blankly American to the point of alienating the idiom from itself – of her fiction:

> She had started the story with her landlady. Her landlady, an old woman from Trinidad, was alone in the downstairs hall talking quietly about the Mayor, while she was upstairs, thinking of writing a letter to the President. Her landlady said the red carpet remnant on the hall floor was given to her by her friend the Mayor. She will probably take out the President and the landlady, but leave in the Bible and the hurricane. Perhaps if she takes out things that are not interesting, or do not belong in the story for other

reasons, this will give it more of a center, since as soon as there is less in a story, more of it must be in the center. (Davis, 2001b, p. 36)

Like the Benjaminian translator, the writer wishes to transcend the noise of everyday language, to 'take it out', make it yield to the Bible's 'language of truth'. Yet as in Blanchot's imperceptible yet decisive adjustment of Benjamin, this desire for transcendence, for a meaning 'beyond all determined and limited meaning', is caught in the very limits it would cross. The center withdraws from her approach and, like the story itself, throws her back on the carpet, the Mayor, the landlady and President. The title names precisely nothing *in* the story, but rather the motion by which the center renders everything extraneous to itself. The center is never present except in its consignment to what is not central, to the 'determined and limited meaning' to which it cannot be reduced, and from which it cannot escape. Just, indeed, as the thirteenth woman, destined to the obscurity of her radical superfluousness, continues 'to live in the town' of twelve women 'without resenting what it did to her' (Davis, 2001a, p. 14).

The thirteenth woman is another name – like the hurricane, dying, faith – for the disaster that 'does not come', except in the form of this not-coming, this life which is only in the mode of the Blanchotian '*pas*' or step/not. Neither here nor beyond, she lives 'curiously unlocated, an odd non-being' (I quote from Davis's description of the translated work, from the Translator's Note to *The Gaze of Orpheus*). Like the empty center of Creed's installation, she is revealed neither in the visibility of the town nor in the invisibility of her unnumbered house, but in the imperceptible difference of the two.

The artwork as material event

What is the significance of the artwork whose content coincides with its own voiding?

In the last chapter of *The Space of Literature*, Blanchot asks why it is that such an art withdraws from any determinate content, and ceases subservience to 'active labour or any of the values upon which the world is built' (Blanchot, 1982, p. 220) at precisely the time that history emerges as the terrain of the Absolute's realization. To rephrase: why does art withdraw from History at the point where History becomes everything (so rendering itself nothing)? At the point where every thought or action is judged in terms of its capacity to be 'put to work', why does art become a 'superabundance of refusal'? (Blanchot, 1982, p. 228) – the refusal we find in Creed and Davis to show anything other than 'showing' itself.

In an important essay on the contemporary condition of art, Jean-Luc Nancy characterizes art today as a 'vestige', an 'almost nothing'; severed from a content with which it could unify itself, art reduces to 'the Idea of art itself . . . like an ideal visibility without any other content than light itself' (Nancy, 1996b, p. 90). The vestige of art is art divested of depth, of a phenomenal presence or content: 'smoke without fire, vestige without God' (Nancy, 1996b, p. 96). If Nancy insists on the proximity of this vestige to the *essence* of art, it is because this almost nothing is what remains once art ceases its subservience to forces extraneous to it (the gods, history, morality).

I want to conclude by offering two different theoretical and, by extension, ethico-political interpretations of the meaning of the artwork's vestigial status. The first comes via Paul de Man, and specifically through the late essays collected posthumously in *Aesthetic Ideology*.

What these essays, orbiting largely around Kantian and Hegelian aesthetics, show is that the category of the aesthetic is structurally doubled. On the one hand, it is a principle of articulation, the means by which a system completes itself. Thus, Kant's third *Critique* joins the first to the second – that is, imagination carries cognition to morality. In Hegel, the aesthetic is the last and necessary staging post in the progress to the absolute universality of the thinking Subject. But precisely *as* a mechanism of articulation, the aesthetic is simultaneously one of *dis*articulation, a means of making a system cohere only by way of an element radically heterogenous to it, which undoes it.

To briefly take up de Man's Kantian example: what assures the passage from beauty to morality in the third *Critique* is the imagination's experience of its own inadequacy to the sublime.[3] The sublimity of the ocean or sky is registered precisely at the point when we see it 'as the poets do', that is, without phenomenological or teleological overlay, as what de Man calls a purely *material* vision, 'purely formal, devoid of any semantic depth and reducible to the formal mathematization or geometrization of pure optics' (de Man, p. 83).

In other words, it is only the passage through this semantic depthlessness, this loss of content, the reduction of the world to pure appearance – Nancy's 'smoke without fire' – that the integrity of Kant's system is secured. For de Man, this intimation of nothingness into the system at its very heart – that is, at the point of its own coherence – is a *material event*, the taking place of the sheer materiality of the letter, divorced from phenomenality.

However – the point about the material event in de Man is that it is indissociable from the system into which it is taken up. Material disarticulation is always and necessarily also phenomenal articulation, inasmuch as the system is secured by what destabilizes it. In the Pascalian terms de Man discusses in a previous essay,[4] the *zero* of the system, which is radically heterogenous to it, can never appear other than as a *one*; the nothing is always taken up into the something.

From this perspective, Davis's stories read as allegories of this doubled logic of the system. The thirteenth woman, for example, is surely the pure materiality of the letter, a surface devoid of any semantic depth, the non-phenomenal excess or supplementarity to the story. *But* – as this excess or supplementarity, she is what holds the story in place; the non-phenomenal thirteenth woman is what defines and makes cohere the phenomenal 'town of twelve women'. The point here is that read this way the story becomes an allegory of how the material event of nothingness is always and inevitably taken up into the phenomenality of narrative and description. Thus what resists the system is always bound up with it, so that the moment of material otherness can never take place as such, but only as a trace inside the system. Looking at Creed's installation from a slightly different vantage-point, it is worth noting that it becomes readable, available to public conversation only at the point the media confer on it the very symbolic content (the artwork as symptom of cultural decadence, emptiness, stupidity) it refuses. The non-content which disarticulates reading simultaneously makes it possible.

A different way of thinking about the vestigial status of the artwork returns to Agamben. In a discussion of Kafka at the end of *The Man Without Content*, Agamben points to Kafka as the writer who discovers in 'the task of trans-mission' nothing less than 'the return of the concrete space of man's action and knowledge' (Agamben, 1999, p. 114). Agamben, following Benjamin directly, finds in Kafka's stories the enactment of *the sacrifice of truth for its transmissibility*. They are identical with their own transmission inasmuch as they 'abolish the gap between the thing to be transmitted and the act of transmission' – the thing transmitted, that is, *becomes* the act of transmission (Agamben, 1999, p. 114). Is not this coincidence enacted in the examples from Creed and Davis? In each case, the 'thing to be transmitted' is sacri-ficed to the act of transmission – the 'lights going on and off' disclose, *are*, nothing other than the passage of light itself, just as the center of the story and the thirteenth woman are nothing other than the passage of language itself, beyond any content.

For Agamben (as, differently, for Blanchot and Nancy – all three have contributed forcefully to the question on 'community'),[5] this 'contentless' art ciphers a community, an ethico-political relation which is bounded by no principle of identity. No pre-legislated content or ideology would draw a line between the included and the excluded in this community. 'A true community', writes Agamben, 'can only be a community that is not presup-posed' (Agamben, 2000, p. 47). Can the strange (non)appearance of the thirteenth woman not be read as the promise of such a community, coming into being in spite of her exclusion by the other ('real' or phenomenal) twelve? Or must we insist, with de Man, that her coming *depends* on her exclusion?

Creed's installation and Davis's stories, in their very 'smoky' slightness, compress one of the most urgent questions facing aesthetic theory today: if the content of art is one with its voiding, just how, in all resonances of the term, can it matter?

Notes

1. See Nancy (1996a).
2. Interest, that is, affective response, marks the key difference between the sublime and the beautiful.
3. See his essay 'Phenomenality and Materiality in Kant' (de Man, pp. 70–90).
4. See his essay 'Pascal's Allegory of Persuasion' (de Man, pp. 51–69).
5. See Jean-Luc Nancy, *The Inoperative Community* (Nancy, 1991); Maurice Blanchot, *The Unavowable Community* (Blanchot, 1988); Giorgio Agamben, *The Coming Community* (Agamben, 1993).

Works cited

Agamben, Giorgio, *The Coming Community*, trans. Michael Hardt (Minneapolis: University of Minnesota Press, 1993).
——*The Man Without Content*, trans. Georgia Albert (Stanford: Stanford University Press, 1999).
——'The Idea of Language', in *Potentialities: Collected Essays in Philosophy*, trans. Daniel Heller-Roazen (Stanford: Stanford University Press, 2000).
Benjamin, Walter, 'The Task of the Translator' in *Selected Writings*, 1 (1913–26), eds Marcus Bullock and Michael W. Jennings (Cambridge, MA: Belknapp Press of Harvard University Press, 1996).
Blanchot, Maurice, *The Space of Literature*, trans. Ann Smock (Lincoln, NE: University of Nebraska Press, 1982).
——*The Unavowable Community*, trans. Pierre Joris (Barrytown, NY: Station Hill, 1988).
——*The Writing of the Disaster*, trans. Ann Smock (Lincoln, NE: University of Nebraska Press, 1995).
——'Translating', in *Friendship*, trans. Elizabeth Rottenberg (Stanford, CA: Stanford University Press, 1997).
Davis, Lydia, 'The Thirteenth Woman' in *Almost No Memory* (New York: Picador USA, 2001a).
——'The Center of the Story', in *Almost No Memory* (New York: Picador USA, 2001b).
de Man, Paul, *Aesthetic Ideology*, ed. Andrzej Warminski (Minneapolis: University of Minnesota Press, 1996).
Kant, Immanuel, *Critique of Judgment*, trans. Werner S. Pluhar (Indianapolis: Hackett Publishing Company, 1987).
Nancy, Jean-Luc, *The Inoperative Community*, trans. Peter Connor, Lisa Garbus, Michael Holland, and Simona Sawhney (Minneapolis: University of Minnesota Press, 1991).
——'Why Are There Several Arts and Not Just One?', in *The Muses*, trans. P. Kamuf (Stanford: Stanford University Press, 1996a).
——'The Vestige of Art', in *The Muses*, trans. P. Kamuf (Stanford: Stanford University Press, 1996b).

17
Form, Reflection, Disclosure: Literary Aesthetics and Contemporary Criticism

Simon Malpas

> Where philosophy stops, poetry has to begin. An ordinary point of view, a way of thinking, natural only in opposition to art and culture, a mere existing: all these are wrong; that is, there should be no kingdom of barbarity beyond the boundaries of culture. Every thinking part of an organization should not feel its limits without at the same time feeling its unity in relation to the whole. For example, one ought to contrast philosophy not simply with unphilosophy, but with poetry.
>
> –Friedrich Schlegel[1]

What is the relation between philosophy and poetry; or, rather, how might the relations in which the two continually find themselves be thought productively through aesthetics? Schlegel's fragment frames the argument I want to develop here, not just by its insistence on a contrast between the two, but in its refusal of a 'kingdom of barbarity beyond the boundaries of culture': it is not a question of protecting the boundaries of culture by defending established notions of poetry and philosophy, but, instead, of exploring the ways in which both continually test the limits that tradition has erected. This, I want to claim, might productively be done by evoking once again the categories of philosophical aesthetics to rethink the ways in which poetry, literature and art have been figured in recent theoretical work, and to reactivate their potentials to transform experience, thought and critical practice.

Culture, commodification and the loss of the aesthetic

To invoke aesthetics might seem an outdated gesture. This problem is noted by Theodor Adorno, who opens his 'Draft Introduction' to *Aesthetic Theory* with the following comments:

> The concept of philosophical aesthetics has an antiquated quality, as does the concept of a system or that of morals. This feeling is in no way

restricted to artistic praxis and public indifference to aesthetic theory. Even in academic circles, essays relevant to aesthetics have for decades now noticeably diminished. (Adorno, p. 332)

Written in the 1960s, this might today be even more relevant. Contemporary literary studies has little time for aesthetic questions, and the very ideas of systematic philosophy and universal morality tend to be treated, often for good reason, with extreme caution. For cultural materialism, if aesthetics is mentioned at all, it is usually discussed as a product of bourgeois culture and ideology. For psychoanalysis and the film theory first propagated on the pages of *Screen*, aesthetic experience is defined in terms of imaginary identification and, again, ideology. Historicism tends to posit the aesthetic as 'historically determined', and therefore a matter best to be elucidated through analysis of cultural context rather than investigated in its own right. In postcolonial criticism, the aesthetic is suspected as a tool of Western domination as rules of art, beauty and representation are imposed through imperialism and the global hegemony of North American or Western European culture. For poststructuralism, the point of departure is always the signifier, and little attention is paid to affectivity or the supposed sentimentality of beauty. Each of these critical approaches mobilizes contingencies, whether of the signifier, of history or of difference, to challenge the closure of the universal system, and with it the ideas of taste, canonicity and beauty that have been associated with aesthetic judgement. As Isobel Armstrong notes,

> The most influential cultural and literary theorists of the last two decades, even when they come from constituencies and traditions inimical to each other, have agreed – and sometimes it is all that they have agreed on – that the category of the aesthetic, together with its foundational philosophers, Kant and Hegel, is up for deconstruction. Marxists, cultural materialists, post-structuralists, and deconstructive psychoanalysts, have converged in what has sometimes looked like a mission of cultural eugenics . . . [and] the concept of the aesthetic has been steadily emptied of content. (Armstrong, pp. 1–2)

While neither the importance of the critical approaches just mentioned nor their contribution to cultural politics is to be underestimated, the emptying of content from earlier concepts of aesthetics serves not to remove it entirely as a category but, rather, to retain its traces in often unquestioning ways. Frequently, the concepts of representation, disclosure and experience that are deployed by critics silently invoke the aesthetic philosophies of the eighteenth and nineteenth centuries, and leave in place categories and notions of art, literature and culture that might helpfully be explored.[2]

In today's culture, the status of art and the aesthetic seems no less precarious than it does in current critical practice, and Adorno's prognostications about the relation between art and contemporary general culture might again offer a useful point of departure:

> For most people, aesthetics is superfluous. It disturbs the weekend pleasures to which art has been consigned as the complement of the bourgeois routine . . . . [A]rt allies itself with repressed and dominated nature in the progressively rationalised and integrated society. Yet industry makes even this resistance an institution and changes it into coin. . . . The consumers, whose naïveté is confirmed and drilled into them, are to be dissuaded from entertaining stupid ideas about what has been packed into the pills they are obliged to swallow down. . . . Ever since the surface of life, the immediacy it makes available to people, has become ideology, naïveté has reversed into its own opposite; it has become the reflex of reified consciousness to a reified world. (Adorno, pp. 335–6)

For Adorno, the potential for good sense that thinkers as diverse as Matthew Arnold and Antonio Gramsci have located at the heart of the common sense of the populace, and which culture's role is to nurture and develop, has vanished with industrialization, thereby turning naivety and immediacy away from truth and authenticity to produce ideological justifications of bourgeois routine. Even if capitalist society has more recently, as many economists and sociologists claim, moved into a post-industrial phase that breaks down the rigidity of the class hierarchies with which Adorno is working, his arguments about the deployment of art and culture remain telling. The superfluity of aesthetics in public discourse about art has never been more apparent than it appears today. Examples of the commodification of contemporary culture are too numerous to discuss here, although one can point quickly to the growth in financial speculation in the contemporary art markets; the current focus on 'accessibility' in many Western governments' arts policies that appear more interested in populism and financial returns than art's potential to challenge or disrupt doxa; and the ever-present idea of art as a leisure activity to be purchased as relief from the continually lengthening working day. Art and culture continue in many public proclamations to be defined as instruments of personal and social improvement, but the justifications for this evaluation become more tenuous as rapidly as the superfluity of aesthetic judgement becomes the norm. Contemporary culture threatens to become, as Jean-François Lyotard argues, a culture of 'Anything Goes', in which the 'realism of Anything Goes is the realism of money: in the absence of aesthetic criteria it is still possible and useful to measure the value of works of art by the profits they realize' (Lyotard, p. 8). Contemporary criticism does little to challenge this, and its complicity in presenting aesthetics as superfluous is both the basis of its many insights and also an indication of its blindnesses. And it is this tension between insight and blindness that drives Adorno's critique of the non-aesthetics of what he calls culture industry criticism:

> Those who have been duped by the culture industry and are eager for its commodities were never familiar with art: They are therefore able to perceive art's inadequacy to the present life processes of society – though not society's own untruth – more unobstructedly than do those who still remember what an artwork once was. They push for the deastheticisation of art.... The humiliating difference between art and the life people lead ... must be made to disappear: This is the subjective basis for classifying art among the consumer goods under the control of *vested interests*. (Adorno, pp. 16–17)

The consumers and critics of the culture industry, according to this passage, have an advantage over the aesthetes: they perceive art's inadequacy to the present. Unlike the aesthete's nostalgic longing for the return of an age when artistic works could still provide the sensuous presentations of a society's ideals and nurture the intellectual and moral outlooks of its citizens, these so-called 'dupes' focus on the present social processes that locate art in society. On the basis of this, they push for art's 'deastheticization', and argue for its consideration and consumption as one commodity amongst others. The result of this process will be an understanding of the vested interests behind art and its inability to resolve the humiliations of people's everyday lives. In other words, one might say that the perspectives of the culture industry's critics act to unmask art's relation to ideology, and challenge its mystification of the life processes of present society. Outlined in these terms, this is, I think, a pretty good assessment of where much theoretical work stands today. And it is not wrong: works of art are commodities to be bought, sold and consumed. As readers of books, students in seminar rooms, audience members in cinemas or viewers in our own front rooms, we are all consumers, and analyses of the political and social economics of artistic and cultural consumption make valuable contributions to our understanding of the cultures we inhabit.

But, Adorno argues, as positive as it might appear, this approach to art and culture serves only to get the artwork wrong:

> The poles of the artwork's deastheticisation are that it is made as much a thing among things as a psychological vehicle of the spectator. What the reified artworks are no longer able to say is replaced by the beholder with the standardized echo of himself, to which he hearkens. (Adorno, p. 17)

The critics and consumers of the culture industry, in responding to art as a 'thing among things', reduce its specificity, and thereby its difference, as they transform it into a psychological vehicle that echoes the drives and desires of the individual, or rather, in the 'reflex of reified consciousness to a reified world', the mores and structures of society. The work is a thing, a commodity, and its reception is subjective, psychological, which is to say that the meaning produced by their interaction will be ideological. Approached in this way, the work might challenge specific ideological positions, but can do so only from the perspective of other, albeit counterhegemonic, ideologies. In critical reading, a similar process is often identifiable: the work becomes a reflection of the theoretical perspective, an object to be shaped and transformed into a 'standardized echo' of the theory that is 'applied'. On this basis, art loses its ability to surprise or shock: always already grasped and comprehended by the spectator or critic, any radical or disruptive potential it might contain is refused, and the roles it has hitherto been given by philosophical aesthetics come to seem at best delusions and, at worst, mystifications of the political and economic forces at work in the world.

This is all very well, but what is being presupposed so far is that the work of art might have such a 'radical or disruptive potential' in the first place, that it might somehow be more than just another commodity caught up in the circulation of capital. So what is it about the work of art that might allow it to resist reduction to economy, instrumentality or ideology?

According to Adorno, the basis of art's resistance lies in the fact that the complexity of its form is at once irreducible to social convention and yet also inextricable from it:

> Art negates the categorical determinations stamped on the empirical world and yet harbors what is empirically existing in its own substance. If art opposes the empirical through the element of form – and the mediation of form and content is not to be grasped without their differentiation – the mediation is to be sought in the recognition of aesthetic form as sedimented content... The unsolved antagonisms of reality return in artworks as immanent problems of form. This, not the insertion of objective elements, defines the relation of art to society. (Adorno, pp. 5–6)

This notion of form as sedimented content is a key premise of Adorno's aesthetics, and is crucial here because it serves to open up the central question of this chapter: why is aesthetics so important for thinking the relations between literature, philosophy and society in a productive, critical and politically engaged manner?

To begin relatively superficially, what Adorno is suggesting in his analysis of form is that the unresolved tensions and anxieties of a society are presented not simply in the *content* of a work, where they can be identified and resolved through instrumental means, but at the level of presentation itself. Artistic form is thereby thought as a dynamic cultural category linked to social relations, economic structures, technological development and the history of art itself. The *form* of an ode or a symphony, what presents its content, allows its communication, is not an abstract, a-historical structure but a dynamic procedure of production and mediation that generates meaning and affect differently for any given community. A reading of the work's 'meaning' that does not take into account this problematic, frequently anachronistic, formal relation to social actuality (which is precisely what generates its aesthetic affects), refuses to read it as a work of art, commodifies it and comprehends it, thereby transforming both work and critical response into ideology.

This notion of form as sedimentation, however, generates a whole set of questions about the relation between the work and empirical existence, history, and the mechanics of presentation, at which a brief gloss of the last passage can only hint. The key point of interest here is the resources that such a thinking of form might offer as an argument for the political–philosophical importance of aesthetics as disclosure rather than representation. In order to begin to see the ramifications of Adorno's thinking of form for contemporary aesthetic criticism, it is helpful to return to and make explicit the earlier notions of philosophical aesthetics to which he is responding. These notions find their most powerful modern formulation in G.W.F Hegel's *Aesthetics: Lectures on Fine Art*.

The end of art and the beginning of aesthetics

Adorno's and Armstrong's complaints are not new: over the last two centuries, at least, the history of philosophical aesthetics has been a history of loss. Modern thought has quite frequently taken refuge in the notion that art is something from the past; or, more accurately, that, at the moment at which reflection about the meaning and nature of art takes place, it appears to have lost the powers with which it had hitherto been invested. Perhaps the most pertinent and influential example of this process is Hegel's declaration of the 'end of art' in his *Aesthetics*:

> just as art has its 'before' in nature and the finite spheres of life, so too it has an 'after', i.e. a region which in turn transcends art's way of apprehending and representing the Absolute. For art has still a limit in itself and therefore passes over into higher forms of consciousness. . . . For us art counts no longer as the highest mode in which truth fashions an existence for itself. (Hegel, 1975, pp. 102–3)

This claim ties art in to a notion of historical progress that identifies the cultural and political transformations that go along with changes in social organization and, in turn, re-evaluate art's relation to a given community.

Its importance, however, goes beyond just the relationship between art and history that it forges. What is at stake is the production of a notion that art can no longer grasp the ideals and beliefs of a society in its own right, but, with the onset of philosophical modernity, has come to require investigation, analysis and definition by the 'higher forms of consciousness' that speculative philosophy will provide.

For Hegel, modern art requires interpretation according to the moving principles of dialectical logic: not a once-and-for-all identification of meaning, but a restlessly negative procedure of re-reading and re-contextualization that explores the continual transformations of meaning that emerge from the flux of modern existence.[3] In other words, according to Hegel, art's 'vocation is to unveil the *truth* in the form of sensuous artistic configuration' by distilling and re-presenting to a society its foundational identifications, beliefs and aspirations (Hegel, 1975, p. 55). He argues that for the apparently fixed and a-historical belief systems of many pre-modern societies, art is able to act as the 'highest mode' of self-understanding and representation, but that with the move into modernity and the increasing complexity of social organization, scientific sophistication and religious understanding, sensible presentation is no longer up to the task of adequately grasping and communicating a society's most vital ideals. The result of this, he claims, is that

> [A]rt, considered in its highest vocation, is and remains for us a thing of the past. Thereby it has lost for us genuine truth and life, and has rather been transferred into our *ideas* instead of maintaining its earlier necessity. . . . The *philosophy* of art is therefore a greater need in our day than it was in days when art by itself as art yielded full satisfaction. (Hegel, 1975, p. 11)

There should be no question of reading this as a claim that philosophy replaces art. Rather, Hegel announces the necessity of a critical analysis of its aesthetic impact: modern art has lost the immediacy of earlier works, and requires interpretation, reflection, exegesis, criticism if it is ever to yield meaning.[4] This is the task he sets himself in the *Aesthetics*.

Hegel's success in producing a philosophical account of art and aesthetics remains debatable. For Adorno, his arguments, by insisting that art is always caught up in the historical–philosophical movement of Spirit (*Geist*), provide powerful means to challenge both the a-historicism that ascribes eternal meanings to art and the sentimentalism that locates aesthetic meaning entirely in subjective responses to a work. On the other hand, though, and in a direct contradiction of these insights, Adorno claims that in Hegel's *Aesthetics* 'the dialectic of art is limited to the genres and their history, and it is not sufficiently introduced into the theory of the individual work' (Adorno, p. 274). The result of this is that, while Hegel presents a historically mutable notion of the importance of art itself, his retention of a classical account of form and genre makes it impossible to think of the individual work in any other terms than those that lead to the very forms of undialectical a-historicism and sentimentalism he set out to challenge. If Hegel provides a compelling analysis of the importance of philosophical aesthetics for exploring art as a mode of experience, the resources for a criticism that might counter the contemporary de-aestheticization of theory must be sought elsewhere.

Between infinities: aesthetic reflection and the literary absolute

A key resource for contemporary aesthetic criticism can be found in the work of Hegel's contemporaries: the Romantics. One of the most compelling recent accounts of the challenges that a thinking of literary aesthetics might offer is provided by Philippe Lacoue-Labarthe and Jean-Luc Nancy in *The Literary Absolute: The Theory of Literature in German Romanticism*. Setting the Romantic theory produced by the circle of writers who came together around the journal *The Athenaeum* against the newly emerging speculative idealism of Hegel, J.G. Fichte and F.W.J. Schelling, this book identifies a 'veritable romantic *unconscious* [that] is discernable today, in most of the central motifs of our "modernity"' (Lacoue-Labarthe and Nancy, p. 15). Against the systems of philosophical modernity that hold out the possibility of comprehending the world through a speculative absolute, Lacoue-Labarthe and Nancy present the possibility of a literary absolute that 'aggravates and radicalizes the thinking of totality and the Subject. It *infinitizes* this thinking, and therein, precisely, rests its ambiguity' (Lacoue-Labarthe and Nancy, p. 15). The result of this is that Romantic aesthetics is presented as figuring a point of disturbance within modernity that 'aggravates' speculative philosophy's drive towards totality and system by bringing the absolute within the scope of dialectical logic, a point that generates a more radical model of subjectivity, which defers the closure of philosophical self-certainty in a writing that incessantly produces 'signs of [a] small and complex fissuring' at the heart of identity (Lacoue-Labarthe and Nancy, p. 15). This fissuring, I want to claim, emerges from a rethinking of the temporality of aesthetic experience.

To develop their case for a literary absolute, Lacoue-Labarthe and Nancy draw on the arguments of, and follow a similar tack to, Walter Benjamin's 'The Concept of Criticism in German Romanticism', which defines Romantic reflection as, 'at bottom, the autochthonous form of infinite positing' that continually transgresses the limits set by Fichte's foundational notion of positing reflection as the moving principle of the dialectical relationship between the I and Not-I that gives rise to knowledge' (Benjamin, p. 124).[5]

According to Benjamin, what distinguishes Romantic reflection from the dialectical, developmental models of idealist philosophy is its form-giving propensity: it is not simply the mediation of a pre-given immediate reality, but, rather, the mediation of reflection takes up, runs through and generates the immediacy of the real as formed experience, and this process is endless. He argues that, while for Fichte, 'the possibility of an intuition of the "I" rests on the possibility of confining and fixing reflection in the absolute thesis', for Romanticism, 'reflection is logically the first and primary.... Only with reflection does that thinking arise on which reflection takes place. For this reason, we can say that every simple reflection arises absolutely from a point of indifference' (Benjamin, pp. 130, 134). In Benjamin's Romanticism, then, reflection is primary: it is the forming agent that brings subject and object into existence, generating knowledge, reality and experience in a manner that is continually open to re-formation and trans-formation. And poetry, as the form-giving process par excellence and the 'point at which reflection arises from nothing', becomes the means to 'raise ... reflection again and again to a higher power'.[6] Put simply, poetry discloses world and subject by reflexively forming experience for thought. The consequences of this apparently simple idea are, however, profound and far reaching.

It is this notion of a form-producing poetic reflection that lies at the basis of Lacoue-Labarthe and Nancy's discussion of aesthetics in *The Literary Absolute*. Analysed in this way, aesthetic experience becomes both destructive of established modes of perception and knowledge, and productive of new forms of experiencing and thinking. Poetry is, they argue, employing a term to which the Romantics have continual recourse, a *Bildung*: it is both 'formation as putting-into-form and formation as culture. Man and work of art alike are what they are only insofar as they are *gebildet*, having taken on the form and figure of what they ought to be' (Lacoue-Labarthe and Nancy, p. 47). It is not a question, then, of aesthetic experience being generated when a pre-formed individual approaches a pre-written literary text to discover a pre-ordained meaning; rather, the reflective relation of reading forms text, meaning and subject anew in each act, and this moment of formation is aesthetic. Moreover, the process of formation, which is the essence of both reflection and aesthetics, is, they argue, 'infinite'.

It is important to define the way the term 'infinite' is being used here, as the notion of infinity is crucial to the presentation of the literature–philosophy relation in both *The Literary Absolute* and 'The Concept of Criticism', and also to an understanding of what might be at stake in the positing of a poetic infinite that 'aggravates and radicalizes' the organized infinity of the speculative philosophical system.[7] To run through this briefly, one of the founding premises of Hegel's dialectics emerges from a distinction between what, in *Science of Logic*, he calls the true and the spurious infinite. The latter account of infinity presents the infinite simply as opposed to or 'beyond' the finite, as *'one of the two*; but as *only* one of the two it is itself finite, it is not the whole but only *one* side; it has its limit in what stands over against it; it is thus the *finite infinite'*, and, by definition therefore, not a true infinity (Hegel, 1989, p. 144). Hegel's true infinity, on the other hand, sets out from this apparent opposition and, by thinking the unity of itself and its finite constituents, 'embraces both itself and finitude – and is therefore the infinite in a different sense from that in which the finite is regarded as separated and set apart' (Hegel, 1989, p. 144). In other words, the true infinite is not presented as opposed to or different from its finite constituents, but is rather the totality of the moments of their continual interrelationships; and these moments, taken together, are the stuff of the infinite movement of speculative thought. This unity of finitude with the infinite, Hegel argues, provides the basis for a thinking of the ways in which the philosophical system can comprehend its constituent aspects (the determinate beings, negations and becomings that make it up) as parts of a whole that does not hover above them in some other sphere, but, rather, runs through them as the necessary and inevitable movement of reason itself. As he states, 'The infinite in its simple Notion can, in the first place, be regarded as a fresh definition of the absolute' (Hegel, 1989, p. 137).

In contrast to this, the infinite of Romantic aesthetics is, as Benjamin argues, 'not an infinity of continuous advance but an infinity of connectedness' (Benjamin, p. 126). Each reflection connects with others, but also re-forms them and their relations, not to generate a speculative result, but to form a totality of fragments that remain constantly open to yet more re-formations. As Lacoue-Labarthe and Nancy argue, at the heart of Romantic aesthetics, one finds fragmentation:

> Fragmentary totality . . . cannot be situated in any single point: it is simultaneously in the whole and in each part. Each fragment stands for itself and for that from which it is detached. Totality is the fragment itself in its completed individuality. It is thus identically the plural totality of fragments, which does not make up a whole . . . but replicates the whole, the fragmentary itself, in each fragment. . . . [T]his is what installs the totality of the fragment as a plurality and its completion as the incompletion of its infinity. (Lacoue-Labarthe and Nancy, p. 44)

The work of art, thought in terms of this notion of Romantic aesthetics, can only ever be fragmentary: it might appear to be complete in and of itself, but as a fragment it must also remain continually open to new reflections, re-readings, re-contextualizations and re-formations. The fragmentary infinity of literary reflection subsists within speculative infinity (without philosophy there is no literature), fragmenting it with 'signs of [a] small and complex fissuring' (Lacoue-Labarthe and Nancy, p. 15) that disrupts closure and result. And this fissuring occurs not only in the artwork, but also in the reader, spectator or critic: aesthetic reflection discloses both subjectivity and artwork as sites that resist the reifications and totalizations of the culture industry's ideologies.

If criticism is to take this into account, it requires a re-orientation around the sort of productive reflection that Benjamin finds in Romantic aesthetics:

> [C]riticism is, as it were, an experiment on the artwork, one through which the latter's own reflection is awakened, through which it is brought to consciousness and to knowledge of itself.... The subject of reflection is, at bottom, the artistic entity itself, and the experiment consists not in any reflecting *on* an entity ... but in the unfolding of reflection – that is, for the Romantics, the unfolding of spirit – *in* an entity. (Benjamin, p. 151)

In other words, rather than reflecting *on* a text by 'applying' a predetermined theory to contextualize and explain it, criticism's task might be conceived as opening theory and text to reflection, being surprised by what is disclosed in the event of reading. Rather than 'explaining' texts, the aim of criticism might be to disclose what in those texts resists the theoretical apparatus that are employed. Thought in this way, aesthetics becomes a site of disruption that continually exceeds and solicits the organization of knowledge into a philosophical system by opening the economy of the speculative present to intimations of a future that is 'absolutely surprising'.[8]

Notes

1. Schlegel, *Ideas*, fragment 48, p. 98.
2. For a particularly astute analysis of this process, see Bowie (2003) and also Bowie (1997).
3. For a reading of Hegel that sees his thought as actively and inextricably caught up in the transformative flux of modern experience, see Nancy (2002).
4. For a reading of the transformation of art from the spontaneous immediacy of religious experience to an ironized 'self-annihilating nothing', see Giorgio Agamben, *The Man without Content*, especially pp. 40–58, as well as Josh Cohen's preceding essay in this book, 'No Matter: Aesthetic Theory and the Self-Annihilating Artwork'.
5. See Walter Benjamin, 'The Concept of Criticism in German Romanticism'. Fichte's notion of reflection is developed most fully in his *The Science of Knowledge* (Fichte, 1982).
6. See Benjamin, p. 150; Schlegel, p. 32 (*Athenaeum* fragment 116).
7. I have explored this idea in more detail in my 'Framing Infinities: Kantian Aesthetics after Derrida' (Malpas, 2000).
8. This notion of the future as 'absolutely surprising' is developed by Emmanuel Levinas in *Time and the Other*. The account of aesthetics to which such a thinking of poetry gives rise is developed in more detail, and from various other perspectives, in *The New Aestheticism* (Joughin and Malpas, 2003).

Works cited

Adorno, Theodor, *Aesthetic Theory*, eds Gretel Adorno and Rolf Tiedemann, trans. Robert Hullot-Kentor (London: Athlone, 1997).

Agamben, Giorgio, *The Man without Content*, trans. Georgia Albert (Stanford: Stanford University Press, 1999).

Armstrong, Isobel, *The Radical Aesthetic* (Oxford: Blackwell, 2000).

Benjamin, Walter, 'The Concept of Criticism in German Romanticism', in *Selected Writings*, Vol. 1 (1913–26), eds Marcus Bullock and Michael W. Jennings (Cambridge, MA: Belknapp Press of Harvard University Press, 1996).

Bowie, Andrew, *From Romanticism to Critical Theory: The Philosophy of German Literary Theory* (London: Routledge, 1997).

—— *Aesthetics and Subjectivity: from Kant to Nietzsche*, 2nd ed. (Manchester: Manchester University Press, 2003).

Fichte, J.G., *The Science of Knowledge*, ed. and trans. Peter Heath and John Lachs (Cambridge: Cambridge University Press, 1982).

Hegel, G.W.F., *Aesthetics: Lectures on Fine Art*, Vol. 1, trans. T.M. Knox (Oxford: Oxford University Press, 1975).

—— *The Science of Logic*, trans. A.V. Miller (Atlantic Highlands, NJ: Humanities Press, 1989).

Joughin, John, and Simon Malpas (eds), *The New Aestheticism* (Manchester: Manchester University Press, 2003).

Lacoue-Labarthe, Philippe, and Jean-Luc Nancy, *The Literary Absolute: The Theory of Literature in German Romanticism*, trans. Philip Barnard and Cheryl Lester (Albany: State University of New York Press, 1988).

Levinas, Emmanuel, *Time and the Other*, trans. Richard A. Cohen (Pittsburgh: Duquesne University Press, 1987).

Lyotard, Jean-François, *The Postmodern Explained*, trans. and ed. Julian Pefanis and Morgan Thomas (Minneapolis: University of Minnesota Press, 1993).

Malpas, Simon, 'Framing Infinities: Kantian Aesthetics after Derrida', in Rachel Jones and Andrea Rehberg (eds), *The Matter of Critique: Readings in Kant's Philosophy* (Manchester: Clinamen Press, 2000).

Nancy, Jean-Luc, *Hegel: The Restlessness of the Negative*, trans. Jason Smith and Steven Miller (Minneapolis: University of Minnesota Press, 2002).

Schlegel, Friedrich, *Philosophical Fragments*, trans. Peter Firchow (Minneapolis: University of Minnesota Press, 1991).

Index